John Diebold on Management

by Carl Heyel

Foreword by Richard M. Cyert
President, Carnegie-Mellon University

Prentice-Hall, Inc.
Englewood Cliffs, New Jersey

A WORD FROM THE AUTHOR

John Diebold's first book — "Automation: The Advent of the Automatic Factory"—was published in 1952. It attracted world-wide attention, and over the ensuing years has been translated into many languages. This lucidly written, compact book (it needed only 181 pages to get its message across) stirred the imagination of business men and political leaders, economists and engineers, and social theoreticians and practical, production-minded executives with its insights into the direction and exciting promise of a new, emerging technology.

Today, looking back at John Diebold writing as he did at mid-century, one is struck by two facts: first, how well it all stands up — two decades later what he wrote seems fresh, logical and rings true — and second, just how unique, at the time, were the insights, perceptions and stands that he took.

Over the two decades that followed, he has done as much as any one person to "make the future work." As pointed out in our opening pages, his views have special significance not only because of the consistency of the philosophy which he has continually voiced from the time when his first book brought him, at an early age, into international prominence; and not only because his views have been borne out by events. For the hard-headed business reader, the significance is that the specifics of his management approaches have been proven in the hard arena of the marketplace. Far from confining himself to ivory-tower generalizations, he has put his ideas into successful practice. He has built up several businesses in high-technology fields, and is head of a far-flung international management consulting firm. The latter is in the forefront of applying computer and related technology to business operations, and handles hundreds of projects a year involving the planning by client businesses for technological change.

To the present author-editor, this combination of commonsense practicality with wide-ranging intellectual sweep and philosophic insight appears as the most outstanding characteristic of his subject. It has been an exhilarating experience to go through John Diebold's many speeches and writings over the past twenty years, to excerpt from them the passages that illustrate the basic themes of his work, and to bring them together in a logically consecutive treatment. The result, if intent is hopefully realized in deed, presents "John Diebold on Management."

Because of the extent of the lode to be mined, the task was no easy one, and grateful appreciation is here expressed to Miss Liesa Bing, General Counsel of The Diebold Group, as well as other members of the firm, and to The Diebold Group's library staff in making available the many publications, research reports, and transcripts that had to be searched, and in assisting in the many processing chores involved.

Carl Heyel

Information Systems for Marketing

The technology of computers and the rapid communications and information processing equipment which this technology makes possible will permit far more extensive analysis of our national economy and business methods, through up-to-the-minute market surveys and extensive research on distribution data and transportation patterns.

Automation: The Advent of the Automatic Factory,
Princeton, New Jersey, Van Nostrand Company, Inc.,
1952.

Systems concepts are inadequate to the problems of the marketing function. Many companies spend sizeable sums to develop technically impressive marketing data bases, information systems, and "corporate models" of all descriptions. But marketing men do not find the information useful. Planning for useful marketing information systems must take on a different definition and focus. Specifically, it is more important to plan the value side of this equation than the cost side.

Press interview on a Diebold Research Program Study,
August 6, 1970.

Management Of the Computer

When you are dealing with equipment that sometimes costs millions of dollars, it is dangerous to be satisfied with anything less than optimum productivity.

"Applied Automation: A Practical Approach,"
Keynote address before the Special Manufacturing Conference of the American Management Association,
New York, New York,
October 10, 1955.

Automation remains a shining promise, and nearly everyone is convinced that for business it does represent the road of tomorrow. But this is little comfort to financial officers who are faced with a computer's ravenous appetite for cash now, and whose earnest efforts to reduce costs by normal efficiency and economy methods seem almost futile in the face of this real fixed cost.

"Automation 1958: Industry at the Crossroads,"
Dun's Review,
August, 1958.

Ironically, naive standards are used in justifying and evaluating the machines which so greatly extend our analytical powers . . . Most companies carefully weigh the decision, consider the alternatives, compare relative costs, and then reach a conclusion – on the basis of the wrong criteria entirely. The problem is not lack of technical knowledge on the part of the experts. Rather, it is the failure on the part of top management to ask the right questions.

"Bad Decisions on Computer Use,"
Harvard Business Review,
January-February, 1969.

Management By the Computer

Computers open to management the possibilities of an entirely new order of magnitude of control over business operations. Savings in clerical costs will be the smallest effect of automation: it is by providing management with better and current information that they will score their greatest gains.

"Automation: A Factor in Business Policy Planning,"
The Manager,
September, 1955.

Through improved communication the span of control can be widened, leading to more efficient organization and to considerable savings . . . Traditional departmental boundaries can be expected to blur as with intricate management-science techniques and common data bases at their disposal, decision-makers are forced to consider problems in their entirety rather than parcelling them out in pieces.

"The Computer's Changing Role,"
Management Today,
January, 1969.

For 15 years I have advocated bringing knowledge of the potential business uses of computers to management. It is now time to apply management's knowledge of business more fully to the planning and evaluation of computers. In allowing technicians to set goals for ADP activity, management has not been facing up to its responsibilities.

"Bad Decisions on Computer Use,"
Harvard Business Review,
January-February, 1969.

Developing of Managers

The machines of automation are only symbols of fundamental developments that are taking place in the way we organize our world. The training of management personnel must reflect this fact. But such education programs as have accompanied automation hardly even begin to reflect it because businessmen who understand this themselves are as rare as whooping cranes.

"Education for Data Processing – The Real Challenge to Management,"
Great Issues Lecture, Dartmouth College, Hanover, New Hampshire,
November 11, 1957.

On the whole, the manager's job will become more difficult rather than easier, for he will need technical skills as well as experience in line functions, an ability to respond to change when everything moves at a faster pace, plus all the traditional entrepreneurial judgment and drive that makes a company dynamic.

"The Computer's Changing Role,"
Management Today,
January, 1969.

John Diebold on Management

by Carl Heyel

FOREWORD

This book contains the writings and speeches of a man who was one of the first to perceive the revolutionary implications of the computer for management and the society. John Diebold has emphasized throughout his career as a manager and entrepreneur the fact that technology is a creator of opportunity for the business firm and that the computer is special in this respect. The computer represents the greatest single technological advance in this century and perhaps in the whole history of man. It is, therefore, proper that it receive the kind of concentrated attention that John Diebold has given it.

A basic change in management began after World War II. This basic change amounted to a shift in attitude which had its origins in some of the approaches to solving the problems of the war. The changed philosophy was characterized by a recognition that a scientific approach could be made to the problems of business management. This radical change in attitude was stimulated by the successful use of operations research techniques to solve some of the important problems of World War II. Following the war the analytic approach was pursued at a few business schools and research institutes. It was, however, the development of the computer that made a scientific approach to management practical and operational. Thus the conditions for a successful revolution in management practice were partially achieved with the advent of the computer.

The final link in completing the revolution, however, was management itself. The need for management to understand that the computer was something more than a desk calculator was the final necessary step. It is in this area of educating management that John Diebold has struggled valiantly. He was an early revolutionary and his commitment to the "cause" has persisted. Nevertheless, continued effort is necessary to help managers recognize the potential of the computer as a management tool.

It is critical, for example, that management recognize technology as a strategic alternative in its planning process. For too long the tendency has been to look upon acquisition as the only strategic alternative to attain the firm's goals. Thus we have had in the last ten years a great growth of the diversified firms. Diebold in this book correctly, however, emphasizes the need for management to regard technological alternatives as part of the planning process. The whole area represented by the interface between management and the research and development process is one that needs continuing attention from management scientists. Management must develop the ability to specify the needs of the company as derived from the planning process in terms of the actions necessary on the part of the scientific personnel to achieve the firm's goals. We must move, in other words, toward a much closer interrelationship between planning and technological research. To meet some goals the firm will require new basic research activities. Other goals may be met by exploiting the opportunities already available from the known technology. Educating management on the latter approach has been one in which John Diebold has played an outstanding role. He has described in operational detail for industry after industry the kinds of opportunities that were available through more intelligent use of the computer.

We are moving in the seventies into a period in which the United States no longer holds a technological advantage over the rest of the world as it once did. It becomes imperative that others at the top management level follow John Diebold's lead in urging American management to greater thought and action to improve technology and in adopting quickly new technological developments whether coming from the U.S. or other countries.

In addition to the loss of technological advantage, the U.S. is in a position where there is need to be concerned about ways to increase exports to improve our balance of payments. The need to deal with this problem raises immediately the question of improving productivity. Productivity must be increased at all levels in American industry. We must find ways of motivating the laborer on the assembly line to increase his productivity, and we must find ways of motivating managers at all levels to improve the way in which they operate so as to improve our overall utilization of resources. Again, one of the major means of increasing productivity at these levels is through the computer. There are many suggestions within this book for ways in which management can improve the job that it does. In particular, the stress on the role of the computer in providing greater opportunities for effective managerial control is a key idea that must be accepted and developed by current and future managers.

As we look at the problems of society we see further opportunities for problem solving through the intelligent use of technology. In education we face a great need to reduce the cost of instruction. This is particularly true at the university level. The steps currently being taken by a few institutions on the forefront of research involve what is called "a multi-media approach." This approach is an attempt to utilize all the modern forms of technology such as TV and computers, as well as the old forms of education such as classroom and books. The aim is to try to determine the tasks for which each medium is superior and then use a combination of media. Hopefully, this can be done in such a way as to reduce the amount of time that an instructor must spend in the classroom and devote to a single class. Thus with the same amount of effort as he currently spends in a single class he may handle several classes. John Diebold's writings on the use of the computer in education will give the reader some interesting insights into this current and important development in education.

In general, these writings represent in a good way the kind of interface that is badly needed within American management. It is the interface between modern technological development on the one hand and current management practice on the other. We need more people who, like John Diebold, have a knowledge of the technology and a knowledge of the problems faced by top management and our society. This book does not represent the writings and speeches of a technician but rather of a man who has comprehended the implications of a technological development for industry and society. Carl Heyel has done a service in pulling these writings together and annotating them in an effective way. I hope the book will inspire other industrial leaders to speak on the same set of problems and that ultimately the effect on the practice of management will be significant.

Richard M. Cyert
President
Carnegie-Mellon University
Pittsburgh, Pennsylvania

TABLE OF CONTENTS

PART I

Technological and Social Change As a Business Opportunity

B15-26 TIL FLYENE
TO THE AIRCRAFT

John Diebold believes the key to benefitting from the forces of change rather than being buffeted by them is a never-ending search throughout the world to keep on top of developments and to assess the new entrepreneurial opportunities which they open. He is seen here traveling abroad putting that philosophy to work – translating ideas into action.

We have the most dynamic and productive economy the world has ever known...As we satisfy the material needs for food, clothing, and shelter, we find that we have created new needs — needs for books, art, travel, music, sports, and for leisure. The continual emergence of new needs is a basic cause of the dynamic qualities of our economy.

"Automation – Its Impact on Human Relations,"
address before the Congress of American Industry, National Association of Manufacturers, New York, **December 3, 1954.**

It is the social changes which, looking back upon them, we see to be the real hallmarks of a "revolution" for which technology is only the agent.

"Technology's Challenge to Management,"
address before the Plenary Session, European Conference of The High Authority of the European Coal and Steel Community, The Commission of the European Economic Community, The Commission of the European Atomic Energy Community, Brussels, Belgium, **December 6, 1960.**

*First, and most obviously, technology changes **how** business operates. Second, and often less obviously, it changes **what** business does...Third, most important and least understood, it changes the **society** that business serves — and thus creates new business opportunities and alters or ends long-established patterns.*

"Automation in the Future,"
keynote address before the 37th International Conference of the Financial Executives Institute, New York, New York, **October 25, 1968.**

Technology as an Entrepreneurial Opportunity

Technology should be viewed as an entrepreneurial opportunity for new business building as well as a means of reducing costs.

Technological change is the central and exciting fact of our times. What problems, challenges, opportunities, and responsibilities does it pose to business management? How will it affect what an enterprise does, and how it does it? Whom will it prosper? Whom will it render obsolete?

1

This book presents the special insights of John Diebold on these questions, as he has given voice to them over the past decade. John Diebold is widely known for his contributions to management thinking and to the formulation of public policy on automation, computers, and related technology. He served as the first witness in the first Congressional hearing on automation in 1955, and has appeared before numerous Congressional committees and other public policy-making bodies since then, as well as serving as a member of the U.S. delegation to the U.N. Conference on Science and Technology for Less Developed Areas, in Geneva in 1963. As a public speaker, writer, and lecturer he commands an international audience.

But what gives John Diebold's views special significance is not only that the general philosophy which he has expressed from the start has been justified by events, but that the specifics of his management approaches have been proven in the hard arena of the marketplace. Far from confining himself to ivory-tower generalizations, he has put his ideas into successful practice. He has built up several businesses in high-technology fields, and is head of a far-flung international management consulting firm. The latter is in the forefront of applying computer and related technology to business operations, and handles hundreds of projects a year involving the planning by client businesses for technological change. This total immersion in business problems has had a multiplier effect with respect to the dissemination and implementation of his ideas. By providing direct policy counsel to the heads of hundreds of major enterprises around the world, he has had significant impact behind the scenes in the setting up of new businesses and in effecting mergers and acquisitions.

Many others have, of course, spoken and written about technology in general, and about automation and computer technology in particular. But what has distinguished John Diebold's speeches and writings on these subjects from the very start of his career is that he early saw and always stressed that the true significance of technology is not the specific innovations in themselves, dramatic as some of them may be, but rather the multi-level impact of technical change itself, and especially of the rate of that change. In the keynote address before the International Conference of the Financial Executives Institute in New York, referred to in our opening quotation, and on other occasions he has elaborated three levels of meaning that technological change holds for business.

First, he says, and most obviously, technology changes how business operates. The traditional use of technology, for example, is to increase productivity — in manufacturing processes, and, latterly, in computerized office operations. The latter, as indicated in later chapters, has had and will increasingly have profound effects on long-established concepts of departmental segregation and organizational hierarchies.

Second, and less obviously, he points out, it changes what a business does, even as it alters processes and methods. When products or the form in which they are distributed and sold are changed, when services are enlarged or offered in different combinations, business policy questions involving marketing and distribution channels, pricing concepts, and other fundamentals become involved.

But there is a third way in which technological change, he says, affects business decisions. This is the social change which is brought about as a result of technological innovation, and which, he contends, opens to business its greatest opportunities and poses the gravest of threats.

The business implications of the first two levels mentioned above are, of course, highly important, and will receive ample attention in the chapters to follow. Here, however, we wish to underscore the entrepreneurial implications of the social changes resulting from technology, which ironically, says John Diebold, while most important are the least understood. As he told his financial-executive audience:

The greatest success stories and the worst tragedies in business history relate to the ability of businessmen to perceive this level of meaning of the technological change going on about them and the opportunities they present. This is more true today than ever before, and it is this impact of technological change on business decisions and policy that requires the greatest imagination and presents the greatest rewards.

> **"Automation in the Future,"**
> *keynote address before the 37th International Conference of the Financial Executives Institute, New York, New York,*
> **October 25, 1968.**

TECHNOLOGY AND SOCIAL CHANGE

The accumulating and ramifying social change, says John Diebold, will in turn result in more profound consequences for business than the specific changes which spawned it. As he told an international audience:

If we adopt the long view of history, it is to the social change brought on by technology that we must look for the real meaning of our current technological revolution. After all, it is to this change that we really apply the word revolution — not to the machines.

The industrial revolution was revolutionary because it created a whole new environment for mankind — a whole new way of life. What it gave to history was much more than the steam engine and the cotton gin, the railway and the power loom. It gave society a whole new tempo, a whole new outlook.

It took men off the fields and out of small shops and put them for the first time into factory life. Hence it gave us mass production, and through mass production the first civilization in history in which luxury was not confined to a few . . .It gave us a sense of material progress, an itch to get ahead, which is unknown in those parts of the world which are still pre-industrial.

In other words, the machines which it produced were agents for enormous social change. No one, least of all Richard Arkwright or James Watt, thought that they were changing civilization itself. Yet for us, looking back, that is precisely what was *revolutionary* about the inventions they made.

The current technological revolution promises to have far wider effects than mere technology. Like James Watt and Richard Arkwright, many of our inventors have no intention of reshaping our entire world. Yet that is what they are unwittingly doing.

> **"Technology's Challenge to Management,"**
> *address before the Plenary Session, European Confer-*
> *ence of The High Authority of the European Coal and*
> *Steel Community, The Commission of the European*
> *Economic Community, The Commission of the Euro-*
> *pean Atomic Energy Community, Brussels, Belgium,*
> **December 6, 1960.**

But what makes the "second industrial revolution" of even greater significance than the first, in John Diebold's view, is the rate of the social changes induced by technology. That is why, as we shall discuss in detail in the following chapter, he has always insisted that the element of change itself must be incorporated as a fundamental part of the management planning process more than has generally been the case. The following observations highlight the need for the kind of social awareness and qualitative interpretation that he has said must form the basis for a systematic program of business innovation:

The continuing increase in the standard of living — despite the drains of war and defense — brought about by technological change, will continue to have a tremendous effect on the demand for discretionary goods — entertainment, travel, sports, books.

Hand-in-hand with this is the continuing increase in leisure, which is creating whole new businesses in the do-it-yourself field, and is providing the time for travel and entertainment which the rise in real income makes possible.

The social unrest caused by the great disparities in the distribution of our increasing material wealth will certainly create continuing and growing problems in the way business is done, in the social responsibilities that must be assumed (e.g., creating jobs for hard-core unemployed, preserving racial balance in work forces, recognizing minority groups in advertising and marketing policies), and in the stance business must assume as regards public and community relations, education, housing, transportation, and the like.

Changes in public taste and concepts of permissiveness in behavior (the pill, a product of twentieth-century technology, has certainly been operative here) will profoundly influence the way in which products are advertised and sold.

A related phenomenon is the shift in population mix, with marked changes in the proportions of the old and the young, which will continue to affect consumer orientation. The so-called "youth market" has been heavily preoccupying the professional platform and press of marketers and advertisers — not only in terms of the demographic change that will soon make half of our population under 25, but also in terms of the increased precociousness of teeners and preteeners whose generous allowances give them a purchasing power to be reckoned with, and the increasing influence of the very young on purchases of food, entertainment, vacations, and even the family car.

"Suburbia" and "exurbia," brought into being by the automobile, are creating ever more elaborate shopping centers and "super-super" markets, with profound effect on the way products must be packaged, priced, and displayed.

The practical disappearance of the servant from urban middleclass and upper-middleclass America (itself a result of technology that has made jobs in factories and offices more attractive than domestic service) has been a powerful stimulus, and at the same time an effect of, the home-appliance industry, and has had an effect on housing, home furnishings, ready — or almost-ready — cooked foods, restaurant dining, and a host of other consumer products and services.

> **"Technology's Challenge to Management,"**
> *and elaborative remarks at meetings of Diebold Research Group sponsors,*
> **January 7, 1965.**

The foregoing listing, which is only a series of snapshots, so to speak, of phenomena in continuing flux, obviously adds up to significant problems in business management. However, the basic point John Diebold makes — and which we in these opening pages and in the immediately following chapters wish to emphasize before addressing ourselves to the administrative aspects of the new information technology — is that the phenomena mentioned present exciting entrepreneurial opportunities for managements who see in technology not only specific innovations to be applied to existing products and processes, but also a cumulative force profoundly changing our entire society.

"RETHINKING" THE EXISTING BUSINESS

It is this insight which led John Diebold to the corollary theme that has recurred in his speeches and writings, and has been recognized as one of his most influential contributions to management thinking. That theme is his continuing reiteration of the need for management to "rethink" its products and processes and in fact the basic function of the business as a whole in light of the opportunities inherent in social changes resulting from technology.

Such rethinking, as shown in Chapters 3 and 4, requires constant re-examination of what a business is and should be in terms of possible current and future user needs. Rethinking, as we quote him later, is an "attitude," the "ability to get outside of a problem and see it in a new and perhaps wholly different way." It is much more than the application of advanced technologies to specific production or data-processing aspects of a business, or improving products for merely existing markets.

Chapter 3 develops in detail, with case examples from the machine-tool and petroleum industries, the concept of "defining the real function of the business." However, to underscore the importance of the concept, some "preview" quotations are well worth offering here. (The first of these, incidentally, points up the inroads of competition from entirely different industries if a given industry is not alert to the need for "rethinking" in terms of its user needs.):

Next week, for example, at the Philadelphia convention of the American Society of Tool Engineers, the Hillyer Instrument Company — an electronics manufacturer — will display for the first time a new feedback-controlled positioning and drilling machine. This machine is similar in function, though not in construction, to the positioning device built by the General Electric Company under a Signal Corps contract. Both these machines are of great importance to the electronics industry in the drilling and punching of short runs of electronic chassis. But the most significant thing about the Hillyer machine seems to me to be the fact that an *electronics manufacturer,* not a *machine tool builder,* is the first to offer for sale a standard line of such equipment. Some of the more farsighted machine tool builders are already deep in feedback work, but other electronics companies are even now deciding whether to enter this market themselves.

> **"The Impact of Automatic Control on Industry,"**
> *address before the Symposium on Automatic Production of Electronic Equipment, sponsored by the Stanford Research Institute and the United States Air Force, San Francisco, California,*
> **April 20, 1954.**

Study the changes in your customer's organization! The emergence of the manufacturing-engineering function is symptomatic of the change that has taken place in the way customers buy machine tools. This development demands serious study in terms of selling capabilities rather than just making machines for use in production. For manufacturing capabilities is what your customers really buy. Your customer doesn't care whether he buys a lathe or a punch press, he just wants to produce his parts in the best way possible.

"The Revolution That Fails to Take Place,"
address before the National Machine Tool Builders Association, Cincinnati, Ohio,
May 3, 1963.

In speaking of necessary management vision, I am speaking of much more than rationalization of existing methods of doing business and of making equipment and procedures compatible, or the doing of business on a more extensive geographical scope.

Something akin to the great entrepreneurial decisions or insights of business definition should be called forth if we are to use the new technology brilliantly. This is not the kind of development we can predict — but we must have ample conceptions of the enterprise if we are to use it properly.

"Management and Railroad Cybernetics,"
address before the Plenary Session, International Railway Union, Symposium on Cybernetics, Paris, France,
November 4, 1963.

While technology may threaten some products and services with obsolescence, it will create opportunities for enterprising companies to engage in new business ventures.

One example is the new data service industry already on the horizon. Several large companies are offering data services to other companies and to universities, not merely to gain a foothold in a new market, but as an exercise in public relations. In Japan, one newspaper company, recognizing that the publishing industry is destined to undergo a fundamental change, has begun transmitting its newspaper directly into the home by television. Similarly, dramatic changes are bound to come about in retailing, banking, warehousing, office equipment manufacturing, education, and many other activities. To take advantage of the opportunities these changes offer, management must fully understand the direction in which information technology is leading.

"The Computer's Changing Role,"
Management Today
January, 1969

NEW BUSINESSES

The same type of thinking applies, of course, to grasping entrepreneurial opportunities in the totally new industries and services that new technology is opening up. The management stance to assume in order to be aware of and plan for these is discussed in detail in the following chapter on planning, and in Chapter 16 which gives John Diebold's observations on the need to develop methods for scientific, technological, and socio-economic forecasting. Again, to put this whole book in the proper, imaginative perspective, some additional quotations are worth giving here in "preview."

The design, manufacture, installation, and maintenance of automatic control equipment has created *a new industry* and *new professions*. Composed of many old and well-established firms as well as many new ones, the automatic control industry is young and incredibly vigorous. This year [1954] some 750 companies will sell about $3 billion worth of control systems, components, and automatic end-products to industry and government. Still in its infancy, and as yet unrecognized by the financial statisticians, its sales figures are often mixed in other aggregates.

> **"Automation – Its Impact on Human Relations,"**
> *address before the Congress of American Industry,*
> *National Association of Manufacturers, New York,*
> *New York,*
> **December 3, 1954.**

Automation will create new industries and give a shot in the arm to some old ones, so that whatever is lost on the swings will be gained on the roundabouts. The most commonly cited new industry that it has created is the manufacture of polyethylene which demands an exquisite precision in timing that is beyond human achievement . . . The manufacture of automation equipment alone will increase employment in such industries as machine tools, electronics, and computer manufacture. Employment in electronics, now [1958] up to about 1.5 million, has grown at least ten times since 1939.

> **"The Economic and Social Effects of Automation,"**
> *address before the 2nd International Congress on*
> *Cybernetics, International Cybernetics Association,*
> *Namur, Belgium,*
> **September 3-10, 1958.**

New industries and new businesses are made possible by developments in information technology. The manufacturing of equipment and components, and the supplying of systems are major and growing fields in industry. Less obvious are the emergence and growth of many service enterprises utilizing the systems: there are already [1961] several hundred data processing service centers; the information retrieval field will produce new businesses; foreign language translation will produce new business; the growth of systems to perform routine tasks such as making hotel and airline reservations will produce new businesses. Businesses based on software, like my own company, are emerging as a new and promising field.

> **"Applications of Automation,"**
> *address before the International Chamber of Com-*
> *merce, Paris, France,*
> **November 21, 1961.**

*Remote-access terminals linked to nation-wide (and already, in a few cases, international) computer "data banks" and communication networks have created the opportunity to sell information in totally new ways. Chapter 13 presents a case study of a whole new industry that has developed in this field — the computer-based information services — which The Diebold Research Program studies quoted there now estimate as doing an annual volume of upwards of $50 million, with a multi-**billion** dollar market in sight. Again peering ahead to Diebold Research Program findings later discussed, in order to dramatize the point here:*

Hundreds of computer-generated indexing services are being offered that help control the printed flood resulting from our "knowledge explosion." A dramatic example is the world's largest medical information storage and retrieval system, MEDLARS, developed by the National Medical Library Association, part of a $3-million center utilizing a large-scale computer that began operations in Bethesda, Maryland in 1964. It currently indexes and cross references some 25,000 issues of medical journals a year, containing some 250,000 articles . . .Projections of The Diebold Research Program analysts indicate that by 1975 over five billion dollars of such services will be provided yearly in the United States alone. These will be primarily for professional users. However, it is expected that in the mid 1970s a significant consumer market for such services will develop.

Diebold Research Program studies,
1965-1966

ENTREPRENEURIAL OPPORTUNITY AS AN "EXTRA"

*In addition to the foregoing approaches, there is one further insight which, on the basis of existing literature, John Diebold has apparently been alone in advancing at professional gatherings and in the business and professional press. This is his many reminders of the highly profitable entrepreneurial opportunities that exist in exploiting, **as new businesses in themselves**, technologies that are at first blush assumed to be fulfilling their maximum potential when applied to speeding up existing operations or reducing costs, or to improving existing products.*

He agrees, of course, that these traditional applications are important in themselves, and deserve all of the attention that competent technicians and other specialists can supply. However, he calls for top management to turn its eyes outward as well as inward when it views new technology:

Many businesses that install automation devices make a serious mistake. When new equipment performs old tasks more efficiently, the executives suppose that they are reaping the full benefits of automation. But they are missing the much more important potential of automation: its capacity for new venture and business expansion.

"Facing Up to Automation,"
The Saturday Evening Post,
September 22, 1962.

While the process industries frequently develop lucrative by-product businesses (often in markets quite unconnected with their main business) — in most industries, he says, managements seems to have a blind spot in this connection which is costly in terms of opportunities lost. And even in processing industries there may be surprising lapses in applying this type of entrepreneurial thinking, as shown by the following example cited by John Diebold:

A case in point is a venerable hundred-year-old drug and pharmaceutical company with sales in the $250 million range. The company had a falloff in profit of almost 33 percent over a seven-year period, in the face of a 77 percent rise in drug industry profits. A leading figure in the industry was brought in as the new chairman and chief executive officer. He immediately overhauled management, started a commercially oriented research and development setup, and launched a strenuous program to cut costs.

His cost cutting extended to the most remote corners of operations. For example, the company normally uses about a million eggs a week in which to grow vaccines. The labs used to throw the unused parts of the eggs away. Now the company sells the yolks to mink breeders and is looking into the possibility of selling the shells as a source of lime for plant food.

> **"Applications of Automation,"**
> *address before the International Chamber of Commerce, Paris, France,*
> **November 21, 1961**

The Hillyer Instrument Company example cited earlier could be considered as falling into this type of opportunity. Another example is the use by International Minerals and Chemicals Company of its marketing simulation, discussed in Chapter 5. There (again we are "previewing") a computerized marketing simulation was developed originally for the company's own marketing analysis. However, information developed by using its economic model of a farm has been developed into a service showing how the farmer can do a better job, including what the best possible blends of fertilizers are for his particular soil condition. While this is not sold as a separate package, it solves problems for customers and is a powerful creative marketing weapon. It is entirely conceivable that developments of this sort could be turned into new saleable items.

Of course, many of the computer-based inquiry services discussed in Chapter 13 are offshoots of information technology initially applied internally in an existing business. In this connection, John Diebold had in earlier discussions pointed to the publishing industry as an example of such opportunities:

When you start dealing with more advanced forms of this technology, the biggest question is: how do you define your need? What kind of installation do you really need *to run the business?* Then you come quickly down to the question of the definition of the business.

Publishing is a good example. Here traditionally one has thought in terms of the mechanizing, advertising, billing, list-maintenance, and so on. But if you look closely at the business of publishing you discover that the business really is dissemination of information, and the consequence of the technology is that you may be able to offer quite new services. I think this has parallels in many industries . . .

> **"John Diebold's Vista of Automation,"**
> *Business,*
> **December, 1965.**

The publishing enterprise is going to take new form, and through it you will offer new editorial services. Your publishing firms will offer new kinds of services to other papers, as well as to the public.

Electronic morgue services and special local and regional information can be sold by publishers over the data transmission facilities of our telephone system . . . Supplementary and specialized publications can be compiled using the extensive material you have on hand and easily accessible in electronic memory systems — doing for newspapers what book publishing is beginning to do for magazines.

> **"The Editor and Automation,"**
> *address before the American Society of Newspaper Editors, Washington, D.C.,*
> **April 9, 1963.**

THE DRAMA OF CHANGE

As John Diebold says, we are living in a world in which only one thing is sure — change, fundamental change. But the paradox is that despite the pace and impact of change, most people instinctively cling to a tomorrow that looks like today. And strangely enough this entanglement with the past is characteristic not only of people in general, but of **business** *people and public policy makers. In times of peace, generals plan for the last war. Corporate managements, even those who are proud of their "long-range planning," are prone to cast projections based on the past into* **patterns** *based on the past.*

In 1953 John Diebold said:

Being accustomed to the innovations of the scientist is one thing; recognizing their significance is another. Taken together these many gadgets form a pattern, and it is a pattern that will have more meaning for our individual lives and for our collective future than the double-mushroom shape of atomic explosions. For the TV baby-sitter cameras, the computing machines, and the self-operating controls are only the first hardware of a new industrial era.

"Factories Without Men: New Industrial Revolution,"
The Nation,
September 19, 1953.

A decade-plus later, he still felt it necessary to call for a greater awareness of the true implications of technological change:

We do not take anything like as far-ranging a view of the future as we could. The data are available to us to anticipate what technological changes will occur over the next ten years. But people have a terrible tendency to believe that the world will stay as it is — even when scientists in the laboratory are working on devices which will make it radically different.

John Diebold as quoted in an article about him, "Mr.
Automation Looks to the Future,"
The Times Review of Industry and Technology,
June, 1964.

The mighty forces of change that are apparent all about us are changing business and marketing management in a most fundamental manner. "New product" programs alone are meaningless symptoms of an effort to cope with this change. It is only when they evolve from a business plan that displays true insight into the nature of the enterprise and its environment that they will have meaning in the future.

"A Short, Fast Step to Tomorrow,"
Printer's Ink,
May 29, 1964.

And only yesterday:

New-product, diversification, and acquisition programs are often a symptom of management groping with a fundamental and environmental change, the real nature of which may not have been identified . . .The fundamental problem is that of coping with a far more rapid and basic change than we have ever known; it presents business with an almost totally new situation, requiring quite new entrepreneurial, as well as managerial concepts.

An interview for the
Financial Times of London,
January 3, 1969.

John Diebold's thesis of the pervasiveness of technologically induced changes, and the opportunities they present, calls for a new function of management — the "management of innovation." In the following chapter we see how he proposes to incorporate this into the process of planning.

Photograph by Marvin Newman

The new business opportunities inherent in technological change have always been a principal theme of John Diebold's speeches, books and articles, and business counsel since the beginning of his career. He is seen here on a 1960 inspection tour through a French computer factory

2

Like the pioneers of the Industrial Revolution in the 18th century, we face a world in which only one thing is sure: change, fundamental change. We are leaving the pushbutton age and entering an age when the buttons push themselves. We should greatly benefit from it. Farsighted and aggressive managements see not only the possibility of decreasing operating costs, but also of entering the field with new products and new services.

"Automation – The Challenge to Management,"
address before the British Institute of Management, Harrogate, England,
November 18, 1955.

In many fields there is no longer time to sit back and profit by a competitor's mistakes. We are already seeing situations in which only the first in the field has a chance to make a profit, not those who copy him, for another basic change in technology is by then already taking place.

"A Short, Fast Step to Tomorrow,"
Printer's Ink,
May 29, 1964.

*We are now beginning to get to the point at which senior management is addressing itself to the question of what to do with the new information technology . . . Senior management is beginning to realize that . . . dramatic things can be accomplished if people **who know the objectives of a business** will take the responsibility of putting these new capabilities to work.*

"Business, Computers, and the Turn Toward Technology,"
address before the Economic Club of Chicago, Chicago, Illinois,
February 24, 1966.

Change as an Active Element in Planning

Technological and social change must be incorporated as an active element in business planning and strategy.

With John Diebold's early insight into the true significance to business of accelerating technology – namely its creation of profound social changes that, along with new problems, create totally new business opportunities, rather than technology's *admittedly important effects upon production costs and management information systems — it is logical that he should always have insisted that change itself, and especially the **rate** of change, must be the central element in business planning.*

THE NEW ENTREPRENEURIAL MILIEU

This recurring motif in his writings and speeches over the years is indicated by the quotations with which this chapter opens. In the Brussels address cited below, he pointed out that technological change and its concomitant effects are indeed the central fact of our times, creating an entirely different and ever-evolving entrepreneurial milieu:

The technological developments which we have witnessed as a steady parade since the end of World War II are not a single burst originating from military work — a spurt from which we will recover. They are but the beginning of a continuum of fundamental change — a phenomenon that will continue at an increasing rate for as long ahead as we can see a future.

> **"Technology's Challenge to Management,"**
> *address before the Plenary Session, European Conference of The High Authority of the European Coal and Steel Community, The Commission of the European Economic Community, The Commission of the European Atomic Energy Community, Brussels, Belgium,*
> **December 6, 1960.**

*The intervening years have amply borne out that observation. However, the rapidity with which innovations become a familiar part of everyday life sometimes makes us lose sight of the suddenness with which they came upon us. In 1945, for example, television, jet travel, and digital computer industries were commercially nonexistent. In 1965, these industries contributed more than $13 billion to our Gross National Product, and an estimated 90,000 jobs. In 1949, television had been in the laboratory about three years, and there were a few thousand sets in use. A short ten years later, the industry reported that television sets, tubes, components, and various materials going into components represented upward of $885 million in business. For 1967 the figure was $2.4 billion, and today (1971) the figure according to **Electronic News** is over three billion dollars.*

This onslaught of technological change, says John Diebold, will increasingly focus attention on the planning process. Some of the basic reasons he has cited are:

Product life is being shortened. The traditional cycle of product innovation is being telescoped — not by planned obsolescence or styling changes, but by genuine technological innovation . . . [If] it is only the leader who has a chance to make a profit [and] a secondary position becomes untenable, the risks of the leader increase. So must the possibility of profit, or he should not enter the field.

The reaction time of management must shorten. The time leeway in adapting to new technologies has disappeared. Companies must keep track of a number of fundamental areas of scientific work and must react rapidly to apply this work when the time is right. They must consciously plan to be the ones who obsolete not only their own products, but their very industries.

The life of business and industrial processes as well as products are being both shortened and changed. Much of the new technology, particularly that part of it dealing with information processing, profoundly changes the manner in which business is being conducted.

The increased complexity and tightened interrelationship of functions within a single organization, together with the ever more complex relationships with other organizations, means that successful — and successful is increasingly coming to mean *rapid* — adjustment to change is impossible without a high order of skill in planning.

> **"Technology's Challenge to Management,"**
> *address before the Plenary Session, European Confer-*
> *ence of The High Authority of the European Coal and*
> *Steel Community, The Commission of the European*
> *Economic Community, The Commission of the Euro-*
> *pean Atomic Energy Community, Brussels, Belgium,*
> **December 6, 1960.**

Innovative Risks

Fifteen to twenty years ago, the average life span between the conception of a new product and its introduction as a profitable item of manufacture was from one to three years. In recent years, this time span for research and development and product introduction has lengthened to three to five years, and sometimes to eight. The marketplace, says John Diebold, will no longer accept just any product. To be successful, a new product today, as he told a client group, must have a higher degree of sophistication, and therefore has longer development and test requirements:

In connection with some products, governmental regulations and test requirements have imposed additional time lags. For example, the length of time required to test a new pharmaceutical drug, because of new Government regulations, has lengthened to three to five years before market sale, not to mention the research and development time required to get the drug in readiness for testing. This lengthening of R&D time is paralleled in many industries. Even where exceptions may be noted — as in the extraordinary speeds achieved in some electronic innovations — the development investment required is enormous.

Durables are especially subject to risk. Six to eight years may elapse between the original concept of a new piece of equipment and delivery of tested units to customers. In that period much can happen to the business climate and to the target market in particular . . .

Many types of research and development programs require almost back-breaking investment before payout. Du Pont, for example, has reported that it invested $27 million in research, development, and plastic facilities for nylon before large-scale production was achieved. Dacron polyester fiber was an $80 million project. This does not mean, of course, that innovation can be carried on only by industrial giants. It does emphasize the need for careful determination of technical and commercial feasibility before extensive projects are undertaken.

> *Opening remarks to a meeting of the senior managers of sponsor firms of The Diebold Research Program — Europe, Mainz, Germany.*
> **September 15, 1970.**

Since time in development and test is equivalent to dollars of investment, increasingly greater blocks of corporate discretionary funds are today being risked on new products. The penalty for error is correspondingly greater. After bitter experience, many firms, as reported in Diebold Research Program studies, have found that helter-skelter product development can be economically ruinous. It follows that a detailed and orderly planning activity, both as to choice of ventures and mode of implementation, is imperative to minimize the risk.

Marketing Risks

*On the other side of the innovation cycle, the average profitable time span for **marketing** a new product has been decreasing rapidly. Managements can no longer count on long profitable runs of stable products as sources of continued growth and income. This means, as John Diebold pointed out in the 1960 Brussels speech cited earlier, that return on investment must be higher in these new fields in order to justify the increased risk. Conversely, he said, business must take bigger risks for sufficient return when technological change is great. In the fast moving computer field, for example, the costs of entering the new industry exceeded everyone's expectation, and* *manufacturers who planned for a low rate of return have been forced out of the business... On other occasions he reverted to this problem of shortened marketing time:*

A 1966 study showed that 50 per cent of the profits of the major chemical firms came from products which had not existed eight years before that, and it was anticipated that at least a similar turnover would occur in the following six years, since the rate of technological change in the industry was expected to increase, not diminish.

"The Use of Computers in Long-Range Corporate Planning,"
Diebold Research Program Report,
September, 1967.

In durables, the foreshortened marketing span can be especially risky and costly. Innovations by competitors may force expensive model revisions and improvements, and even total withdrawal from the market, only a few years after introduction. General-purpose computers offer a dramatic example. Introduced only twenty years ago, they have gone through three "generations" and are on the brink of the fourth. The high obsolescence rate of computers is emphatically shown in the length of time manufacturers have kept computer models in production before superseding them with later designs. The periods have ranged from 18 to 20 months. I note by contrast an estimate attributed to a Ford executive that the original Ford engine cost $50,000 to develop, and had almost 20 years of useful life with minor modification.

"Youth and Business"
commencement address presented upon receipt of an honorary Doctor of Engineering degree, Newark College of Engineering, Newark, New Jersey,
May 27, 1970.

Related to the foregoing is the shortening life span of entire industries, and the impact upon them of new technologies which drastically change profitability patterns and survival strategies. John Diebold touched upon these developments in the remarks cited above:

TV changed the entire economic balance of Hollywood moviedom, as well as, of course, the total character of radio network programming. It contributed heavily to the survival problem of the mass publishing industry (where are *Liberty, Colliers,* and *The Saturday Evening Post*?). The publishing industry as a whole – newspapers, books, and the trade and technical press – is currently going through convulsions because of its delayed and cumbersome response to shattering *social* changes wrought by technology, and because of its failure to avail itself of automation and information technology in its internal operations.

Network TV, a key villain in the piece, is itself now under a technological threat of which many in the industry are apparently unaware: The proliferation of ultra-high frequency channels, coupled with Government-controlled (and available to competing communications outlets) output from communications satellites, providing instant news and special events coverage from all parts of the globe, will inevitably change the whole pattern of TV network programming.

> **"Conversation with John Diebold,"**
> *Script for interview with Harry Reasoner, released with long-playing record by Listening Library, Record No. AA3321,*
> **1968.**

Even the side effects of technological change are posing serious threats to entrenched industries, as witness, for example, responsible voices raised not long ago in the California legislature proposing to ban categorically all internal combustion engines from that state because of the growing concern over air pollution. As regards the problem of air pollution itself — belabored by ecologists and concerned citizens for many years before it became a vociferous public issue — the automobile industry (and it is not alone in this respect by any means) has until very recently taken what John Diebold has said could only be described as "an ostrich's-head-in-the-sand posture." But the problem, he adds, will definitely not be made to go away by not looking at it. (His views on this and related issues, which he began calling to managements' attention long before there was public discussion of the subject, are taken up in further detail in the concluding chapter of this book, on business and public policy.)

THE IMPACT OF INFORMATION TECHNOLOGY ON STRATEGIC PLANNING

The use of management science, computers, and information technology in general for strategic, long-range planning is still in the infant stage. However, findings of The Diebold Research Program indicate that usage will markedly increase within this decade.

Present applications of ADP to strategic planning have been in those areas more accurately characterized as *tactical* planning, where operations research techniques have been successful. These include essentially short-term problems such as optimizing distribution patterns, optimal short-term employment of equipment and capital, short-term market changes and forecasting, and the like. Strategic planning in the sense of explicating corporate goals and searching for new opportunities is just beginning to be addressed by computer techniques.

Figure 2-A

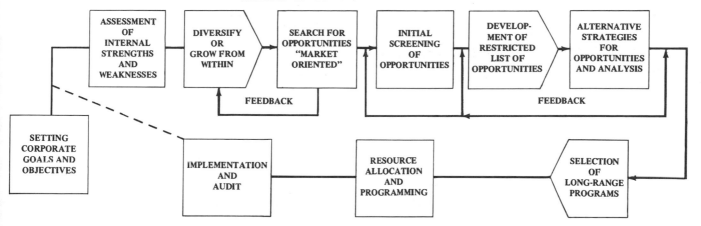

STAGES OF LONG-RANGE PLANNING

Source: The Diebold Research Program

Figure 2 A represents the long-range planning process in a form susceptible of being viewed as an information flow. It is presented here as a backdrop for comments on the present "state of the art" and future potentials and opportunities as regards adding the information-technology dimensions to traditional strategic planning processes. In this light, long-range planning can be viewed as comprising ten distinct operations, with feedback loops cycling the results back into the system:

1. Setting corporate objectives and goals.

2. Assessment of internal strengths and weaknesses.

3. Diversity of grow-from-within decision.

4. Search for new opportunities.

5. Initial screening of opportunities.

6. Development of a restricted list of opportunities.

7. Development of alternate strategies for opportunities and analysis.

8. Selection of long-range programs.

9. Resource allocation and programming.

10. Implementation and audit.

"The Use of Computers in Long-Range Corporate Planning,"
Diebold Research Program Report,
September, 1967.

There is as yet no single, integrated corporate long-range planning model which will encompass all of the stages of the planning cycle here depicted. As a matter of fact, John Diebold has felt it necessary to "play down" some exaggerated notions which have gained currency:

Still in the realm of science fiction is the scene of the chief executive in the board room with a conversational terminal display device tied into a central computer — with the latter containing a "universal" data base consisting of the company's total economic and market environment and its variables, the product-line attributes, the continually updated internal corporate data, and the formulae and analytic programs for processing the data. In this scene the chief executive propounds in rapid fire — a series of "if we do this, what then?" questions, and in response to this voice input the computer in conversational mode supplies estimates of markets, sales, probable profits, and probable return on investment, together with a measure of the degree of uncertainty inherent in any of the alternative strategy lines.

> **"Business, Computers and the Turn Toward Technology,"**
> *address before the Economic Club of Chicago, Chicago, Illinois*
> **February 24, 1966.**

The Diebold Group does not mean to imply that there are no plans for completely comprehensive models in the minds of today's management theoreticians, or that respectable portions of the long-range planning process have not been augmented by management science techniques or the use of ADP. The point is that during this decade, corporate managements will be well advised to build market-product models and financial analysis and summary models with inherent risk-analysis capabilities, rather than attempting the synthesis of a total corporate model covering the complete range of corporate activities.

The Diebold Research Program believes that any company with sales greater than $100,000,000 can afford and easily justify the expenditure of $100,000 to $200,000 on a financial model with risk-analysis capabilities. A comprehensive market-product, alternate-strategy model is more expensive and can cost as much as $800,000. Where R&D allocations are of an order of magnitude greater than this amount, such a model can also be satisfactorily justified. A total corporate model could easily cost well over $1,000,000. It would appear that the present state-of-the-art does not promise an adequate payoff for an expenditure of this order.

> **"The Use of Computers in Long-Range Corporate Planning,"**
> *Diebold Research Program Report,*
> **September, 1967.**

Stages 1 through 3

Very little effort has thus far been devoted to applying advanced information technology to Stages 1 through 3. The first, setting corporate goals and objectives, is by and large still done on a highly intuitive basis. Top managements, say the Diebold analysts, still invariably couch corporate goals in such general terms ("to achieve maximum growth in profits," "to broaden the product base to provide increased stability") as to be useless to the theoretical model builder. However, the setting of quantified corporate goals is, they and John Diebold insist, fundamental to the long-range planning process.

The process of assessing internal strengths and weaknesses (Stage 2) is primarily a qualitative one. However, advanced storage and retrieval techniques must and will be used increasingly to provide company data to support overall qualitative assessments. Even so, this stage will in general not be susceptible of dramatic ADP assistance.

Stage 3, the decision to diversify or grow internally, is the first of three major decision levels, and markedly affects the next three stages. The choice between diversifying or growing internally is not strictly a go or no-go decision, and hence not primarily one for computer analysis. It may, however, utilize the computer output of Stage 4, the search stage, as feedback to help determine those areas where diversification is feasible.

> **"The Use of Computers in Long-Range Corporate Planning,"**
> *Diebold Research Program Report,*
> **September, 1967.**

The risks of diversification are high, and many diversification moves are unsuccessful. For example, during the past ten years, several aerospace firms attempted to capitalize on their aluminum-fabrication skill to produce aluminum-based products for the consumer market. However, the consumer market requirement for highly efficient, low-cost production was totally antithetical to the method of building airplanes and missiles, and the diversification attempts failed. In retrospect, the decision to diversify was made prior to a true assessment of the aerospace companies' strengths and weaknesses, and the results were painfully expensive.

> **"A Short, Fast Step to Tomorrow,"**
> *Printer's Ink,*
> **May 26, 1964.**

Stage 4

The search for opportunities stage is an area in which management science will make major contributions over the next ten years. The Diebold Research Program expects that gross models of the economy will be constructed and equipped with specific search mode capability. Such models will systematically isolate those areas of economic growth where the projected volume and profit potential coincides with requirements stated in the quantified corporate goals:

Highly sophisticated developments are in the offing. Market research firms and a number of universities have begun to do substantial work in modeling total segments of the United States economy. M.I.T., for example, has a gross dynamic model of the consumer market. Other progressive work is going on at Carnegie Tech and the University of Chicago . . . Numerous sophisticated methodologies are being explored which will result in models, that will, for example, assess the characteristics that enable one technology to displace another, and predict the changes in and effects of these characteristics over the planning horizon of the firm.

> **"The Use of Computers in Long-Range Corporate Planning,"**
> *Diebold Research Program Report,*
> **September, 1967.**

Stages 5 and 6

Initial screening, Stage 5, identifies the critical variables in each opportunity, and reduces the list to manageable proportions for further detailed analysis and selection. This stage will be markedly improved through management science, with impressive gains projected by The Diebold Research Program for the first half of this decade. Using enterprise models and simulations, companies will with greater precision establish initial cutoff profitability rates, together with other decision rules by which to screen identified opportunities.

With simulation models, management can test the most outlandish schemes emanating from "brainstorming" sessions with little expenditure of time and manpower. By asking "what if" questions about changed attributes or parameters of a product, it can quickly obtain the kind of information needed to decide whether a given product idea is feasible.

> *Diebold Research Program findings.*

At Stage 6, the planning group presents its ranked list of opportunities to top management, relating them to the goals and objectives of the firm, and offering recommendations based on its simulation analyses. The resultant output is a management go or no-go regarding further detailed analysis.

> *Diebold Research Program findings.*

Stage 7

In this development of alternate strategies and analysis stage The Diebold Research Program expects the greatest progress to be made in the early years of this decade:

Management science techniques will take the form of linking models which derive specific market and sales potentials for specific products and strategies, coupled with models which will generate cost factors and financial returns. These linked models will have the capability of varying the magnitude and timing of product development, introduction, and sales for scientific assessment of return potentials and risk . . . Game theory mathematics will permit the structuring of a limited multi-company market-price model. All management-science techniques will be applicable, from linear programming to sophisticated decision-tree analysis and Monte Carlo simulation.

"The Use of Computers in Long-Range Corporate Planning,"
Diebold Research Program Report,
September, 1967.

Stage 8

The final decision stage, selecting those long-range products, projects, and strategies that the company will pursue, will never, in John Diebold's view, be fully "automated," although some prophets continue to promote this concept.

Stages 9 and 10

Once decisions are made on products and strategy, management has made the commitment to implementation. Stages 9 and 10 are therefore concerned with drawing up detailed step-by-step plans, determining the time sequencing involved, and allocating dollars to each detail step. Much management science work has been done in these areas, especially during the past five years, and much is presently in process. The substance of Stages 9 and 10 is operational, and further discussion of management science applications in connection with them will be reserved for applicable chapters to follow.

THE CHALLENGE TO MANAGEMENT

The "innovation imperatives" of the type to which John Diebold calls attention obviously call not only for more than alertness to technological change in a given industry and its component activity areas. Also needed are imaginative insight into *the effects of existing and over-the-horizon innovations that may at first glance be considered too far removed to have any discernible impact upon a business. What is called for here, he says, is a new approach – in fact, a new discipline, a new management function, already to some degree formalized in some companies – which he terms **technological forecasting**. This concept is discussed in further detail in Chapter 16. The applicability, in this connection, of "marketing data bases" which have evolved from developments in information technology are discussed in Chapter 5.*

*But an indispensable collateral approach is also required, he hastens to add – that of "rethinking" and redefining the nature and purpose of a business. This concept is further developed in Chapters 3 and 4, and in the case-example chapters of Part IV. Actually, he says, this approach does not begin with technology at all. Quite the contrary – it removes the mental blinders by which an over-preoccupation with its own technology may have narrowed management's thinking. It continually reviews the functions of the business, redefining it in broad and flexible terms related to ultimate user needs. The dividend will more often than not be the discovery of previously unsuspected **new markets** which may have been opened by technology – unsuspected because the applicable technology may have hitherto been considered only in connection with improving internal processes and procedures.*

PART II

Achieving Maximum Value from New Technologies Often Requires Rethinking and Redesign—of the Product, of the Process, and of the Business Itself

Redefining the functions of a business in terms of its current and future markets is central to John Diebold's management philosophy. He sounded this theme long before there was interest in or general understanding and acceptance of that concept and of its impact on business strategy.

3

Rethinking must be done on an extremely broad basis — viewing the objectives of the entire organization as a whole. It cannot be confined to the product design or engineering department. It must be an attitude, a state of mind, permeating the entire organization.

"Automation:The Advent of the Automatic Factory,"
Princeton, New Jersey: Van Nostrand Company, Inc.,
1952.

When you start having a lot more data available, you may find the best manager is the one who can ask the right questions.

"What Comes Next in the Computer Age,"
Interview with John Diebold, U.S. News & World Report,
June 26, 1967.

Functional Definition of the Business

The nature and objectives of the enterprise must be defined in a way that allows it to capitalize on new opportunities or consciously pass them by . . . The functions of a business must be re-examined in terms of the widest possible current and future markets.

*Innovation means more than the development and application of **new** concepts. It calls for the collateral and even precursive discarding of **old** concepts. Thus John Diebold has always been highly articulate about the over-riding need for "rethinking" traditional ways of doing things if a business is to take full advantage of advancing technology.*

*In his professional consulting practice, begun shortly after the publication of his widely quoted, widely translated **Automation: The Advent of the Automatic Factory**, he became concerned with the whole field of management, over and above the problems of factory and office automation. He soon saw that the concept of "rethinking" had to be applied to the very fundamentals of the business as a whole, and especially to its basic marketing objectives.*

What is involved, he repeatedly pointed out to client groups and other professional audiences, is much more than the application of advanced technologies to specific production or data-processing aspects of a business. That, he insisted, is basically a problem for technicians, not for top management. What is required, he said, is a strategic assessment of the problems and opportunities inherent in social changes resulting from technology in general:

As the goals, aspirations, needs, and wants of the individual shift, and shift again and again through the human social change induced by automation, the economic realities that sustain the enterprise will change . . . Rapid and major social shifts mean an entirely new and more day-to-day role for strategic planning in using the enterprise. For here lies the heart of business – ascertaining and filling human need – not the mere *techniques* of management, however important the latter may be.

> **"Automation: Perceiving the Magnitude of the Problem,"**
> *address presented at the 5th Annual Salute to the Alumni, Columbia University, New York,*
> **June 3, 1963.**

"Rethinking" cannot be put off with impunity. It must address itself (perhaps for the first time) to defining (1) the real nature and function of the business and (2) how the business relates to the unfolding advances in technology in general with their concomitant social changes. And it must be remembered that social changes will affect the desires and needs not only of individual consumers, but of industrial customers as well, since the latter will adjust their own market objectives in accordance with the changing needs of *their* customers. Only when all of these factors are added to the equation will management be in a position to take advantage of new technology in its R&D, production, and marketing activities.

> **"How Can Executive Management Maximize Its Ability to Use Data Processing?"**
> *address before the Executive Forum, 1964 International Data Processing Conference, Data Processing Management Association, New Orleans, Louisiana,*
> **June 24, 1964.**

DEFINING THE REAL FUNCTION OF THE BUSINESS

Such esoteric concepts as "defining the real function of the business" may, John Diebold concedes, be intuitively understood by successful entrepreneurs. However, he adds, the high rate of product failure indicates that they may be more widely misunderstood.

The essence of the approach called for, as he sees it, is (1) a sensitive awareness and response to the way in which customers perceive their needs, both in consumer and industrial markets; and (2) an alertness to perceive how technological change will inevitably change the habits and ways of doing business of existing customers, and so open up wholly new entrepreneurial opportunities in areas still unperceived by the users themselves. This is far different from the approach which has been traditional in business and industry generally and which (because of what has been termed "marketing myopia") has been characterized by product rather than customer orientation, and heavily locked into a company's and an industry's existing technology.

Redefinition of the basic function of the business in terms of customer need is the prime tenet of the "market concept" now increasingly discussed in professional marketing meetings and in marketing literature. It continually poses the question, "What is the customer really buying?" It is the kind of thinking that must be done by any far-sighted management before it even begins to think about the direction its research, product diversification, and acquisition program are to take.

In consumer markets, for example, it is being recognized that characterizing oneself as being part of the "food industry" may lead to an unconscious and costly narrowing of vision and goals. Consumers, as marketers see them now, do not buy food: they buy nutrition, good taste, gustatory gratification, social status, ceremony, time-saving (prepared foods), and many other *benefits* . . . They do not buy insurance, they buy anxiety reduction. In this connection, a recent example is the broadening of the concept of traditional life insurance, in recognition of anxieties about inflation — the packaging of equity investment with standard life insurance . . . Consumers do not buy *fuel oil*, they buy warmth and good health.

"Automation in the Future,"
keynote address before the 37th International Conference of the Financial Executives Institute, New York, New York,
October 25, 1968.

The Carborundum Company is an example of this type of thinking in the industrial field. Founded in 1894, the company was content for many years to sell abrasives, with an extremely broad line of grinding wheels, coated abrasives, and abrasive grain. The focus was on product. But in the mid 1950s, management saw that the market for abrasives could be broadened considerably if, looking at abrasives through the customers' eyes, it perceived the product as fitting into *metal-polishing, metal-cleaning,* and *metal removal systems.* The company is now concerned with all aspects of abrading — the machine, the contact wheel, the work piece, the labor cost. Above all, it is concerned with the *customer's needs* — not abrasives per se, but rather the creation of certain dimensions, type of finish, or required shapes. To meet this need, it set out to supply a *complete system.*

Based on remarks made before the Diebold Group Professional Development meeting, New York, New York,
June 2, 1969.

Much of the new technology, particularly that part of it dealing with information processing, profoundly changes the manner in which business is conducted. Companies must keep track of a number of fundamental areas of scientific work and must react rapidly to apply this work when the time is right. They must consciously plan to be the ones who obsolesce not only their own products, but their very industries.

For example, the American Telephone & Telegraph Co. expects that communication between machines in different cities will soon exceed voice communication over telephone lines. The consequences of such a change are staggering, not only for the telephone system, but for the procedures by which the remainder of U.S. business is conducted. It is only by a high order of planning that such a rate of change can be made to benefit a firm rather than its competitor.

The increased complexity and tightened interrelationship of functions within a single organization, together with the evermore complex relationships with other organizations, mean that successful — and successful is increasingly coming to mean rapid — adjustment to change is impossible without great skill in planning . . . For these reasons, and many more, planning as a process is a subject to which more attention must be given by business management. It begins, however, with a proper definition of the business.

> **"A Short, Fast Step to Tomorrow,"**
> *Printer's Ink,*
> **May 29, 1964.**

*In the above light, we can get a new insight into the high failure rate of new products. In this light, also, we can see the reasons for the stagnated growth of companies and industries, which, as John Diebold shows, are attributable not to failure of new products, but failure to do **any** imaginative innovation at all beyond the traditional parameters of their time-honored existing products and markets.*

In this whole matter of defining oneself into a market, or out of it, some Diebold observations on specific industries are illuminating:

Machine tools provide a prime example of an industry that has accumulated severe problems as a result of the inability to come to grips with its own role — with a true understanding of the essence of its business. Although machine tools are defined in general terms as power-driven machines used to shape or form, by cutting, impact, pressure, or electrical techniques, the machine-tool industry still tends to view itself as builders of *metal*-cutting and *metal*-forming machines. There is a strong resistance to widening the definition to "manufacturing" machines, and the emphasis is on boring machines, milling machines, lathes, punch presses, and similarly functionally specialized equipment.

The very term "builders" conveys much about the way machine-tool people think of themselves. Not as "marketers" to industry, but "builders" — builders for "orders." They incessantly talk of *filling* customer *orders* with a high-precision product designed for the craftsman.

What is wrong with such a view? It is too limited. A viable business is built with the customers' basic and underlying problems, as well as their craftsmen, in mind. The machine-tool industry has defined its business in such narrow terms that it has painted itself into a corner — of ever-decreasing relative size in American business — despite cyclical swings of prosperity. In spite of the industry's growth in absolute terms, *its customer industries have grown much faster.* The hard fact is that the machine-tool industry is not getting its attainable share of the capital-goods market. In fact, metal-cutting and metal-forming are techniques which its customers tend to engineer out of their products and processes. The latter, relying on the engineering support of *nonmetallic* material suppliers, are extensively replacing metal with other materials in their product designs.

What does definition of a business have to do with this? I would say that the industry leaders should give thought to defining their businesses as *suppliers of manufacturing systems and capabilities to all industries.* For example, in a recent year some $3 billion was spent for automated equipment — special machinery, process machinery, and package machinery — much of which could better be manufactured by machine-tool builders . . . Customers' needs should dictate the business, and the businesses should be market-oriented and receptive to technological inputs from any quarters. The aim should be to provide customers with a *manufacturing capability* – not only a particular, functionally oriented metal-working tool, but also the ability to make a product. Metal-cutting and metal-forming exclude many important manufacturing processes — welding, casting, molding, extruding, and powder metallurgy. The growth of plastics such as nylon, Teflon, delrin, polyethylene is important in industrial output.

The machine-tool industry has lost much of its business because it has refused to supply what the customer wanted. One survey showed that 83 percent of machine-tool customers engineer-build all or some of their new manufacturing equipment. Where applicable equipment is not available, in-plant engineers design and build it themselves . . . But much of it they are obtaining from other industry sources.

In short, the machine-tool industry has many new competitors because other industries are today fulfilling their customers' needs. The most threatening competitors are thus not located in Fond du Lac, Milwaukee, Bridgeport, Springfield, Cincinnati, or Rockford — traditional machine-tool centers. They are in Los Angeles, Seattle, San Diego, Detroit, Philadelphia, Pittsburgh, Wilmington, and along Boston's Route 28 and in Long Island, the centers of electronics automation. Their case is like the earlier one of the textile industry — whose members for years thought of competition as the firm across the street in Lowell or Fall River, but woke up one morning to realize that their customers' needs were being filled by a chemical manufacturer in Wilmington, or a man-made fiber company in Markus Hook, Pennsylvania.

In this connection it is interesting to note that of the six most important developments influencing metalworking since World War II, only one, shear spinning, originated with the machine-tool industry. Numerical control, electron beam, high energy rate forming, electric chemical machining, and electrical discharge machining were all developed outside of the machine-tool industry. Numerical control and electrical discharge machining were the only two innovations in whose development the machine-tool industry even participated — and this after the appearance of the innovation itself.

> **"The Revolution that Fails to Take Place,"**
> *address before the National Machine Tool Builders'*
> *Association, Cincinnati, Ohio,*
> **May 3, 1963.**

The petroleum industry has a history of defining its business to serve new markets created by technological change. Its largest single product today is gasoline, to serve the age of the automobile. At the turn of the century it was kerosene for illumination. A continuing redefinition is taking place to provide a wide range of energy products and petroleum derivatives such as synthetics. The industry is, in fact, beginning to think of itself not as a "petroleum" producer and marketer, but as a supplier of energy and a producer and marketer of the whole broad range of hydrocarbon products. This shift in the conception of the industry from product-orientation to use-orientation is accelerating. Example: Humble, when it renamed its Esso gasoline outlets, elected the brand name ENCO — Energy Company.

That the petroleum industry is finely attuned to the challenges and opportunities of advanced technology is evidenced by the record: In addition to its achievements in the laboratory and its translation of these into processes and products through applied engineering, it has pioneered in the use of computers and information technology in administrative processes, and in the application of operations research, linear programming, and other management-science techniques in management decision-making.

In the era confronting it, it cannot afford to lose any of this momentum. Gasoline and fuel oil, which now account for over 80 percent of the petroleum market, are not in any immediate danger of being replaced. Nevertheless, it is clear that the prime uses of petroleum — motive power, electric-power generation, fuel — are all undergoing fundamental changes. Some of these are already under development, and others are yet to be conceived. While the latter cannot be precisely predicted, their broad outlines must be continually subjected to intelligent surmise. As the inevitable technological breakthroughs come, their impact will be explosive. The industry will not have sixty years to adapt to the next product change as extensive as that brought about by the internal combustion engine. The day after the nuclear-power tanker is economically profitable, it will be obsolete as a carrier of bunker oil and of other currently used petroleum products.

> **"Petroleum Industry Management in the New Era of Information Technology,"**
> *address before the American Petroleum Institute,*
> *Chicago, Illinois,*
> **November 11, 1963.**

*The lesson from the foregoing examples is obvious: Creative business planning, says John Diebold, begins with a sensitivity to and an understanding of **customer needs** — needs viewed in the widest possible perspective.*

*In this connection a new product (new-services) program is widely prescribed as an indispensable part of management activities in any for-profit enterprise. However, he has repeatedly warned that without the basic "rethinking" here advocated, too many deceptively business-like new-product efforts are more a **symptom** of a problem rather than a start at the **solution** of a problem, properly identified and understood. For example:*

A new-product program may be a manifestation of a healthy business that is intent on staying competitively and continuously responsive to new needs and changing desires of its customers. On the other hand, a new-product program — even a well-staffed and imaginatively managed one — can also be a sign of a business in serious trouble trying to make up for a lack of a sense of mission or lack of a genuine definition of direction in its business by groping for "new products."

Too many companies fall in the second category. Some of the most unbelievably inappropriate moves have been made by otherwise successful business managements. (At the end of World War II, some of the major airframe manufacturers even went into the bathtub and casket business, rationalizing that they were using war-found skill in handling sheet metal.)

> **"A Short, Fast Step to Tomorrow,"**
> *Printer's Ink,*
> **May 29, 1964.**

On the other hand an outstanding example of imaginative planning is furnished by a Diebold client, North American Aviation. Realizing, some fifteen years ago, that it was faced with problems in many ways similar to those of the machine-tool industry, it made a careful analysis of customers' needs that were being met in new ways, and set about building its own capacity in these areas — in electronics, in atomics, in rocket engines. The company established divisions in each of these fields. Today the electronics division alone accounts for a volume of annual business nearly as large as the entire machine-tool industry.

> **"The Revolution that Fails to Take Place,"**
> *address before the National Machine Tool Builders'*
> *Association, Cincinnati, Ohio,*
> **May 3, 1963.**

RELATING TO TECHNOLOGICAL AND SOCIAL CHANGE

Viewing needs in the widest possible perspective, says John Diebold, calls for an "unblinking alertness" to change.

*With respect to **industrial markets**, he points out, this means an alertness to changes over a wide spectrum of technology as the industrial users of the firm's products and* *services advance their own technology, and as they adapt products and modes of operation to the changing needs and desires of their own customers, the ultimate consumers.*

*With respect to **consumers**, he adds, it means a highly developed appreciation of the social changes being produced by technology, and how these will affect the demands of consumer segments that form part of the firm's immediate market. Taken together, these approaches constitute entrepreneurial innovation.*

With respect to both industrial and consumer markets, enterpreneurial innovation focuses on two specific lines of management action:

1. Fostering of an attitude throughout the organization that looks outward, not inward — a "washing of the corporate windows" to provide a better view of what the customers need and want.

2. Establishment of an organizational structure that not only makes possible, but actively encourages technological innovation, and that sees to it that there will be inputs of technological intelligence from many sources, from outside of the company and outside of the industry.

> *Remarks at a meeting of Diebold Research Program sponsors,*
> **September 9, 1969.**

*"Defining the business" to fit the needs of industrial customers in wide perspective means helping customers analyze their needs, and helping them solve their problems, rather than merely selling them products. As a matter of fact, as John Diebold points out, in many highly successful companies the distinction between whether they are selling a **service** or a **product** is becoming increasingly hazy. For example:*

Computer manufacturers have created their enormous volume of new business by letting their customers know they want to help them analyze and solve their business needs. They early saw the need to set themselves up not as purveyors of computing equipment, but as creators and purveyors of integrated management information systems. IBM, for example, has specialists in a wide variety of industries completely conversant with each industry's special problems of marketing, production, materials control, payroll handling, and the like, as have NCR and Burroughs in banking, retailing, and general manufacturing.

In the computer field today, "software," and not "hardware" represents the single most important determinant of sales. As to the hardware itself, communications devices and input/output and other peripherals — the devices that change computing *equipment* into an information *system* — represent (as of 1970) between 75 and 80 percent of the value of an installation, an exact reversal from the situation that existed in the mid 1950s at the beginning of the computer age.

"The Next Vital Step to Management Control Systems,"
keynote address before the International Meeting of the Data Processing Management Association, San Francisco, California,
November 20, 1964.

Management has always known that changes in social structure change consumer demand. But as the rate of such social change increases, management must be able to anticipate shifts and react with increasing speed. As indicated in the discussion in Chapter 1, John Diebold early called attention to this sweep of change to show the need not only for the kind of social awareness and qualitative interpretation that must form the basis for systematic business innovation but also for making this effort a conscious part of the business planning process.

"One Valid Definition of a Business Purpose . . ."

The need for a posture that stresses innovation need hardly be belabored further . . . In his book, **The Practice of Management,** *Peter Drucker makes the point that "there is only one valid definition of a business purpose: to create a customer . . . any business enterprise has two — and only these two — basic functions: marketing and innovation."*

If John Diebold's thesis — that we must link the customer-oriented "market concept" with an abiding awareness of and response to technological change — is accepted as the indispensable ingredient of corporate philosophy, the definition of business purpose will be adhered to and the two basic functions will have every chance of fulfillment.

Maximum value from new technologies can be achieved, says John Diebold, only by rethinking and redesign — of products, processes, and perhaps the entire business itself. He has emphasized this message ever since the days of his graduate work. He is shown here inspecting a client facility.

Product and process redesign ... the analysis of processes in terms of **functions** *rather than in terms of the steps that are now being performed ... rethinking of the* **entire** *operation – all these are necessary, important, and often difficult problems which must be solved before business can begin in any real way to take advantage of the Aladdin's lamp which technology holds forth.*

"Automation: The Advent of the Automatic Factory,"
Princeton, New Jersey: Van Nostrand Company, Inc., **1952.**

In a consumer economy as dynamic as ours, the producer who is wedded to one product because of heavy machine investment soon finds himself in an untenable position ... It is his agile competitor, capable of changing and altering his product with every swing of market demand, who runs off with the business.

"Automation – Its Impact on Industry,"
address before the 7th Annual Industrial Engineering Institute, University of California, Berkeley and Los Angeles, **January 28–February 1, 1955.**

We are grossly underutilizing information technology. We have largely converted old data collection and control systems to computerized operation rather than designing new systems to utilize the potential of the new technology. Like the early auto-makers who thought they were making "horseless carriages," we are still thinking along the lines of "humanless bookkeeping systems."

"Impacts on Urban Government Functions of Developments in Science and Technology," Governing Urban Society: Monograph No. 7,
American Academy of Political and Social Science, Philadelphia, **May, 1967.**

Redesign of Products and Processes

The products and processes of a business must continually be reviewed, and often redesigned, to be sure the business will be able to meet new demands upon its systems, organizations, and products ... and such review and design must often be done before the new demands are even palpable.

One of John Diebold's earliest – and continuing – major contribution to the developing concept of automation was his insistence that in order to make full use of technological innovation, it is usually necessary to redesign the product or process, or both. Simply mechanizing past processes or applying advanced technology to products in their existing form, he reiterates, does not tap the real potential of the new technology. Even worse, as costly experience has amply demonstrated in office as well as factory automation, such an approach, undertaken in the name of modernization and up-to-date efficiency, may defeat its own purpose by locking a company into cumbersome and perhaps fatal rigidity.

The essence, as he sees it, lies in "rethinking" products and processes — producing and assembling parts in a factory into a finished, tangible product, or processing data in an office to produce information — completely untrammelled by prior concepts. For example, as he pointed out in his first book, which was concerned with factory automation:

If a product or process does not lend itself to automation, perhaps it may be redesigned so that it performs the same functions in a different way — a way that *does* lend itself to automation.

Rethinking is an attitude. It is an ability to get outside of a problem that seems insoluble and approach it in a new and perhaps wholly different way. It is a constant re-examination of whether the problems we are attempting to solve are the problems we really should be trying to solve. It is asking ourselves: Should we produce this product differently? Should we try to produce a different product that will serve the same purposes? Rethinking is a constant awareness of the end functions of a product and a continual questioning of whether those functions can be performed better or equally well by a slight variation in the product or perhaps by total change to a new product that can be produced automatically.

> **"Automation: The Advent of the Automatic Factory,"**
> *Princeton, New Jersey: Van Nostrand Company, Inc.,* **1952.**

And he elaborated upon this point shortly thereafter when he spelled out the basic difference between "automation" and mere "mechanization". (As indicated later, this concept includes office operations.)

In approaching automation problems it is highly important that one does *not* think of automatic production as a process of automatically duplicating the hand motions of present machine operators. It is often possible to devise a workable Rube Goldberg mechanism that duplicates exactly the motions of a machine operator. But the remote-controlled mechanical hands developed by the Atomic Energy Commission for the handling of radioactive materials, although worthwhile for laboratory use, represent an ideal example of how *not* to automate a production line.

Not only does the approach of mechanizing present operations fail to yield the most efficient solution to the task at hand, but it often leads people to think of certain operations as entirely inappropriate to automatic control when in fact the opposite may be true. By contrast, rethinking involving redesign of the process, the product, the machinery, or perhaps all three, may produce results even greater than anticipated . . .

> **"Automation – The New Technology,"**
> *Harvard Business Review,*
> **November-December, 1953.**

The Processing Industries

The processing industries, from oil refining and chemical manufacture to the production of fissionable materials, present an excellent example of the manner in which the redesign of production processes can lead to automatic manufacture. At the beginning of this century, both oil, refining and chemical manufacture were entirely batch processes. Today, instruments monitor a continuous flow of raw materials through automatic processing equipment, and the finished product flows from the plant in an uninterrupted stream. The entire process is fully automatic.

> **"Automation – The New Technology,"**
> *Harvard Business Review,*
> **November-December, 1953.**

Yet even in the 1950s, when we were only on the threshhold of sophisticated computer development, John Diebold pointed out that oil refineries, while "fully automatic" in the sense of pre-automation technology, would soon stand to benefit from further imaginative rethinking:

An oil refinery where instruments and controls far outnumber the human workers gives the impression of being highly automated. Compared with an automobile factory, that is true. Refineries have achieved what fabricating is still struggling for – conversion from batch to continuous processing so that operation can be made automatic. But they are only beginning to feel the full impact of a second, more significant, state of automation, *when the automatic operations themselves* will be automatically controlled.

The intricate controls that run a refinery *almost* by themselves are in a large sense not really running it at all. As things stand, the variables of processing – temperature, pressure, level, and rate of flow – can be maintained at desired values without human intervention through the use of feedback control devices. But the *values themselves* must still be selected and the control instruments adjusted accordingly. In many cases, it is not possible to determine the relationships among these variables that will hold true throughout an entire process. This means that an operator cannot come to work, set his controls, and go home. He must reset them every time a test of the product being processed shows that changes are needed. Thus, it is the operator who does all the decision-making.

To achieve genuinely effective process plant automation, all the plant's individual controls will have to be integrated into a single, coordinated, self-regulating system. Just as a single machine designed on the feedback principle notes and corrects variations in its output, so an integrated self-regulating system will note and correct variations in the end-product of an entire plant, making precise and instantaneous adjustment whenever the product itself shows any variation from optimum quality. Since the control of a number of variables to produce a desired end is essentially a calculating operation, the integrated operation of the process plant of the future will depend upon an electronic computer to analyze, correlate, and correct the operations of the individual control device.

> **"Automation and the Manager,"**
> *address before the XIth International Management Congress of the Comite International de l'Organisation Scientifique, (CIOS), Paris, France,*
> **June 26, 1957.**

By 1964, digital computers were beginning to be applied to process control along the lines outlined in John Diebold's Paris talk. With increasing computer speeds and advanced programming methods, a new dimension was being added to total systems that included automated manufacturing based on real-time response from sensors on processes in the plant. In this method, a digital computer is directly connected to the process, receives information on pressure, temperature, speeds, and so on; makes logical decisions based on these data in the light of programmed alternatives; and gives output command signals to open and close valves, change temperature settings, and the like.

Discrete Manufacturing

But in the manufacturing of discrete units, aside from certain large-scale automotive installations, managements are still struggling to achieve significant integration, the first step in automation. Again, what John Diebold said as early as 1959 is still largely pertinent today:

In discrete-unit manufacturing, operations are still on a departmental or step-by-step basis, and the manner in which the work is performed still adheres to the principles of the division of labor. And even after the problem of integrating the production process into a *system*, or an overall process, is solved, there still remains the task of achieving automatic control.

In the most modern factory, machines have taken over the routine assembly line jobs. However, with a few exceptions like some of the tape-controlled machine tools, the machines do not yet control their *own* performance. Thus a badly adjusted machine tool in an automatic engine line will activate a cut-off switch which stops the machine and prevents it from ruining engine block after engine block. But a human worker still has to adjust the tool. This is automatic operation, but is not *automation* — it is not the high level of automatic control that can be achieved by self-correcting systems.

> **"Automation: Its Impact on Business and Labor,"**
> *Washington, D.C.: National Planning Association,*
> *Planning Pamphlet No. 106,*
> **May, 1959.**

Integrating all the separate stages of the production process into a single smooth-running system cannot be done simply by designing a machine to help a worker do his job more effectively. It can be done only by *questioning each stage in the production process* and finding out whether it is really necessary, whether it must be separate from other stages, and whether it can be performed without the help of a human operator . . . As R.H. Sullivan, a Ford Motor Company vice president early observed, in the days when "automation" was first being bruited about: "The trouble with our [former] manufacturing methods was that, like Topsy, they 'just growed,' and nobody had taken time out for a long view. What they needed was a complete rethinking of the problem — a whole new philosophy of manufacturing."

> **"Automation: Its Impact on Business and Labor,"**
> *Washington, D.C.: National Planning Association,*
> *Planning Pamphlet No. 106.*
> **May, 1959.**

"RETHINKING" PROCESSES IN TERMS OF "BUNDLE OF FUNCTIONS"

One of the major blocks to widespread automation in the early 1950s was the feeling on the part of many that extensive self-regulating mechanization utilizing automatic feedback under programmed control had only limited applicability — namely to large-scale process industries or to manufacturing operations consisting of long runs of identical (or only slightly varied) products on fully automatic single-purpose machines. John Diebold worked valiantly to overcome this block by stressing the concept of viewing a machine tool group as a "bundle of functions" which would then be contained in one machine or one group of machines operating as an integrated system:

In many fabricating operations a clearly definable group of functions is usually performed upon a related grouping of products. For example, there may be a series of turning operations, followed by a drilling operation. If these could be performed at the same time in the same machine, a saving in machining time would be achieved. This would also save equipment cost, because it would not be necessary to transfer the product from one machine element to another. This comes down to something like our present-day production machines.

Production machines are the midway stage between the hand-operated machines such as drill presses and lathes and the fully automatic machines common in the packaging industry . . . performing a series of machining functions semi-automatically. The *chucking machine* is an example . . . it has a number of spindles, or heads, arranged in a circle. Each spindle holds a workpiece for machining and spins individually; but all may be revolved around the common center without changing their positional relation to one another. The machine performs a series of turning and cutting operations on each workpiece.

By holding a number of workpieces — typically four, five, six, or eight — in as many heads (or chucks), it is possible to perform a series of machining operations simultaneously upon the workpieces . . . The machining operations on each piece are performed in a series of stages . . . The tools that perform the operations are held at each index position so that the workpiece is moved from one set of tools to another and finally back to the starting position where it is removed from the machine and replaced by a new workpiece . . .

In designing flexible machine units for an automatic factory, the starting point would be a group of functions commonly performed on a class of product. These units would be built into a machine that could handle a limited size-range of workpiece and perform its functions automatically. This solution, of course, represents a compromise between a fully automatic machine and one that performs a rather wide range of functions. But it is a compromise that lends itself economically to many of the tasks of American industry . . .

If we could couple a group of production machines, or similar machines designed around the *bundle of functions* concept, by some form of inexpensive and flexible materials-handling equipment, and add a control mechanism to do the work normally done by the operator, we would have a factory completely automatic in terms of direct operation, although there would still be need for considerable indirect labor.

"Automation: The Advent of the Automatic Factory,"
Princeton, New Jersey: Van Nostrand Company, Inc.,
1952.

THE FLEXIBLE STANCE

*The line of thinking, of course, underlying the "bundle of functions" approach was that concentrating upon functions rather than specific end products would make it possible to couple the safeguard of **flexibility** with the dramatic savings in labor costs made possible by the continuous, uninterrupted run on an automated line. Two years before the classic failure of automation at the Granite City, Ill. frame plant of A.O. Smith Corp. (a $4- million, 600- ft. long single machine designed to rivet more than*

200 automobile frames an hour, that was scrapped after running for only a few months of its trouble-laden three-year life), John Diebold was preaching the following philosophy:

True enough, the producer with heavy machine investment is able to produce at low cost because of his highly automatic plant. But his magnificent machines, incapable of producing a variety of products, rust before they are paid for while more conventional manual equipment owned by the shop next door operates to capacity. It is his agile competitor, capable of changing and altering his product with every swing in market demand, who runs off with the business.

It is this very situation, happily, that automation now promises to alter. Through *flexible automatic* control, machines can be made versatile as well as automatic. No longer must the benefits of automatic production be limited to large operations. Now the job and semi-production shop – which actually accounts for the largest volume of our national production – can enjoy the fruits of automation.

"Automation – Its Impact on Industry,"
address before the 7th Annual Industrial Engineering Institute, University of California, Berkeley and Los Angeles,
January 28-February 1, 1955.

And even earlier he was able to preach the doctrine of flexibility and versatility, especially as he saw the possibility of implementing his "bundle of functions" concept with the emerging tape-controlled machine tools.

Until now, the economics of automation has required long runs of non-varying products. It is the automotive industry that has been able to make the most of automation to date, and it is the suppliers to the automotive plants who possess the bulk of automatic machinery today.

But we live in a dynamic economy. Automatic screw machines have their place. Automatic machines for handling engine blocks have theirs. But these represent special cases. In very few areas of the economy can we afford to risk investing in special-purpose machinery of this kind which requires the guaranteed output of at least five and six million units to amortize the investment. The bulk of production in the United States is in smaller lots. Even though end output may be numbered in millions, variations in style, size, and model mean that average runs are far smaller.

Automatic machinery that can be varied is of course available. By changing the cams in the screw machine you can change the output. But the time required for setting up such automatic machine tools is a significant part of the cost of a product produced in limited runs.

"The Challenge of Automation"
address before the American Society of Tool Engineers, Philadelphia, Pennsylvania,
April 26-30, 1954.

Most of American industry depends upon short runs of product. About 89 to 90 percent of all American production is in lots of less than 25 individual pieces. It is impossible to build special-purpose machines to manufacture these, because the character of the product changes too frequently. This is where the second meaning of factory automation comes in. In such a "job-shop" operation automation is just beginning to be achieved, in the form of tape-controlled machine tools — machines for which instructions can be provided in a flexible and variable form. This kind of automation is just beginning to have an impact.

> **Extracts from testimony on Automation and Technological Change,**
> *Subcommittee on Economic Stabilization, Joint Congressional Committee on the Economic Report, Washington, D.C.,*
> **October 14, 1955.**

"RETHINKING" OFFICE PROCESSES

Long before the new vistas of "management information systems" were opened by the third-generation computers and related communication technology (to which we shall address ourselves in Chapter 6), John Diebold saw the need for looking at office automation in the broadest possible terms — not merely as an extension of office machines that would further speed up administrative operations by "putting wheels under" existing systems and procedures.

Again he was concerned with the "systems" approach — and in this connection he stressed not only the unifying of office systems into an integrated whole, but meshing office operations as a whole into a unified system that embraced other functions of the business:

One result of treating the computer as just another tabulating machine and not integrating it into the business system is that high costs of data preparation are encountered and often seriously negate the dollar savings of automatic data processing.

This is one of the principal reasons dollar savings have been so disappointing in existing computer installations. On virtually every project my firm has worked on, one of our principal sources of savings has been the automatic derivation of data from a process as a by-product, and the elimination of extensive key punching or other data preparation costs encountered when the computer is treated as just a new, faster, and more automatic addition to the tabulating room.

It is through just this process of reaching out into production and other business processes for automatic collection of data that the office and factory are being drawn more closely together.

"Pitfalls to Business Data Processing,"
address before the University of California Conference on Automation, San Francisco, California,
January 9, 1957.

*When we recall that John Diebold's **Automation: The Advent of the Automatic Factory** appeared as long ago as 1952, we appreciate the prescience of his following remarks in the chapter, "Automatic Handling of Information":*

We have discussed automation of the plant. What about automation of the office? It is probably there that the most immediate, widespread, and fruitful application of the new technology will be made . . .

In the plant, the materials-handling problems are formidable obstacles to effective automation. In the office, materials handling is the *basis* for use of the new technology. We may deceive ourselves into thinking that the materials handled in the office are papers and cards, but actually the basic material being handled is *information.* The new technology was developed primarily for the effective and rapid handling of information.

As business grows and becomes more complex, the need for detailed, up-to-the-minute, accurate information increases enormously. Better methods of production control and market analysis, a growing body of government regulations, complex payroll deductions — all these are placing an increasing burden on office procedures. Although we have developed some extraordinary machines for handling information, between 1920 and 1950 there was a 53 percent increase in the number of factory workers as against 150 percent increase in the number of office workers.

"Automation: The Advent of the Automatic Factory,"
Princeton, New Jersey: Van Nostrand Company, Inc.,
1952.

Preoccupation With Equipment

But over the years, as he personally assumed a continually more important role in the application of computer technology, John Diebold warned against preoccupation with equipment — the "hardware" of ADP — at the expense of "rethinking" the problems of information in the broadest possible terms. In the chapter on information handling in this earliest of his books he wrote:

This chapter might have been entitled "The Automatic Office." Although the temptation was great, it was felt that this phrase might distract attention from the fact that the new technology will ultimately bring many of the office functions into closer contact with the production functions. In manufacturing firms, the function of the office is fundamentally related to the function of the plant. Recognition of this fact is of considerable importance to a fruitful analysis of office methods. When this basic relationship is overlooked, the introduction of new machinery often perpetuates existing procedures instead of eliminating or replacing them . . .

Most writing on the subject of applying computers to the handling of business information has emphasized speed and accuracy as compared with present methods. But the new technology can do far more than improve speed and accuracy.

With proper analysis and development, the control circuits that are used to operate the production machinery can be directly linked to the equipment whose function it is to schedule production. Thus the routine supplying of production data by hand, the recopying of this information, and its transfer to punched cards can all be eliminated. With proper storage systems the information-handling equipment can retain all of these data in its own storage system, printing only the portion that management must have to make decisions, and retaining the raw data for automatic comparison with, for example, production planning schedules for future operations. In addition to eliminating many clerical operations, data can be provided for management more quickly and in far more useful form than at present. To accomplish this, however, special analysis of the particular information functions of each firm is necessary.

> **"Automation: The Advent of the Automatic Factory,"**
> *Princeton, New Jersey: Van Nostrand Company, Inc.,* **1952.**

The spectacular growth in computer use for business applications — The Diebold Group estimates that some 60,000 computer systems for administrative (as distinguished from scientific and engineering) applications are in current operation in this country — has certainly borne out John Diebold's prediction as to "immediate, widespread, and fruitful applications." Yet as he watched the lag on the part of even advanced managements to keep pace with the versatility, sophistication, and capacities of computer systems, John Diebold felt it necessary to stress again and again the need to "rethink" information needs so that the new machines would be used to their full potential — and that the rethinking must be done on a continuing basis. Excerpts from speeches and writings over the years are illuminating:

1957

The hard truth of the matter is that we have hardly begun to learn how to put these splendid new machines to work . . . Surprising as it may seem, even in this new field, most management thinking has already become rigid and cluttered with stereotypes that stand in the way of real progress. New insights are needed. It is up to management to do a good deal more original thinking and to learn to question traditional patterns of operation . . . It is dead wrong to equate the bewildering array of hardware shipments of recent years with true progress in the use of automation.

"Automation and the Manager,"
address before the XIth International Management Congress of the Comite International de l'Organisation Scientifique (CIOS), Paris, France,
June 26, 1957.

1958

What is one to make of it . . . when a major utility company announces publicly, a year after installing a large-scale computer, that the program – two years in preparation – has been scrapped and the machine returned to the manufacturer, because those responsible for the installation had underestimated the running time of the daily billing cycle?

"Automation 1958: Industry at the Crossroads,"
Dun's Review,
August, 1958.

1964

We are beginning to have the ability to do economically whatever we want to do in the handling of information . . . But as more powerful systems, more nearly paralleling the real flow of information in an organization come into their own, as they have, the paucity of our understanding of what it is management needs in the way of information processing begins to become clear . . . We need a synthesis of existing and some as yet undeveloped techniques leading to an imaginative new approach to analysis of information needs and a basis for information systems design.

"The Next Vital Step to Management Control Systems,"
keynote address before the International Meeting of the Data Processing Management Association, San Francisco, California,
November 20, 1964.

1969

Now that computers are becoming useful at a higher level of management and for more sophisticated tasks, top executives should use different yardsticks in evaluating and planning for them. But this is not being done; the old criteria are still in general use. By concentrating on savings in data processing costs and on added efficiencies in routine operations, management exposes itself to serious errors of omission and commission . . . Naive standards are used in justifying and evaluating the machines which so greatly extend our analytical powers.

"Bad Decisions on Computer Use,"
Harvard Business Review,
January-February, 1969.

Stories in the financial pages of the first half of 1970 echo John Diebold's refrain that there has been insufficient "rethinking" (or even proper thinking?) on the part of top managements as regards computerized information systems. The Penn-Central debacle has made history. Serious discussions of the merger of the New York Central and the Pennsylvania Railroad had been going on for a decade and more before the union was consummated in 1968. Yet in discussing "Bad Management or Ailing Industry?" Robert E. Bedingfield in the June 28, 1970 edition of The New York Times reported as follows: Stories about the deteriorating service to shippers, and reports of spiraling costs and mounting railroad losses spread almost from the first day (February 1, 1968) the two railroads began unified operation. The computers of the two systems were incompatible, and there were horrendous tales for months about the misrouting of freight cars and the mislaying of thousands of waybills, in addition to a serious lack of motive power. There were even the impossible story that one freight train "just disappeared."

*In an earlier story, Leonard Sloane in the same publication discussed the events leading up to the traumatic $23-million deficit, for the year ending March 31, as announced in a "stark, one-paragraph statement" in the preliminary financial report issued by a leading travel and credit-service agency, and had this to say in part in the July 5, 1970 edition of The New York Times: There was, for example, the question of its computers, which process the monthly bills to customers and the semi-monthly payments to member establishments. They were simply unable to cope with a blizzard of paperwork ... The growth in the physical volume, particularly in the summer of 1969 when the airlines had their seasonal bulge, just inundated the computer system introduced in 1965. "The system was designed strictly to get the bills out," (quoting a senior executive) "and **couldn't supply the credit division with the information it needed to collect the money.**"*

We have added the italics to the sad commentary ... and refer the reader to Chapter 6.

"RETHINKING" PRODUCTS

Redesign of a process, whether plant or office, can only go so far. Often the product, too, must be redesigned before full advantage can be taken of the new technology. John Diebold has always coupled this aspect with "rethinking" of processes:

Product design for the purpose of automatic production takes many forms. It may be as simple as the designing of a small nipple or small jog of metal or glass on the part. For example, the way many manufacturers of glass bottles have switched the printing of two or more colors *on bottles* to an automatic basis by simply designing a small nipple of glass that sticks out at the bottom of the bottle and positions it under the printing screen. Before, it was necessary to hand position it, to insure that the color would be applied in the proper place.

> **"The Automatic Factory: Mechanization vs. Work Effort,"**
> *address before the California Personnel Management Association and the Personnel Section of the Western Management Association, Berkeley, California, Management Report No. 151,*
> **1952.**

Product design engineers have, of course, always devoted prime attention to designing for ease of manufacture, and John Diebold claims no credit in connection with the concept beyond that of continually publicizing the need for it in all thinking and "rethinking" regarding possibilities for automation. And the end result may even be a better product — for example, an ice cube designed with a hole in the middle, he has pointed out, allows fully automatic production, and by providing a larger cooling surface is actually a better product. The consumer does not object to the hole.

*Always he has hammered on the theme that in product design, as well as in automation of processes, the need is to approach the problem **de novo** from the point of view of end function, without being hampered by tradition or preconceived ideas. In his 1952 book on the automatic factory, he illustrated this by citing the significant breakthrough in the then state of the art of radio manufacture provided by the novel concept of printed circuits (since then, of course, superseded by electronic technology's microscopic miniaturized circuits and other solid-state developments):*

If an attempt were made to automatize radio circuit assembly by mechanically reproducing the hand operations, a Rube Goldberg device of stupendous proportions would again be necessary . . . Coupled with this fact is the knowledge that the whole device must be flexible enough to permit continuous changes in the design of the circuits. However, by thinking of circuits in terms of their functions rather than their present physical form, it has been possible to solve the problem by designing the wiring circuit in the form of flat planes, and using *printed* circuits . . . The design of circuits with printed, punched, or painted patterns is truly revolutionary and an ideal example of product design for automatic production.

> **"Automation: The Advent of the Automatic Factory."**
> *Princeton, New Jersey: Van Nostrand Company, Inc.,*
> **1952.**

IN SUMMARY: "IMAGINATIVE THINKING"

*What does one do in order, in John Diebold's words, to "get outside of a problem" and approach it "in a new and perhaps wholly different way"? What is required, he says again and again, is "imaginative thinking-through of technology" to make entirely new processes and procedures possible. One may readily visualize the application of many of the computer and automatic control techniques here discussed. But it does take a "Diebold jolt" to think of the kind of **additional** twist that might change the whole substance of the business operation itself — such as the following thought which he tossed off to one of his audiences:*

For example, certain items can now be mass-produced by inserting a magnetic tape into a computer which guides the machine in the manufacturing process. Instead of manufacturing such items at headquarters and shipping them where required, it may be cheaper to ship the magnetic tape and manufacture the items in the market areas.

> **"Computers, Program Management, and Foreign Affairs,"**
> *Foreign Affairs,*
> **October, 1966.**

He has expressed it neatly in the following summing-up of the meaning of automation — again stressing the need for a broad thinking-through rather than a preoccupation with specific equipment and controls:

Automation is much more than the technology of feedback. We have had that for many years. It differs from mechanization in the very way it regards the problem of production. Automation requires us to view the production processes as an *integrated system* and not as a series of individual steps divided according to the most economic distribution of human skills — or even of individual machines.

Automation is a way of thinking, a way of "looking at . . ." as much as it is a way of doing or a specific technology. It is an attitude — a "philosophy" of production, if you will — rather than a particular technology or particular electronic devices. It is a conceptual breakthrough, as revolutionary in its way as Henry Ford's concept of the assembly line.

> **"Applied Automation: A Practical Approach,"**
> *keynote address before the Special Manufacturing Conference of the American Management Association, New York,*
> **October 10, 1955.**

It is "imaginative thinking" in action!

Photograph by Burt Glinn

In view of the rapid changes in information technology, John Diebold has always stressed the need for systems methodology characterized by a systematic rather than a piece-meal approach to systems design, permitting prompt modification of systems in responses to changes in demand.

5

The technology of computers and the rapid communications and information processing equipment which this technology makes possible will permit far more extensive analysis of our national economy and business methods, through up-to-the-minute market surveys and extensive research on distribution data and transportation patterns.

"Automation: The Advent of the Automatic Factory,"
Princeton, New Jersey: Van Nostrand Company, Inc.
1952.

A characteristic which today makes for success in management is the ability to make the right decision on too little data. As we enter a world in which we can increasingly have all the data we want the premium is on an ability to ask the right questions and properly interpret the results. Will a different kind of man then rise to the top? What will be his characteristics? What kind of training and development will he need?

"New Rules and Opportunities for Business — As We Enter the Post-Industrial Era,"
keynote address before the Third Tri-Annual International Productivity Congress, Vienna, Austria,
October 28, 1970.

Information Systems for Marketing

Marketing information systems must be useful today and adaptable to the effective assimilation of future improvements.

For some time now the protagonists of the new information technology have been trying to make as substantial an impact on marketing as they have on accounting, production control, and the broad spectrum of administrative functions. Indeed, with the advent of remote-access computers with large-scale memories, many firms have in recent years spent sizeable sums in developing technically impressive market data bases and information systems and models of all descriptions. Nevertheless, in John Diebold's view, the results have been generally lamentable, at least from the point of view of marketing men trying to use them.

*But more important than the general inadequacy of marketing information systems, developed to date, he has repeatedly pointed out, has been the lag in awareness that, used **imaginatively**, computers offer a powerful opportunity for improving the marketing competitiveness of a firm. Too much of marketing's use of the new technology has been in the mundane area of speeding up clerical and administrative functions, and, as far as analysis is concerned, issuing the same **types** of reports improved only in the sense of greater timeliness, comprehensiveness of data, and accuracy. While these accomplishments are not to be denigrated, they nevertheless do not represent basic "rethinking," and are, again, merely an exercise in "putting wheels under" existing procedures.*

This persisting tendency to use computers in marketing for hardly more than totalling sales by various categories is understandable, since the business use of computers was from the start primarily accounting oriented. Consequently, where the marketing organization has truly wanted to use the new tools, it has often been forced to confine its use of information processing to an analysis of current products and markets rather than of potential ones. Thus as late as 1966, John Diebold still had to couch his discussion of computer potentials in marketing in terms of opportunities ahead rather than solid accomplishments achieved:

The computer has been used mainly to do things more efficiently and at less cost. Again, only recently have people used the computers to do things that couldn't be done before, especially in terms of business functions. Now we are beginning to do very much in the way of breaking new ground.

The marketing area holds some of the greatest potential in terms of the utilization of computers and related management science capabilities, although the present use of computers in marketing doesn't tell you much about what the potential is, which is vastly greater than the present utilization would imply.

> **"Marketing's Role in the Coming Age of Automation,"**
> *Sales Management,*
> **October 1, 1966.**

The following colloquy in the same article neatly sums up his doctrine of the broader and more imaginative application of computers and related information technology to marketing, which he had been expounding for a decade and a half:

SM: Can you make some guesses as to the potential to be realized in the marketing area in the future?

Diebold: The computer will be used as a control device for the sales organization and the marketing operation. It will allow much more ready access throughout a business to the information that is relevant to controlling the marketing operation.

Second, the computer is an enormously powerful tool to use in the analysis of marketing operations, distribution and marketing costs, customer patterns, buying patterns, shopping patterns, time delays, and changes.

Third, it can be of major importance in market planning, as a means of helping you allocate resources in different patterns and in different ways. Media-planning models that are used in advertising, where you determine the alternative media plans, are one example.

A fourth area is going to be the use of the computer as a competitive tool in pricing. For example, you can build a model of your customer's business in the computer. We have some clients doing this, on large orders. The suppliers make a model of their customer's business and work out very complex orders where, for example, they are delivering natural-resource chemicals or other materials, or are committing themselves for a long period ahead.

The whole approach to pricing of these contracts is a major area for modeling and for coming up with a much more precise knowledge of what will benefit you and what kind of price combinations will work best.

"Marketing's Role in the Coming Age of Automation,"
Sales Management,
October 1, 1966.

Further along in this question-and-answer interview, John Diebold put his finger through the surface-answer to the question posed, and touched upon an underlying uneasiness, a "fear factor," which psychologically may have been the main reason for the time-lag mentioned earlier:

SM: Many a marketing man, when talking about computers or models, will say that there's nothing like intuitive judgment, because marketing is too complex, with too many imponderables, to follow predictable patterns. How do you answer that argument?

Diebold: I have great sympathy for that feeling.

I don't in any way believe that the statistician or the mathematician will ever take the place of a great marketing man or a great salesman. But the marketing manager should use these tools to do a much better job, just as he uses the telephone and all the modern means of transportation, communication, and display.

"Marketing's Role in the Coming Age of Automation,"
Sales Management,
October 1, 1966.

"Praising With Faint Damns"

But admitting the defensive uneasiness to which John Diebold alluded, perhaps marketing people have had some more tangible reasons for appearing, at least to bright-eyed management-science enthusiasts, to be dragging their feet. In this regard the following observations of a Diebold Research Program group are illuminating:

Typical reactions of marketing men have ranged from praising with faint damns to resigned lip service to outright hostility . . . The market research head of one major broadcasting company, for example, expressed the view that most marketing information systems are geared to provide the most data for the most trivial questions, and almost nothing relevant to the important ones . . . A leading professor has in similar vein criticized the application of management science to marketing problems – which should play an important part in any advanced marketing information system – complaining that marketing "models" are solemnly discussed at professional management meetings and even advertised and sold, without reference to application limitations, true development costs, and experience with false starts.

Another common complaint of marketing men is that there is not enough *good* information and too much *bad,* arriving too late, from too many different sources, and without any indication of even relative credibility.

Various reasons have been advanced for this lack of success relative to the measurable accomplishments from utilizing the technology in other areas of the business. Some marketing men have claimed that their work is an art which cannot be captured in a mathematical equation. Systems analysts, on the other hand, have countered that the marketing men who claim this are unimaginative traditionalists trying to save their jobs until retirement . . .

In many cases the issue has been resolved by allowing the systems group to develop larger and more complex "corporate information systems" (often justifying added costs under the head of "intangible benefits") while permitting the marketing manager to ignore the outputs of these systems beyond routine sales accounting and data processing services.

> **"The Marketing Data Base,"**
> *Diebold Research Program Report,*
> **January, 1968.**

This is hardly a fruitful state of affairs. The dynamic techniques of modern information processing, the attacks upon uncertainties made possible by the new management sciences, and the scope and timeliness of marketing information offered by emerging marketing data banks represent more than opportunities that can be accepted or postponed at will. Instead, they pose challenges that must be accepted not only by marketing management, but by top management as a whole if the business is to survive. For, as John Diebold has always emphasized, the world does not stand still, and the company that chooses to ignore what technology has to offer will soon find itself in a strange new harsh world of strong competitors and reluctant customers.

In the new age, managers of a company may or may not know more about the world — depending upon their own attitude and effort — but the world will certainly know more about their own company. Competitors will have a much clearer view of its traditional products and customers, its strengths and weaknesses, and even its response or lack of response to moves of their own. Customers and prospects will be more aware of substitute products and alternate suppliers, and the extent to which they can press bargaining advantages.

It is apparent that marketing operations will be altered drastically by an environment in which customers have a far wider and more knowledgeable view of suppliers, and in which suppliers have in-depth intelligence about markets or market segments which they formerly defaulted to competitors because of a lack of information.

Added to these factors is the greatly reduced management-adjustment time occasioned by the shortened life-cycle of established products in almost every field.

> *Remarks before a meeting of Diebold Research Program sponsors,*
> **November, 1969.**

Broadly speaking, we may break down into the following five categories the areas within which, in his speeches and writing, John Diebold has indicated that marketing management, through computers and information technology, can realize a new order of magnitude of effectiveness:

1. *Improved administrative and accounting controls and the analysis of and reporting upon traditional types of sales data. (Already fairly widely achieved in practice.)*

2. *A step above (1), enlarged scope of analysis and new kinds of analyses, made possible by "rethinking" the information needs of the company and of the company's customers to improve existing service. (Some degree of achievement in practice.)*

3. *Greatly increased scope and timely availability of **marketing intelligence** embodied in the development of a comprehensive **market data base**. (As yet only negligibly realized in practice.)*

4. *Linked to (3) above, development of realistic marketing models and the application of "management sciences" – advanced concepts and techniques of decision-making. (Now carried on in a fairly sophisticated degree in a small number of companies, but in the infant stage of general application.)*

5. *The development of new information services for customers, related to existing products, to make it more convenient and or profitable for them to **remain** as customers, and to enlarge their requirements and hence their purchases. (Also linked to the use of models and simulations, and thus also in the infant stage of general application.)*

MARKETING'S ADMINISTRATIVE FUNCTION

In recent years, an increasing number of companies have shifted their primary orientation to marketing (as alluded to in the discussion of the "market concept" in Chapter 3), realizing that the most efficient administrative operation in the world will not guarantee profits, since "a penny saved is a penny earned, but only if a sale is made!" In spite of this shift, however, John Diebold has always deplored the lag in the progress of ADP applications in marketing, apart from the more mundane clerical and accounting functions. A decade ago he was outlining the possibilities in purely administrative areas:

Detailed cost analysis of salesmen's efforts by computing the time spent in selling each of the products in the company's product line, of the product's contributions to profits, and of expenses incurred during the sales effort will enable a company to maintain a profit-and-loss statement on every salesman – showing each salesman's individual contribution to the profitability of the company.

Going a step farther, based on the types of cost data cited above, it will be possible to devise idealized schedules for salesmen's calls, using linear-programming techniques. Distribution points for products could be determined using the same techniques. A quantitative approach has even been attempted in the determination of advertising budgets, based on analysis of advertising costs, percentage of market obtained with past expenditures, market objectives of the company, and strategic considerations.

> **"Industrial Applications of Heuristic Machines,"**
> *address before the 3rd International Congress on Cybernetics, International Cybernetics Association, Namur, Belgium,*
> **September 12, 1961.**

The purely administrative functions of marketing – customer records, warehouse allocations, payroll analysis and distribution to products and territories, compilation of territorial analyses and traditional statistical reports of salesmen performance and product movement – will inevitably improve, says John Diebold, as the corporate data base and the corporate-wide information system improve.

According to Diebold Group studies, the corporate information system will establish and control all interrelationships between the various levels and departments. In this system, an action taken, say, in production will generate information in the accounting inventory files, set up purchase orders, and the like. Also, since the new systems will typically be on-line time-sharing, the decision-maker or the person in charge of a specific marketing operation will be able to interrogate the central data base regarding the status of any given process, order, or function at any given moment.

The thrust of the application effort in this area, in most companies, will be directed toward the establishment of an order entry system. The order entry will be the process around which accounting, marketing, production, purchasing, and even engineering applications will evolve. The order entry will initiate production requirements, update the financial records, set up invoicing mechanisms, adjust marketing plans, and cause recognition of expected shortages.

The mode of entry of an order will vary from one industry to another. Companies which market their products in small blocks through the use of salesmen will use dial-up mechanisms to initiate entry. Where dealerships are dominant, terminals will serve to transmit the entry. In cases where delivery requirements necessitate a short turnaround-time system, accessing will be in a true real-time mode. Otherwise some alternative patterns of data entry, e.g., through incremental tape, will be instituted, depending on economic and service considerations.

In production-oriented companies such as heavy machinery or aerospace manufacturers, the order entry may not be computerized. In these companies, the information system will concentrate on production requirements, scheduling, parts inventories management, and the like.

> *Remarks before a Diebold Group Professional Development Meeting,*
> **September 23, 1968.**

ENLARGED SCOPE OF ANALYSIS

Even without the application of esoteric management sciences, a "rethinking" of information needs can, with the utilization of readily available hardware and software, step up by several orders of magnitude the administrative controls for marketing. While decrying the lag in such utilization, John Diebold was always glad to point to the exceptions to prove his rule that much was possible. Thus, in 1960 testimony, he pointed out the following examples to show the opportunities ahead:

A textile manufacturer in New York uses a computer almost entirely for information on inventory, sales analysis, and material available for sale. Not only has this been found to be profitable, but the company is developing new applications and further information requirements that will call for a larger system in the next two years . . . A major oil manufacturer is developing a complete program for marketing accounting that will not only reduce costs, but will provide marketing managers with up-to-date information on sales and sales tendencies all over the country . . . A drug and consumer goods manufacturer is using a computer to keep constant track of area sales in relation to a national index of purchasing power for a given area. As soon as discrepancies are detected between actual sales and sales that should be expected, corrective action is taken and the results can be measured on a week-by-week basis.

> **Testimony before the Subcommittee on Automation and Energy Resources,**
> *Joint Economic Committee, United States Congress,*
> **August, 1960.**

And he always stressed the need to keep information requirements of customers in mind, as well as those of the company itself, so that there would be an optimum, integrated information linkage for the entire sales transaction. An example is the point he made specifically with respect to wholesalers:

I think that you are going to be having direct connection with the retailer on orders. I think, though, that these are going to concentrate on variances. You are going to do much more in the way of anticipation of their requirements, so that you're not responding to individual, specific orders, but you're able to get variances on these orders. You will be connected directly to them electronically.

If I were running a wholesale business in this field, I would make every possible effort to become the prime supplier to the retailers in my particular area by making it possible for them to order directly over the telephone system, through these mechanical means that I've been talking about.

> **"What Automation Can Mean to the Drug Industry in the Next Ten Years,"**
> *address before the National Wholesale Druggists Association, Las Vegas, Nevada,*
> **November 16, 1966.**

THE MARKETING DATA BANK

I have noticed that the marketing data bank as such rarely comes up when the data base concept for management information systems is discussed. Conceptually, the marketing data bank is the next logical step in marketing data processing payoff.

> **Remarks before Diebold Research Program sponsors in introducing "The Marketing Data Base,"**
> *Diebold Research Program Report,*
> **January, 1968.**

*In broad terms, the marketing data bank contains all information pertinent to the marketing decision-making function of a company. As such, says John Diebold, it is logical to include it in any long-range information management plans. In particular, he points out, the marketing data bank could well be the basic building block for the corporate data base. In terms of objectives, the marketing data bank represents no radical departure from the current objectives of data utilization. The innovation rests in the data organization and accessing. Data are structured by **marketing** use, as opposed to source, and accessing is speeded up to the point at which it is no longer a problem.*

The initial task to be accomplished in developing a marketing data bank must be the analysis of the information system currently serving the marketing manager.

This is not a statement of the obvious. It is my experience that many efforts in computerized market systems development fail at the outset because the system developers assume that the marketing manager operates almost solely by intuition, and that *any* information will constitute a useful improvement. This is far from true. Any product or marketing manager worth his salt knows an enormous amount about his product, his market, and his competition, even though he receives this information through informal and often haphazard channels. In fact, it may be said that most current systems are capable only of describing the rough magnitude of an occurrence which has already been brought to the attention of the marketing manager through his *own* "information system" – his customer and supplier contacts, his trade periodicals, feedback from his men in the field, and his own seasoned sizing up of industry and economic developments.

Current information sources used by marketing management are extremely complex and diffuse structures that go far beyond the capabilities of any accounting-based system. The reason for this diffusion and complexity lies in the basic nature of marketing; for marketing is a function which is creatively engaged only as it is able to impact new products, and new markets. Information on *internal* matters, such as the company's own sales, is useful, but it can serve an imaginative creative purpose only if it can be combined with information from other sources.

This is not to say that all large organizations should feverishly begin the construction of complex data bases. It does, however, suggest that the marketing data base, with whatever information, will be most useful if it is designed to complement other sources of information rather than attempting to replace or ignore them.

> **"The Marketing Data Base,"**
> *Diebold Research Program Report,*
> **January, 1968.**

From time to time marketing periodicals have contained schematics of marketing information systems. However, these are adequate only to illustrate the general concept. They do not define the data *interrelationships* which are, of course, essential in developing a complementary data base . . . Perhaps the best definition would begin by analyzing the types of information that belong in a system. For if a system is a method of organization, the information it organizes should not be defined simply as "data" or "facts," but rather as *knowledge that was not previously known to the receiver."*

The current marketing information system is shown in matrix form in Figure 5-A. Inputs are shown vertically and outputs horizontally. Thus, all uses for accounting data are shown below that heading, and all inputs to sales management reports are shown to the right of that entry.

The matrix indicates the variety of sources outside the normal definition of marketing information. For instance, all the "window" departments dealing with the outside world may be sources of valuable information if the appropriate communications channels have been established. Thus purchasing agents often learn of the competition's new packaging ideas from salesmen who try to use this information as a sales argument. Similarly, the advertising department may learn of a competitor's promotional plans.

Figure 5-A

THE CURRENT MARKETING INFORMATION SYSTEM

INPUT TO / OUTPUT OF	Accounting	Purchasing	Advertising	Sales Force	Finance	Marketing Manager's Experience	Government Data and Update Services	Industry Association	Consumer Panels	Warehouse Movement and Store Audit	Interviews	Trade Periodicals	
Sales Management	Comparative Results by Salesmen		Territorial Advertising Campaigns	Sales Activities		Salesmen and Territorial Characteristics	Personal Income Business Indices	Sales by Product					Salesman Evaluation
Packaging	Current Costs	Competitor Plans	Competitor Plans	Competitor Activities		Market Characteristics	Regional Consumer Profiles		Test Results	Competitor Sales	Test Results		Package Planning and Evaluation
Pricing	Fixed and Variable Costs	Material Costs and Availability	Competitor Plans	Competitor Activities	Competitor Plans	Market Characteristics	Demographic Trends		Purchase Patterns	Test Results	Purchase Plans	New Products and Competition	Price Planning and Evaluation
Advertising and Other Promotion	Budgets and Expenditures	Competitor Plans	Competitor Plans-Media Evaluation Target Markets	Competitor Activities		Market Characteristics	Demographic Trends		Purchases	Competitor Sales	Consumer Response		Promotion Planning and Evaluation
New Product Design	Current Product Sales	Material Costs and Availability	Competitor Plans	Customer Requirements	Competitor Activities	Market Characteristics	Technological Trends		New Product Entry	New Product Entry		New Products and Product Uses	Product Planning and Evaluation
Distribution	Distribution Costs and Sales			Competitor Activities		Market and Channel Characteristics	Demographic Trends			Competitor Sales		Competitor Penetration Into New Markets	Distribution Planning and Evaluation

Source: *The Diebold Research Program*

65

Periodicals are used as an extremely important source of market information, although this might seem ridiculous to the professional systems developer, who is by nature a "quantifier." However, the developer of a well-known and complex economic input/output model cited trade publication advertising as an indicator of technological change in the use and substitution of raw material . . . The initial appearance of advertising by a certain chemical company in a trade journal for bakers, for example, might indicate the beginning of a significant shift in raw material requirements for the entire baking industry.

The data matrix indicates that the accounting system is a valuable but not primary source of marketing data. While this may seem to be a truism, the point has nonetheless been largely obscured in the current debate over whether systems should be designed on an integrated corporate level or a functional one. It is fairly obvious that a system should be integrated as much as possible from the data input side in order to optimize the cost and utility of data which have common significance to various functions. It is also true that certain problems are corporate in scope so that certain types of data should be available in an integrated structure and format.

Data in a management information system need not be common for all departments. Instead, functional departments will develop information systems using the corporate data base as an input which will be expanded as still other functions investigate the feasibility of acquiring additional data. Thus, for example, the marketing data bank will certainly include sales reports originating from the accounting system, and might add information from the purchasing system should it appear that forecasted shifts in material prices and availability constitute a reasonable indicator of competitors' positions. Additionally, it might include data from the research department on new technical developments or the appearance of new or potential competitors.

> **"The Marketing Use of Information Processing Systems,"**
> *Diebold Research Program Report,*
> **May, 1966.**

Data Accessibility

Data retrieval must not be allowed to become a major problem in any decision-making activity. Speed of accessibility in a marketing data base is a function of hardware and software. As to hardware, today, the utmost flexibility and desired degree of sophistication are possible in the storage and retrieval of information, as printouts, hard-copy reproductions from microfilm, displays on screens, voice response, and the like, as earlier indicated.

> **"The Marketing Use of Information Processing Systems,"**
> *Diebold Research Program Report,*
> **May, 1966.**

Figure 5-B   CONCEPTUAL FLOW OF DATA BANK DATA ENTRY AND USE

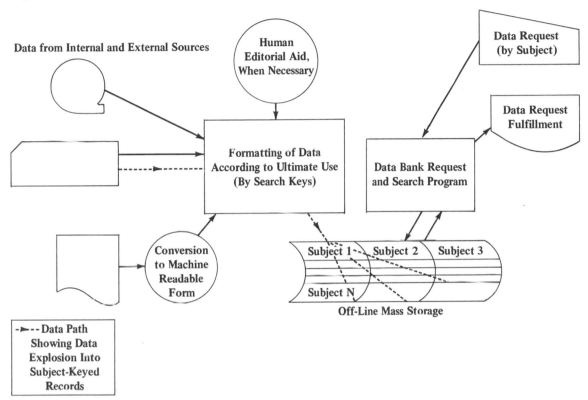

Source: *The Diebold Research Program*

Figure 5-B is a conceptualization of the marketing data base. As data enter the system a header label tells the system how to arrange the data in storage. This might be as simple as reading the data in card or tape image. However, there are many conceivable situations in which human examination of the data will be necessary in order to add editorial content . . . When the data are in the proper format they are entered into the memory medium of the system.

As shown, the entry of one piece of data can generate many data base entries since, in the data base, they are keyed to usage and their ultimate use determines their format . . . The choice of memory medium is extremely important and Diebold studies suggest that there is no justification for storage of this information in an on-line mode. What is more proper is that this information be stored in a low-cost random-access medium such as magnetic cards. The time requirements of a marketing data base are not so critical as to require real-time responses.

Various companies have in the past attempted to set up marketing data bases, and have found that the job is not one that can be accomplished in a matter of months. It is more commonly measured in terms of years.

One company, for example, planned to set up a marketing data base as a complete marketing intelligence system. Salesmen, distribution men, service personnel, etc. were requested to transmit all information which had any possible relevance to the marketing function to central facility on a daily basis. After a period of three years, this effort has not succeeded. Failure was not traceable to the conception of the system but to the fact that the people, involved in the creation and entry of data as reporting sources, were not properly trained nor convinced of the importance of the system.

If such a system is to succeed it is necessary to convince the ultimate user of the system – the *marketing management* – of the data base's practicality. This is much easier to accomplish when marketing management is part of the planning and implementation staff than it is when the system is handed to it by systems designers as a *fait accompli*.

> **"The Marketing Use of Information Processing Systems,"**
> *Diebold Research Program Report,*
> **May, 1966.**

MARKETING MODELS AND MANAGEMENT SCIENCE TECHNIQUES

Since the advent of Operations Research during World War II, there has been an expanding use of mathematical tools in the marketing area, in some of the very large corporations. Earliest applications were in the fields of economics and long-range planning. Since that time these techniques have found acceptance and use in such diverse components of the marketing function as pricing, product testing, market research, advertising effectiveness, sales planning, and competitive strategy. John Diebold considers some of the questions that have been raised about them.
(See Figure 5-C)

Models

At the heart of the use of information processing in the marketing function, as in nearly all functions to which these processes are applied, is the concept of the mathematical model.

The existence of perfectly good sophisticated modelling techniques in the form of multiple regressions, optimization models, game situations, etc., is admitted by even the strongest critics of the use of these methods. However, a common question is raised by many of them: "What good are the techniques if the data we have are not properly structured, not collected, or, in some cases,

Figure 5-C **APPLICABILITY OF COMPUTER TECHNIQUES TO MARKETING FUNCTIONS**

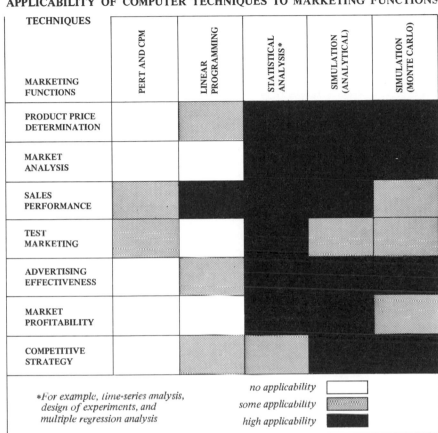

Source: **The Diebold Research Program**

unreliable?" This is a realistic appraisal of one of the more significant hindrances to the widespread use of these techniques . . . Additionally, there is a strong feeling in both industry and the university segments that most market modelling attempts assume too much about the situation and, as a result, do not accurately represent the situations they are supposed to be modelling.

There can be no argument with the fact that the data required for a particular analysis may not be in the format necessary, and that in many cases, this lack of data is a handicap we cannot ascribe any validity to this as a reason . . . While there is no area of the marketing function which can be said to be making the fullest use of the available advanced information processing techniques, examples of successful applications can be found, albeit with a great deal of digging, in nearly every industry and product.

"The Marketing Use of Information Processing Systems,"
Diebold Research Program Report,
May, 1966.

Market Simulation

We believe, in general, that information processing techniques do have wide areas of application in marketing. Furthermore, they are areas of high potential payoff. Perhaps the technique which is the most important, in terms of potential use and payoff, is the simulation of the market.

In a market simulation the factors which enter into the description of the operation of the market are qualified in the form of equations. Varying one or more factors in the model is akin to varying the conditions which play upon the market. Thus, evaluation and quantification of market changes can be made without the risks incurred in the "real world." Admittedly this is easier to talk about than to do, but it has been done and the prospects for further work in this area are good.

> *Remarks at a meeting of Diebold Research Program Sponsors,*
> **January, 1970.**

Simulating Competitive Action

The marketing area where John Diebold sees perhaps the greatest potential payoff is that of "competitive simulation," known also as "market simulation" and "competitive strategy" simulation. When a competitive simulator can be shown to work there is no problem in selling it to management, on any level. The aim of a marketing simulation is to represent the characteristics of the market, normally too diverse and complex to represent by familiar statistical and/or analytical methods, in an algorithm easily manipulated by a computer.

Simply stated, a competitive simulator is based on past actions and reactions of the competition, on the basis of which it forecasts future reactions to given actions. This, of course, calls for more data collection, analysis, and validation than anything ever before done in the marketing area — one reason The Diebold Research Program cites for the lack of substantial progress on the practical level in the development of competitive simulators. It is also, John Diebold adds, a reason for the development of the data base discussed above.

Successful simulators have been developed by some of the major companies which require bidding for jobs as a major part of their income. Records of past bids, both won and lost, and the bids of competitors, as well as detailed information on the specifications on each bid are kept. The specifications of a new job are then used as input to a bidding simulation run, and the output is a series of possible bids with the profit as well as the probability of winning . . .Similarly, pricing models have been built which determine the probability of obtaining a particular share of the market at a particular price.

The construction of competitive simulators describing complex marketing and competitive environments is no small undertaking. There must be a willingness to invest large sums for development, with the realization that the payoff, though potentially very large, will not come in the short-range, but more likely will show up in a three to five year time period after implementation to particularized situations. Moreover, much work has to be done for an individual simulator.

The cost of a competitive simulator will vary from about $400,000 to over a million dollars, depending on the nature of the industry (number of competitors and the product involved), the history of the company with regard to data collection, the degree of accuracy desired, the quality of the personnel involved in the project, and the cooperation given at all levels of management. However, it should be noted that a competitive simulator has many uses aside from competitive behavior. These include determining best strategies, product introduction, pricing, and potentials of warehouse and distribution center location.

Remarks at a meeting of Diebold Research Program Sponsors,
January, 1970.

ADDITIONAL SERVICES TO CUSTOMERS

The fifth category of computer opportunities in marketing, John Diebold has stressed is in using the computer technology as a competitive weapon in expanding service to customers. This may take the form of simply providing quicker and more conveniently obtained information for consumers, as when a public utility uses computerized audio response to provide accurate, up-to-date answers to inquiries about service restoration after a blackout. In its most sophisticated form, for business customers, it involves the development of computerized models that simulate the customer's activities, providing him with new insights on how to operate more profitably, and hence use more of your products. Here are two of his examples:

You should think in terms of developing models of retail-shop operations, being able to provide them with much better information about the conduct of their own business as additional services There will be more and more effort of this kind — using vast amounts of computer-based simulation.

"What Automation Can Mean to the Drug Industry in the Next Ten Years,"
address before the National Wholesale Druggists Association, Las Vegas, Nevada,
November 16, 1966.

. . . For example, the kinds of things that International Minerals and Chemicals has done where they sell fertilizer to distributors. They build an economic model of the farmer's farm, and the distributor goes over a very extensive questionnaire with the farmer. International Minerals and Chemicals then runs the information about the farm on its computer and comes out with all sorts of helpful guides as to how the farmer can do a better job, including what the best possible blends of fertilizers are for his particular soil conditions.

"Marketing's Role in the Coming Age of Automation,"
Sales Management,
October 1, 1966.

There are opportunities for this in many, many industries, says John Diebold, where a company can help its customer by giving him a better understanding of his needs through the simulation of his business and of his buying patterns. "Using the computer as an analytical marketing tool," he says, "you can come back to the customer with suggestions for improved kinds of services and combinations of your product. This, I think, is one of the most important areas: Getting a much better understanding of your customer and doing a major analysis in depth of his operations."

*Summing up the use of computers in marketing, in all categories, John Diebold puts the objectives in these terms: Get away from the stereotype of thinking about the computer as a high-speed data processor to develop information about what **has** happened. Look upon it in terms of **making** things happen — by changing the behavior of your own organization, the behavior of your customer, and the behavior of your competitors.*

PART III:

Developing a Firm's "In-House" Resources to Meet Future Needs and Opportunities

Photograph by Marvin Newman

Computers can provide new insights and thus open areas for new customer services as well as fundamentally changing business operations. Here John Diebold visits a German mining complex where his firm made new customer services possible through creative use of computer technology.

6

Computers open to management the possibilities of an entirely new order of magnitude of control over business operations. Savings in clerical costs will be the smallest effect of automation: it is by providing management with better and current information that they will score their greatest gains.

"Automation: A Factor in Business Policy Planning,"
The Manager,
September, 1955.

Decision points no longer need to be governed by physical or geographical considerations. Through improved communication the span of control can be widened, leading to a more efficient organization and to considerable savings . . . Traditional departmental boundaries can be expected to blur as, with intricate management-science techniques and common data bases at their disposal, decision-makers are forced to consider problems in their entirety rather than parcelling them out in pieces. Departmental structures will thus become more closely integrated.

"The Computer's Changing Role,"
Management Today,
January, 1969.

For fifteen years I have advocated bringing knowledge of the potential business uses of computers to management. It is now time to apply management's knowledge of business more fully to the planning and evaluation of computers. In allowing technicians to set goals for ADP activity, management has not been facing up to its responsibilities.

"Bad Decisions on Computer Use,"
Harvard Business Review,
January-February, 1969.

Management By the Computer

New opportunities for management: management *by* the computer provides tighter controls, and at the same time opens opportunities for new and improved services to customers.

John Diebold was among the first to recognize the impact the new information technology would have upon traditional forms of the internal organization of a business, **when not trammeled by departmental parochialism**. *Even before the actual* *"hardware" became available (as it has in recent years), he began to sound the need for considering the management impact of what the developing computer systems would incorporate: massive memories, on-line ready access, flexible programming incorporating company precedents and decision rules, and the like.*

*With imaginative implementation of these features, he repeatedly pointed out, automatic data processing could be made to assume responsibility for many of the routine functions of top and middle management. High-level executives would then be freed to devote most of their attention to their basic **business** functions — creative innovation and entrepreneurial exploitation, subtle aspects of strategy, financial planning, acquisitions and other expansion programs, and the like — in addition to their administrative responsibilities not susceptible of standardized formulation and programming, such as marketing policy, labor relations, public relations, and executive development.*

But the operative words in the above approach are "imaginative implementation." He saw that in the long run, the computer's impact would inevitably be as thoroughgoing and far-reaching as anything that could be imagined — altering almost every aspect of business organization and management. However, for the individual firm, the computer's potentials would not be realized until management began to think in terms of an information system that would transcend the traditional compartmentalized structure of business organization based upon functional specialities. This obviously called for more than merely copying and speeding up existing systems. And it certainly ran counter to the current management literature on computers, which concentrated on payroll and bookkeeping applications, and almost universally focused on clerical costs in discussing the economics of use. Thus:

"As the installations of these equipments are accomplished, I think we will begin to notice where automation is introducing changes in our concepts, our ways of thinking about management. The organizational structure of business [will] start to shift." This opinion, which I stated in 1955, I still hold today. My feeling now is that the restructuring trend will continue in business organizations. As I said in my earlier testimony, "This makes for many changes in the requirements of what people are doing in firms. It again calls attention to education, and to areas where it is necessary to understand precisely what is happening."

Testimony before Subcommittee on Automation and Energy Resources,
Joint Economic Committee, United States Congress,
August, 1960.

We now have the ability to organize our work in closer relation to reality. We no longer need to make the organization of paper work as much of an abstraction from day-to-day happenings as it has always been.

In order actually to do this, however, the businessman is faced with a wholesale reorganization of work, the likes of which he has never before even had to contemplate. If he uses the new machines of automation just to do more rapidly tomorrow what he is already doing today, he will not have come to grips with the problem; worse, he will have let slip the opportunity of his business lifetime.

> **"Education for Data Processing – The Real Challenge to Management,"**
> *Great Issues Lecture, Dartmouth College, Hanover, New Hampshire,*
> **November 11, 1957.**

Now, suddenly, information technology arrives. Suddenly you have the capability to handle the entire flow of information within a business, and to take into account instantaneously the ramifications of change in any part of that business, or in any of the environmental forces affecting it.

What we are struggling with now is the problem of how to begin to apply this technology properly. It calls for quite a different departmental structure. We are working within older departmental structures, and we are going through the transitional period, beginning to cope with the problems it presents. You can see roots of it beginning to emerge.

In each business it will vary . . .

In each kind of business, the kind of problems, the kind of systems you install, are going to be different. You can begin to see it, for example, in certain utility companies. The installation of a computer system has substantially changed the way in which relations with the customer are handled. In another case, there has been a complete shift in the departmental structure as a result of the computer system; there has been a different line-up of departments because of functional change. All we can find today are the roots. And, because this is a major problem, few people think about it — about the organizational effects involved.

> **"A Review of Computer and Data Processing Problems for Management,"**
> *keynote address before the Administrative Management Institute, New York, New York,*
> **May 16, 1962.**

The technical changes will have a deep effect on the very nature of management operations and on the form of corporate organization. You will see operational dividing lines crossed, by-passed, and even eliminated, because the new information technology demonstrates that division of labor and separation of function not only do not have the validity they had for manually operated systems, but, more often than not, are impediments.

> **"Petroleum Industry Management in the New Era of Information Technology,"**
> *address before the American Petroleum Institute, Chicago, Illinois,*
> **November 11, 1963.**

Despite his enthusiasm about potentials, John Diebold has been realistic in cautioning against expecting too much too fast — not because of limitations of the underlying technology, but because of the problems inherent in traditional management approaches and the still-to-be-resolved problems of systems methodology.

The third-generation computer systems which have now been available for some years have all the speed and capacity for the executive functions for which automation has been visualized. Such features as time-sharing, graphic display, remote access, and real-time operation give all levels of management the capability to become intimately involved in advanced management-information systems.

Nevertheless, as Diebold Research Program studies show, certainly insofar as top management is concerned, computer systems in general are still a long way from the "total management systems" visualized in the advanced literature on the subject. Only a handful of the most advanced companies are utilizing anything approaching the relevant technology — or, in John Diebold's view, have even fully grasped the underlying concept. Moreover, there are many dozens of "automated management information systems" that have been disappointingly slow to begin functioning. Forging truly top-management information systems out of more or less mechanistic data processing is in almost every case taking a good deal longer than anticipated.

It is interesting to read the following statement John Diebold made in the Harvard Business Review in 1964, and to note that five years later, in the same publication, he still felt constrained to sound the same theme:

1964

The new information systems will not be merely more mechanized versions of today's "computer applications," which are themselves simply perpetuations on tape of yesterday's punched-card runs.

The on-line multiprocessing system, linking together many remote sites through a digital communications net, is a *total* departure from today's computerized tab rooms . . .

Business imagination, analytical ability, and entrepreneurial flair will have to be exercised to apply these new systems effectively. No longer will the methodical copying of earlier procedures determine the success of an ADP installation.

Unfortunately, most experience thus far provides no proper basis for entering the new world of ADP. Most managements are, in fact, improperly prepared for ADP to a degree that is alarming.

> **"ADP — the Still Sleeping Giant,"**
> *Harvard Business Review,*
> **September-October, 1964.**

1969

Childhood must end. In view of the massive investment now taking place in the acquisition and application of computer systems to business, more sophisticated approaches are called for . . . When we consider the computer's potential for major impact on a company's position in competition, judgments on how, where, and when the investment should be made assume special importance. In addition, technology itself is changing so that those analytical techniques currently being applied are in many cases no longer appropriate to the task.

The problem . . . is the failure on the part of top management to ask the right questions. It is the failure in particular to seek quantitative measurement of the very real benefits of automatic data processing to a business. I do not mean cost displacement, but rather increased management capacity to *control* and *plan*. Such benefits are not being considered in a serious and meaningful way; yet they are today the principal reason for computer use and for moving computers out of accounting and into operational use.

The problem goes deeper still. Because top management has not asked the right questions, researchers have not yet addressed themselves sufficiently to producing useful methodologies for solution. Technicians, too, have overemphasized system costs and given relatively little attention to system benefits to the company as a whole.

> **"Bad Decisions on Computer Use,"**
> *Harvard Business Review,*
> **January-February, 1969.**

The "Technician Syndrome"

One of John Diebold's most persistent themes has been his inveighing against what he has termed the "technician syndrome" which has led to the over-preoccupation with

equipment *rather than with* **management systems** *— a preoccupation which he has always deplored. A decade-and-a-half ago he said:*

While the major problems of automation in the plant are technological, in the office they are managerial. There are many problems that have handicapped a full realization of the potentialities of automation, but on the managerial side I think that the problems reduce themselves to two:

> *The first mistake* is made when the businessman concentrates his attention on the hardware or individual machines of automation rather than the system.

> *The second major error* is that because the businessman has been impressed into thinking of automation as a scientific or engineering problem, the important decisions have often been delegated to technicians, rather than dealt with as essentially managerial problems.

Many other troubles originate from these two initial mistakes.

"Pitfalls to Business Data Processing,"
address before the University of California Conference on Automation, San Francisco, California.
January 9, 1957.

The lesson is apparently taking a long time to sink in. A recent survey of more than 2,500 executives was undertaken on behalf of the 140 U.S. and overseas companies sponsoring The Diebold Research Program. The survey, which John Diebold reported upon in the **Harvard Business Review,** *indicates that* **technicians** *are still setting goals for computers, rather than* **management** *setting goals for* **information systems.** *(See Figure 6-A)*

From all indications, computer activity in most companies does not receive the serious top management attention which one would expect in view of the magnitude of the investment and its potential benefits. Nor are the strategic importance and sensitive nature of the investment generally reflected in top management reporting, control, and operations planning. This raises the question: *Are the right people setting goals for the company's ADP activity?*

Management's over-deference to technicians is one of the prime reasons why companies often fail to realize the true potential from their data processing investment. Communication between top management and senior ADP executives is obviously far from adequate. Figure 1 shows graphically the division of responsibility for decisions among the respondents to The Diebold Research Program Survey.

"Bad Decisions on Computer Use,"
Harvard Business Review,
January-February, 1969.

Figure 6-A

DIVISION OF RESPONSIBILITY FOR ADP

(Responses of 2,557 executives)

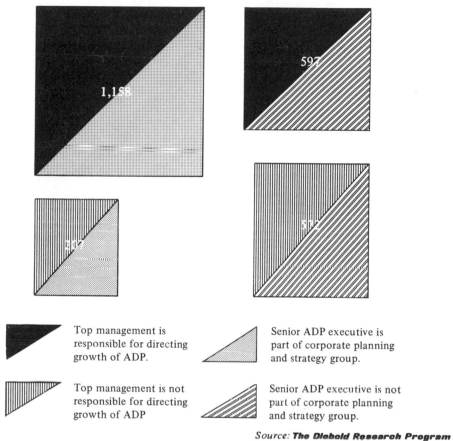

Top management is responsible for directing growth of ADP.

Top management is not responsible for directing growth of ADP

Senior ADP executive is part of corporate planning and strategy group.

Senior ADP executive is not part of corporate planning and strategy group.

Source: **The Diebold Research Program**

THE NEW MANAGEMENT INFORMATION SYSTEMS

The nature of management information systems, the purposes to which they are applied, the technologies involved, and the relative economics of different facets of ADP are all rapidly changing, and will continue to change. The accompanying exhibits (Figures 6-B(1) and 6-B(2)) developed by The Diebold Research Program, and discussed by John Diebold in the **Harvard Business Review** *cited above, show that the level of abstraction at which computers make their greatest impact is constantly rising.*

Figure 6-B (1) shows how the computer, limited no longer to the routine, structured, operational problems of as recently as 1965, is now tackling the less structured, more

THE CHANGING ROLE OF THE COMPUTER

Management application

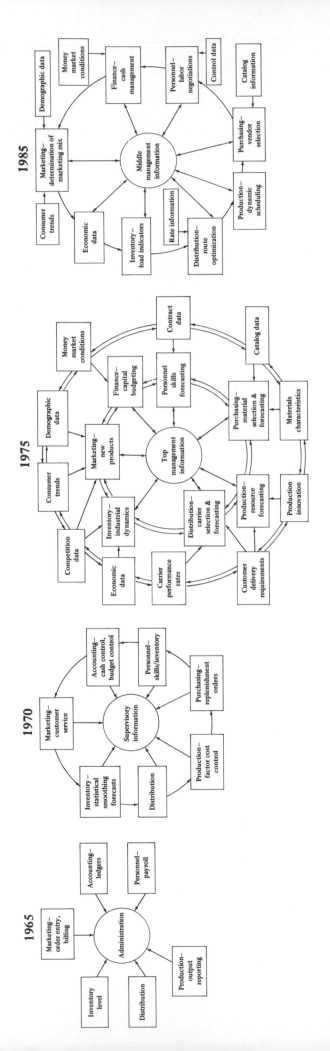

Figure 6-B (1)

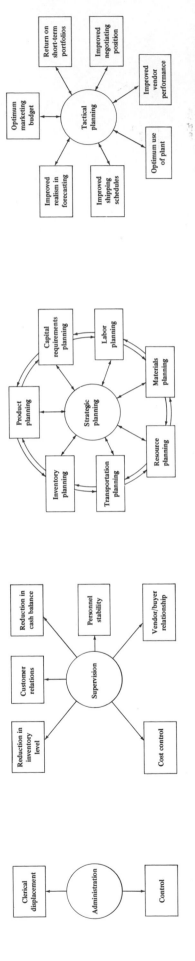

Figure 6-B (2)

Source: The Diebold Research Program

abstract, and more important problems which are the real concern of the top levels of management.

*Figure 6-B (2) shows that the evolution in application of computers requires us to keep broadening the scope of the criteria used in their evaluation. Displacement of clerical costs, an appropriate measure as recently as 1965, has already been superseded as the most relevant criterion. John Diebold's point is that as the computer becomes **more and more the servant of top management** in the years ahead, the criteria employed in its evaluation will have to be those relevant to its contribution to **policy-making** decisions. By 1985, the computer will, he says, have become "central to the nervous system" of the corporation. Again, he emphasizes that the "rethinking" required far transcends the domain of the technician:*

The subtleties of interpreting realistically the requirements of top-level management users go far beyond the ordinary procedures of systems analysts. The design of outputs is still in a fairly early experimental stage. Among the questions currently being wrestled with are the following: What sort of information do various executives require — and in what detail? To what extent should the information system be programmed for exception reporting? What sort of inquiry capability should be built into the system?

In theory, programs could be written to deliver answers to any question a manager might conceivably ask, but obviously that would be exorbitantly expensive and time-consuming. Should the system make management decisions? Or should it diagnose trouble and suggest a limited number of possible solutions?

Because of common business-oriented computer languages and easily operated terminal devices, the gap between the executive and the machine is getting steadily smaller, but it is likely that for many years to come specialists will continue to interpret management's immediate information requirements. Up to now these specialists have fallen into the general category of programmers and systems analysts — technicians who understand how to derive specific information from the system. But in the future, as executives interface more closely with the machine, the bulk of the interpretive work will have to be done by men trained primarily in business and only secondarily in data processing.

"The Next Vital Step to Management Control Systems,"
keynote address before the International Meeting of the Data Processing Management Association, San Francisco, California,
November 20, 1964.

Makeup of the Management Information System

Research by The Diebold Group indicates that the makeup of the management information system of the mid-1970s will be almost totally different from the computer system of the mid-1950s, and also from the data processing system of the late 1960s. These shifts represent the impacts of developing information technology and provide new-dimensional capabilities in data and information collection, processing, interpretation, and dissemination. Thus:

Basic to the problem of methodology is the qualitative change that is taking place in mechanized information systems as a result of rapid changes in information technology. For example, we have always thought of the computer or the central processor as being, by and large, the major part of the dollar value of an information system. In 1955 it accounted for 75 percent to 80 percent of the dollar value of the system. Today this is changed surprisingly, and in the early years of the 1970s we shall have an absolute reversal of the situation that existed in the mid-1950s. In other words, between 75 percent and 80 percent of the dollar value of a typical business computer installation will be in peripheral equipment – in the traditional input/output equipment, in communications, and in such new areas as image files. The computer central processor will have dwindled to about 25 percent of the system. (See Figure 6-C.)

"The Next Vital Step to Management Control Systems,"
keynote address before the International Meeting of the Data Processing Management Association, San Francisco, California,
November 20, 1964.

Figure 6-C CHANGES IN COMPUTER SYSTEM COST DISTRIBUTION 1954-1974

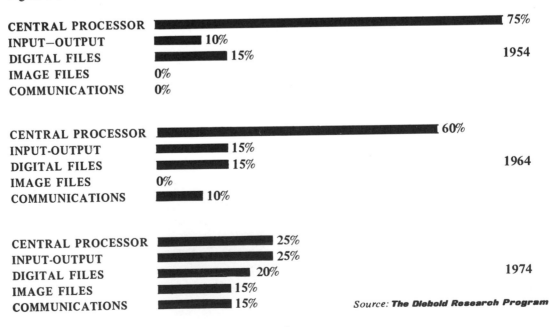

CENTRAL PROCESSOR		75%
INPUT–OUTPUT	10%	
DIGITAL FILES	15%	1954
IMAGE FILES	0%	
COMMUNICATIONS	0%	
CENTRAL PROCESSOR		60%
INPUT-OUTPUT	15%	
DIGITAL FILES	15%	1964
IMAGE FILES	0%	
COMMUNICATIONS	10%	
CENTRAL PROCESSOR	25%	
INPUT-OUTPUT	25%	
DIGITAL FILES	20%	1974
IMAGE FILES	15%	
COMMUNICATIONS	15%	

Source: The Diebold Research Program

New equipment and capabilities: New machine systems providing increased capabilities will change the nature of management information systems . . . Increasingly, management information systems will permit direct interface between management and the computer, permitting direct "conversation" between the manager and the system. This is being made possible by *display equipment*, ranging from inexpensive desk-top devices to elaborate wall-type displays now used in defense systems, and by *inquiry devices* that permit posing of questions from a desk keyboard. (Voice recognition devices are still in the future.) These developments are making currently used printed reports obsolete in many cases. Additionally, optical character recognition and other hardware developments for the *capture of data at the source* – the factory machine, the sales counter, the warehouse, the teller window – are contributing significantly to the "ideal" system through the reduction of keypunching and manual paperwork.

Developments in communications: Communications, terminals, and switching systems make it increasingly possible to have the machine system more nearly parallel to the real flow of information within the organization. Conversation will be carried on between man and machine at nearly all management levels. (See Figure 6-D.)

Executives must be especially careful that they do not purchase, manage, and evaluate the new equipment using standards developed for older, conventional systems. They cannot afford rigidity in this field now any more than they could when data processing was new.

> **"Bad Decisions on Computer Use,"**
> *Harvard Business Review*, **January-February 1969** *and*
> *Diebold Group Report,* **"The Changing Role of the Computer in Business."**
> 1970.

Needed: New Methodology in Systems Analysis

In advocating the full use of available technology, John Diebold has been fully aware of and has called attention to a little discussed problem in connection with the new management information systems – the pressing need for an improved methodology of systems analysis. He took occasion to spell this out in detail in his keynote remarks at the International Meeting of the Data Processing Management Association:

If we are adequately and wisely to use the plethora of technological developments that are descending upon us, we must synthesize a basis for analysis of enterprise information needs. This is our next vital step.

To be absolutely candid, there is today no adequate methodology for systems analysis in general use or on the drawing boards. There is no way to estimate with precision the real current and future information needs of an enterprise in terms necessary properly to use current and future technological capabilities. Nor is there a way systematically and efficiently to translate goals into action. As a result, systems are inadequately planned in relation to the present and future potential that is at our disposal.

Figure 6-D   TYPICAL MULTIPROCESSING COMPUTER COMPLEX

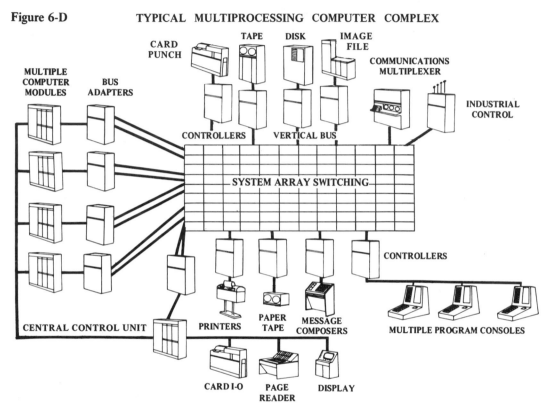

Source: The Diebold Research Program

The complexity of individual problems of systems design serve to obscure the universality of some basic needs. Briefly stated:

1. We need a synthesis of existing and some as yet undeveloped techniques leading to an imaginative new approach to analysis of information needs and a basis for information systems design.

2. We need to formulate such questions and such suggestions — which will enable management to think imaginatively in terms of what is really required — of just what it is we really want to do

in order better to further the ends of the enterprise, rather than to use our newfound and impressive capabilities simply to do by a more advanced computer system what we are doing today.

3. We need to combine the results of the synthesis with management's new thinking, in order to formulate a methodology which will organize enterprise resources to reach enterprise goals while — very importantly — modifying and expanding these goals to take advantage of newly realized systems capabilities.

4. We need to assure that the data processing manager is aware of considerations of top management policy so that he can achieve a new organizational role as a contributing member of management itself.

The task is an enormous one. In the effort to create and implement a systems methodology we must not only draw upon and synthesize the large amount of work that already has been done, but we must evaluate the past efforts and the reasons for their partial failure.

> **"The Next Vital Step to Management Control Systems,"**
> *keynote address before the International Meeting of the Data Processing Management Association, San Francisco, California,*
> **November 20, 1964.**

WHAT THE FUTURE HOLDS

From the foregoing it is obvious that the computer information system will encompass more and more of the business structure. We are now on the threshold of the commercial perfection of man-computer communications. Programming languages are increasingly becoming more like everyday language. Visual display is already a standard form of output, as are convenient desk terminal devices for keying input. Voice communication is already here for many types of output, and its achievement as input is on the horizon.

In his periodic meetings with Diebold Research Program sponsors and with client and professional-staff groups, John Diebold has indicated the challenges and opportunities for the future as he sees them. His insights of earlier years have had a high "realization index." Here are highlights of his more recent observations — developments still in the process of unfolding:

The distinction between the control system of the plant — where overall "on-line" computer control is already a reality in electric utilities, steel rolling mills, and petroleum refineries — and the ADP system in the office will disappear. One management information system will feed the entire business. This system will comprise the arteries through which will flow the life stream of the business: market intelligence, control information, strategy decisions, and feedback for change.

The direct dialogue between the manager and the system will reduce the need for intermediary assistants and supervisors. Further, the integration of previously separate activities, and a reduction in the number of divisional and departmental units, will mean fewer positions for management development. Nevertheless, more general or project managers will be needed, and at a much earlier stage. On the whole, the manager's job will become more difficult rather than easier, for he will need technical skills as well as experience in line functions, an ability to respond to change when everything moves at a faster pace, plus all the traditional entrepreneurial judgment and drive that make a company dynamic.

The data processing center that currently receives information and transmits reports will change into an activity that reaches into nearly every corporate activity, from data collection on the factory floor to an on-line display in an executive office . . . We shall see extension of automatic data processing into areas in which input costs were formerly prohibitive, where memory costs formerly prohibited the allocation of enough file or operating memory, and the like. Additionally, there will be extension of information processing to more complex areas, such as complex production scheduling, for which older systems were not sufficiently sophisticated.

The coming information system will be a combination of data processing and "built-in" operations research techniques. A production scheduling system, for example, will receive input in the form of data on orders, inventories, and current schedules. It will apply to these data the appropriate mathematical approaches to inventory level optimization and shop simulation and will develop a plan and schedule whose output will take the form of production and material orders.

Heuristic, or self-organizing, programs will allow computerized information systems to develop their own problem-solving methods best suited to the management analysis or problem at hand. These systems will help achieve the goal of dispensing with formal programs altogether for certain decision-making processes handled by machine. The machines will tend more and more to "think" in the accepted meaning of that word.

The advances made in communications, among machines as well as people, already allow for direct, cheap, and immediate flow and feedback of information among any geographic points. Management therefore will be able as never before either to centralize or decentralize its decision functions. Whether or not centralization is appropriate will vary with the situation, but the decision will no longer fall automatically to decentralization merely because an organization's operations are complex and far-flung.

The role of middle management will change as the function of allocation of resources is performed by computers. Indeed, some predict the disappearance of middle management as a *line* function, and the growth of a new staff function – the analysis and continuing appraisal of the computer models and of the assumptions on which they are based, in order to keep the system sensitive and receptive to change.

New systems capability [as discussed in Chapters 3 and 4] will increasingly provide the basis for new services to customers, to promote the sale of existing products, or to broaden the range of services offered.

The rate and magnitude of the impending changes will, Diebold points out, dramatically highlight the indispensability of top-management participation in ADP planning. Managements must not delude themselves by viewing these developments as "the natural evolution of new generation business machines." The developments will comprise a conceptual revolution, not an improvement in "hardware."

Truly, in John Diebold's words, "Management will never be the same again!"

Photograph by Alfred Statler

Computer systems and communication networks become ever more complex, calling for ever greater commitment of resources to equipment and the necessary skilled personnel. Here John Diebold discusses new costing techniques for measuring the effectiveness of a large computer

7

When you are dealing with equipment that sometimes costs millions of dollars, it is dangerous to be satisfied with anything less than optimum productivity.

"Applied Automation: A Practical Approach,"
keynote address before the Special Manufacturing Conference of the American Management Association, New York, New York,
October 10, 1955

Automation remains a shining promise, and nearly everyone is convinced that for business it does represent the road of tomorrow. But this is little comfort to financial officers who are faced with a computer's ravenous appetite for cash now, and whose earnest efforts to reduce costs by normal efficiency and economy methods seem almost futile in the face of this real fixed cost.

"Automation 1958: Industry at the Crossroads,"
Dun's Review,
August, 1958

Ironically, naive standards are used in justifying and evaluating the machines which so greatly extend our analytical powers... Most companies carefully weigh the decision, consider the alternatives, compare relative costs, and then reach a conclusion – on the basis of the wrong criteria entirely. The problem is not lack of technical knowledge on the part of the experts. Rather, it is the failure on the part of top management to ask the right questions.

"Bad Decisions on Computer Use,"
Harvard Business Review,
January-February, 1969

Management Of The Computer

New demands on management: management *of* the computer calls for new managerial capabilities and imposes new organizational disciplines.

By 1975, Diebold Research Program studies indicate, the typical medium- and large-user company will be spending more than twice as much for information systems equipment and activities as it did in 1965. However, in such companies the computing and data processing capability will increase approximately seventeenfold during the same period. Clearly the problems of organization, direction, and control of these new capabilities will take on ever-increasing importance.

In the preceding chapter we discussed John Diebold's continuing emphasis on the need for top management involvement in the determination of the type and extent of management information systems, in order to participate intelligently in the selection and evaluation process that must underlie the heavy commitments of corporate resources to computer systems. These are the determinants of decisions in the area of management **by** *the computer.*

Similar involvement, he has always contended, is needed in the area of management **of** *the computer: the place of the computer activity within the corporate organization, the caliber and status of the person heading up the activity, criteria for the selection of personnel to staff it, and, importantly, continuing evaluation of performance within the broad parameters of total information needs (as against the narrow view of cost displacement alone) as set forth in the preceding chapter.*

However, management involvement, he has said, should not consist of a compulsion to learn programming – which most attempts to educate management have always emphasized and continue to emphasize. His point is that management must take the trouble to understand what the new technologies make possible, and what is necessary in order to apply them effectively and imaginatively. Only in this way will it be able to make its approval of basic equipment choices meaningful, and only in this way will it be able to provide for computer-organization leadership of requisite competence and to accord it commensurate status. In addition, he has always urged top management to arrange for meaningful dialogues between senior computer technicians and senior management personnel, in the interest of continuing communications and mutual education.

He made this point of management involvement forcefully in an interview for a top-management readership audience conducted over a dozen years ago, when computer installations were just beginning to come into widespread use for business applications:

Caught with their budgets down and with the responsibility of enforcing cost reductions on the rest of the organization, many comptrollers are red-faced about the cash drain of their own computer centers . . .

A case in point is that of a West Coast aircraft parts manufacturer which bought nearly every piece of equipment produced by its tabulating machine supplier. The company progressed from electromechanical calculators to electronic punched-card calculators and finally to an intermediate-size computer. By simply transferring previous routines to the computer without changes in procedure or results sought, conversion to the computer was accomplished very smoothly. The tabulating supervisor in charge of the conversion was basking in praise from all sides for the unusual ease of the changeover.

Finally, however, the controller got a look at a comparative expense statement — which showed that although the computer was apparently not producing any new data, or even producing data faster than the previous system, departmental expenses had risen by more than $4,000 per month. After a year of study and some $50,000 in wasted rentals later, additional applications of the equipment provided justification for the higher rental.

> **"Automation 1958: Industry at the Crossroads,"**
> *Dun's Review,*
> **August, 1958**

DATA PROCESSING PLANNING AND DIRECTION

It early became clear to John Diebold that the status within the organization of the executive heading up the data processing activity is vital. The person with top responsibility for this function, he insisted, certainly had to be sufficiently broadgauged to be accepted in management councils if management was to participate in total systems planning to the extent advocated in the preceding chapter. The most effective way of involving top management, he said, was for the head of data processing to report directly to top management. However, by this he did not mean the machine-room supervisor, but rather the individual responsible for setting overall information-processing goals and developing overall systems design. In fact, in his view this responsibility for planning the role of the computer in the business was entirely distinct from the responsibility for operating the equipment, which could well report elsewhere.

This organizational concept, which he consistently advocated from the start, flew in the face of practice as it emerged in the early days of computerized business data processing, when it was traditionally lodged in the controller's organization, and frequently at a relatively low level. John Diebold recognized this organizational placement as an understandable evolution, but spelled out its shortcomings:

Deterring factors differ from installation to installation. Sometimes – but rarely now – the equipment is at fault. In most cases the problem can be laid right on management's doorstep:

Inadequate planning, for the most part parochial rather than corporate-wide in scope.

Not enough fresh thinking, and too much reliance on canned approaches.

Selection of the wrong people to plan the installation – technical specialists who fail to acknowledge or even appreciate their limited understanding of business practice.

Overemphasis on hardware and underemphasis on the design of comprehensive systems.

But the basic problem lies deeper: *we still have no place for ADP in our organizational structures.*

Machine accountants were the first to become aware of computer potential because computers were originally manufactured and supplied mainly by the builders and sellers of punched-card accounting equipment. Accountants attended the manufacturers' "schools," learned the new vocabulary, and became "computer experts." They thus became a ready-made repository for the ADP function.

Conversion of existing punched-card applications seemed to be the natural avenue to the world of tomorrow. (Payroll handling was the favorite for conversion, despite the already high efficiency of tab methods for it.) The case seemed closed; the responsibility for ADP was "logically" assigned to the assistant controller in charge of machine accounting.

Plausible as the move may have seemed at the time, it has got many companies into trouble. The assistant controller may do a commendable job in the areas for which he is normally accountable. But his new ADP role frequently places him in an unfamiliar position where he can do neither himself nor his organization much good. True, some computer systems can be justified on the basis of their clerical savings, which are usually the assistant controller's prime preoccupation. However, it is the vision of improved management control (as spelled out in the preceding chapter) through a highly responsive, organic business information system that has attracted *imaginative* management to the new world of computers.

Assistant controllers, equipped with the best computers in the world, are not going to make the vision of applied information technology a reality very often. They are buried too deep in one leg of the business. They lack status. They lack authority. Their departmental position arouses the antipathy of their peers, to say nothing of that of the thrice-removed functional vice presidents, the even tenor of whose ways ADP must inevitably disturb. But, most important of all, they lack the entrepreneur's view of the enterprise as a whole.

We can only speculate on the final outlines of the solution. Probably a new management function will arise which will consist of the design, installation, programming, continual reprogramming, and operation of the *total* business information system, and which will link the traditional activities of market analysis, product development, sales effort, and accounting control. Whether this will be a staff or a line function is a moot and perhaps academic question. But it will surely be a senior-management function staffed by the ablest men the business can find. Only if conceived and organized in this way can it help the organization realize the full potential of ADP.

"ADP – The Still Sleeping Giant,"
Harvard Business Review,
September-October, 1964

Caliber

The executive with top responsibility for data processing as here conceived must obviously be a seasoned, technically knowledgeable man of high caliber, since he must be acceptable as a member of the management team when management becomes involved in decisions on information systems of the scope discussed in the last chapter. Similarly, he must be able to assume responsible internal line responsibility for the efficient conduct of the increasingly complex computer installation itself. John Diebold points out that the myriad configuration possibilities of the proliferating peripheral equipment that will form roughly 80 percent of the systems previously described will require highly sophisticated cost-evaluation concepts, standards, and controls-to say nothing of the supervisory skills called for in managing an organization largely composed of highly creative, professional personnel. He has outlined some of the management specifications as follows:

The [top data processing executive] must become deeply involved with the major problems of management throughout the company. He must be knowledgeable about issues concerning sales, finance, manufacturing, and other areas, as well as accounting. Furthermore, he should be able to think and make decisions on the basis of top management considerations — considerations which involve an understanding of economic and general public policy issues.

It is essential that [he] develop a highly responsive network to provide information of a common utility to all areas of management. He must therefore play an effective role in the research and development of the enterprise itself. He must be given complete freedom to explore in depth the problems of management information systems. In short, the activities of the data processing manager must be intimately integrated into the work of top management itself.

"The Next Vital Step to Management Control Systems,"
keynote address before the International Meeting of the Data Processing Management Association, San Francisco, California,
November 20, 1964

STANDARDS AND EVALUATION

*"Computers," as John Diebold has always insisted, "are too important to businessmen to leave to the technicians." Because of the mystique that early surrounded computers, there has been a tendency not merely to delegate operation to technicians — obviously something that must be done — but also to **abdicate** to the technicians the performance evaluation and controls which management customarily applies to other areas of business. One result of this, as indicated in the previous chapter, has been a narrowgauged view of the opportunities presented by computer-based management information systems, and on resultant narrow cost-displacement. Worse, as he points out, present criteria for allocating resources to ADP are based on outdated data processing operations or on rules of thumb, and do not take into account the ability of computers to contribute to profits, and/or to cut operating costs **outside** of ADP:*

The benefits accruing from any management information system, whether computerized or not, may be seen to fall into three categories:

1. *Cost displacements* — i.e., savings in data processing cost because of reductions in the clerical workforce and other changes.

2. *Operational gains* — i.e., efficiencies in corporate operations resulting from the application by managers of information received through the system — for instance, data on inventory reductions and faster production.

3. *Intangible benefits* — i.e. improvement in customer service, corporate planning and forecasting, the ability to sustain growth, and other advantages which may not be present without the system but which depend on management's astuteness in using it.

Many companies estimate the payback period or make a return-on-investment calculation before authorizing ADP capital expenditures. However, such studies are generally based on cost-displacement savings. It may be acknowledged that operational and intangible benefits will accrue, but serious attempts at measuring the value of these benefits are usually lacking . . . Management may gain important improvements in customer service, in planning and forecasting skills, in its ability to sustain growth, and in other ways.

How can management take into account both the operational and intangible benefits? There is one thread common to both: each of them is derived from information supplied by the system to various classes of recipients — management, customers, salesmen, production supervisors, and others. Instead of starting with costs of processing data, why not start with the positive value of the information produced by that processing? . . . The value of information from ADP is not what it costs to obtain, but rather what it can do for management. Costs have their place, but in a different part of the equation.

"Bad Decisions on Computer Use,"
Harvard Business Review,
January-February, 1969

DATA PROCESSING PERSONNEL

Along with his insistence upon intelligent investment criteria and performance-cost standards for computer installations, John Diebold has called for greater top-management concern about the selection and performance-evaluation of computer-department personnel:

If many companies are weak in financial criteria for judging the business value of the machines, they are even more handicapped by the lack of criteria for judging the performance of computer personnel. The miserable experience some companies have had in this area has produced high costs. These costs are going to increase at a disproportionate rate. Recent studies by The Diebold Group indicate:

> While the share of hardware costs in the total ADP mix has declined during the past five years, the share of personnel and software costs has substantially increased. These costs often amount to twice the annual hardware cost of the computer system.

> The number of positions for programmers and systems analysts in the United States is expected to rise from 317,000 in 1967 to approximately 560,000 by 1970.

> Lack of standards for selection, classification, compensation, training, and measuring the performance of such personnel does not argue well for either quality or cost. Too often, for example, a systems analyst is a programmer whose resume is captioned "systems analyst."

> Computer personnel are quickly becoming the major cost of ADP in the United States. This cost needs to be more clearly related to the corporate benefits realized.

"Bad Decisions on Computer Use,"
Harvard Business Review,
January-February, 1969

The manning of ADP is indeed a key management concern, and John Diebold has contributed significantly to the literature of ADP personnel planning and control. He has continually stressed the need for management, in an age of technology, to address itself to the management of creative professional personnel, of which ADP personnel forms an increasingly significant part. Additionally, of course, with the growing prevalence of computer-based management information systems, ADP personnel of the proper caliber is a prime resource for top-management talent. These matters are considered in detail in the two following chapters.

MANAGEMENT PRACTICE

Continued reiteration of John Diebold's organizational philosophy for ADP has, apparently been striking responsive chords – at least in the larger, more ADP-sophisticated organizations. This is indicated by findings of a Diebold Research Program study of fifty large organizations in the United States, undertaken to determine (1) the place of the ADP activity within the corporate organization structure, and (2) the historical and future trends of the relationship between the ADP activity and other functions within the corporation. (In the companies surveyed, five levels of applications sophistication were identified, ranging from historical accounting operations to highly integrated management information systems.)

Emergence of ADP as a High-Level Function

The Diebold Research Program survey indicates that there is a definite trend towards major organizational changes which elevate the **ADP** function in the corporate hierarchy. This trend appears to be independent of applications sophistication, although there is a correlation between applications level and reporting level: as the applications level becomes higher, the **ADP** activity reports at a level closer to the Chief Executive Officer.

More than half the companies reported that **ADP** organizational changes have either been made or are planned. In cases where **ADP** already holds a relatively high position in the company, such as reports being made directly to the Vice Presidential level, the **ADP** Manager himself is being given Vice Presidential status, or reports directly to the Chief Executive Officer.

Even in companies in which **ADP** presently is low in the corporate hierarchy, it is being elevated to higher reporting levels, generally within the financial area.

*However, The Diebold Group emphasizes that organizational elevation of the ADP unit of itself does not insure successful high-level applications development. This, adds John Diebold, is a more complex problem, requiring **experienced and forward-looking personnel in the data processing function**. It requires a management which has been educated to the uses and capabilities of data processing, with a history of successful and cost-effective use of data processing throughout each applications-level stage.*

Applications Sophistication

In the comments below, levels of applications sophistication are defined as follows:

Level 1 – Historical Accounting. At this level, only historical accounting functions were accomplished with ADP equipment, usually related to payroll and labor distribution, sales accounting and reporting, or financial control.

Level 2 – Current Accounting–Operations. Here a firm has achieved means for supporting the main operating departments of the firm on a current, rather than an historical basis. Such applications would likely include production control and scheduling, inventory control, daily cash accounting, etc.

Level 3 – Departmental Operating Summary (Some Management Reporting). At this level a sufficient scope of operating information has been mechanized to permit management reports to be created for at least some of the major departments or functional activities in the mainstream of the firm's business.

Level 4 – Departmental Operating Statements (Significant Amount of Management Reporting). With this general level of data-base availability, operating statements for each major department and functional activity in the firm would be available for use not only at the departmental level, but at the Executive Vice Presidential level as well. These reports would be used mainly for diagnosis of problems, rather than for identifying current or potential problems.

Level 5 – Departmentally Integrated Management Information System. At this stage of applications development, the basic transaction activity information within all major functional areas of the firm are being captured and introduced into a data base. This serves the many departmental and executive information needs of the firm without duplicating or overlapping files that are maintained specifically for individual departments. The data with suitable computer manipulation are available to management for evaluation and allocation of resources across departmental lines.

Sophistication and Reporting Level

With the increasing level of applications development, there is a corresponding increase in the frequency of the ADP organization reporting to the senior executive level (Vice President or higher).

Of all companies surveyed, more than 70 percent already have the ADP organization reporting to a senior executive. In the remaining firms, the ADP unit reports to a lower-level executive in the financial area. Almost half of the companies in the survey are in the higher applications level group.

Of these twenty-four firms at applications level 4 and 5, seventeen have their ADP functions reporting to the chief financial executive, and the remaining seven report to an administrative or operations executive.

Based on the information provided by the respondents regarding firm plans for increasing the level of applications, and intentions of changing ADP organizational lines, it was found that, as companies become more sophisticated in the use of data processing, there is a strong tendency to reorganize the ADP function and the organizational level to which it reports.

Increasing Degree of Corporate Control of ADP

Those firms with a high level of applications sophistication and a high level of reporting also have centralized control of company-wide data processing activities and, as applications sophistication increases, corporate control of divisional ADP activities tightens.

Of the fifty companies surveyed, twenty-four have complete control of company-wide data processing activities at the corporate level. This includes companies in which all ADP work is done by the corporate ADP department, as well as companies in which the divisional data processing activities report directly to the corporate ADP department. In twenty-one of these twenty-four companies, the ADP function reports to an executive at Vice Presidential level or higher. Fourteen of the companies are at high levels (levels 4 and 5) of applications sophistication.

Another thirteen companies reported that, while they did not directly control divisional ADP activities at corporate level, a close functional relationship was maintained between these groupings, in which overall policy responsibility resided with the corporate group. The degree of functional control varied from company to company, ranging from coordination and standardization of activities to complete corporate systems responsibility. This includes the performance of system-analysis and/or programming for the divisions, with only the day-to-day operations of the departments being independent.

In only four of the companies surveyed were the corporate and divisional ADP activities entirely separate and independent.

It is interesting to note that the centralization of data processing activities is independent of the centralization/decentralization organizational concept of the company. The Diebold researchers found centralized control of ADP in highly diversified and decentralized firms, as well as in companies with a homogeneous product line and centralized control of operating functions. (The definition of centralized ADP did not encompass process control, or scientific, or special-purpose computers.) The Diebold Group did find, however, that those industry leaders which have an extremely high level of successful applications sophistication also had early scientific process control and manufacturing data processing experience. The management information and financial reporting activities were thus based on a strong and successful history of technology and applications in the operating area of the firm.

Lines of Reporting

"Companies are generally reluctant to make radical organization changes," observes John Diebold, commenting on the implications in the recent DRP findings. "This appears to be true not only in the case of ADP, but in all major functional areas."

Since it is difficult to change historical precedent, and as the ADP function usually starts out in accounting, it tends to evolve at higher levels within the financial area . . .

However, it has become clear that when a company has had a long experience of successful data processing usage, a broader range or executive-level personnel become familiar with the techniques and capabilities of ADP. It is at this point that the ADP function tends to move out of the financial area to an area considered a "more neutral" place from which to serve effectively a wider range of information needs of the company.

From Diebold Group surveys, this new area appears to be the "Vice President of Administration," although we have found a tendency to advance the ADP function to even higher levels, as it plays a still more important role in the corporation. In several large companies the data processing function now reports, or will soon report, directly to the President; in one case, reporting to the Chairman of the Board is contemplated; in two other cases reporting to the Senior Executive Committee is either accomplished or under consideration.

foregoing extracts and commentary based on Diebold Research Program Report,
"Corporate Organization and the Computer Issues Facing Management,"
August, 1966.

SUMMARY . . . AND NEW DIRECTIONS

The organizational changes being wrought by the computer development and information technology point straight to the conclusion that the corporate information systems activities must increasingly command the attention of top management. Diebold Group findings may be summarized as follows: (Typical organization formats are shown in the accompanying charts.)

A LARGE FOOD PROCESSING AND DISTRIBUTING COMPANY

CORPORATE ORGANIZATION

Application Level:

– Integrated Management Information System

– Significant Amount of Management Reporting

– Some Management Reporting

– Operations (Production, Inventory, etc.)

– Accounting, Statistical Reporting

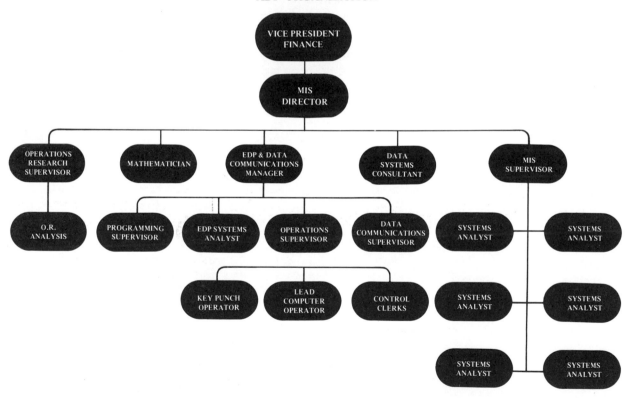

ADP ORGANIZATION

ADP Reporting Level:

The Information Services Division reports to the Vice President-Controller and is two levels below the President.

Recent changes have been made internal to the ADP activity in which accounting applications have been separated from information systems, and "data cells" created to serve specific areas and divisions.

Centralization/Decentralization of ADP Activities:

The Information Service Division has corporate-wide responsibility for all data processing – three divisions have their own computers, but report functionally to the corporate department. The intent is to close down these centers and consolidate all ADP activities at the corporate level.

Definition of Information Needs:

The Information Systems Division is in the process of testing different systems for providing information at top management, and operating management level. The Division is making suggestions and recommendations and evaluating reports based on user reactions.

Although a recent study was conducted to establish a distribution information system, no corporate-wide MIS study is contemplated for the near future.

Source: The Diebold Research Program

A LARGE, DECENTRALIZED, DIVERSIFIED FOOD PRODUCTS COMPANY
CORPORATE ORGANIZATION

Application Level:

- – Integrated Management Information System
- – Significant Amount of Management Reporting
- – Some Management Reporting
- – Operations (Production, Inventory, etc.)
- – Accounting, Statistical Reporting

ADP Reporting Level:

The Director of Management Information Services reports to the Vice President of Finance.

Centralization/Decentralization of ADP Activities:

At present, ADP activities are decentralized. Divisions and subsidiary companies have a loose working relationship with the corporate department, but the trend is toward tighter control. A communications-based, integrated data processing system is being planned which will coordinate divisional, financial, and operations reporting.

Definition of Information Needs:

This company has expanded its activities through an acquisition program. Systems studies have been made for divisions and subsidiaries, and as control over divisional data processing tightens they will be integrated into an overall management information system.

Source: The Diebold Research Program

103

A MAJOR PETROLEUM AND CHEMICAL COMPANY

Applications Level:
– Integrated Management Information System
– Significant Amount of Management Reporting
– Some Management Reporting
– Operations (Production, Inventory, etc.)
– Accounting, Statistical Reporting

CORPORATE ORGANIZATION

ADP ORGANIZATION

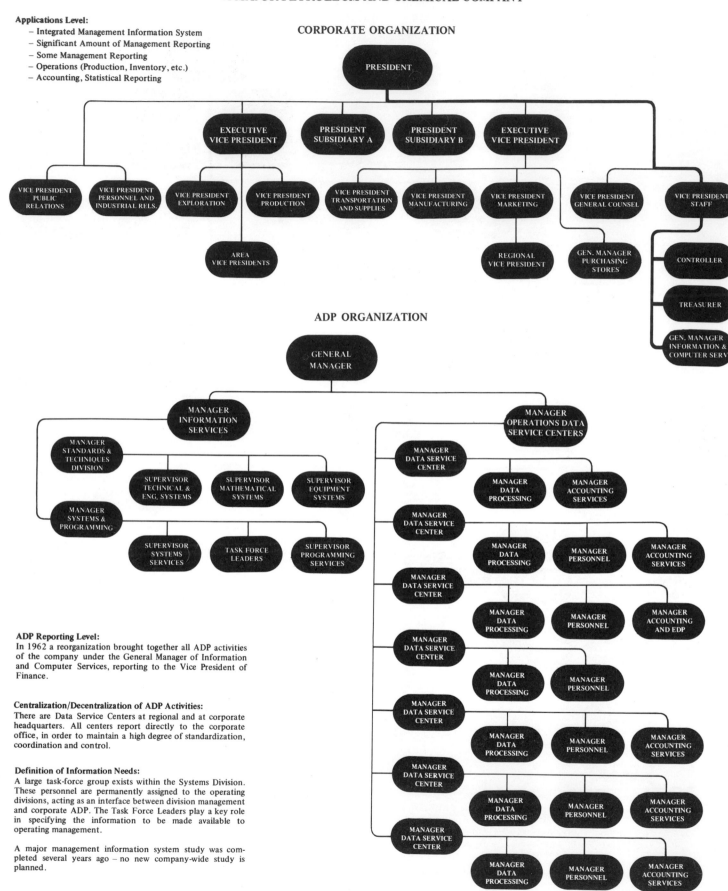

ADP Reporting Level:
In 1962 a reorganization brought together all ADP activities of the company under the General Manager of Information and Computer Services, reporting to the Vice President of Finance.

Centralization/Decentralization of ADP Activities:
There are Data Service Centers at regional and at corporate headquarters. All centers report directly to the corporate office, in order to maintain a high degree of standardization, coordination and control.

Definition of Information Needs:
A large task-force group exists within the Systems Division. These personnel are permanently assigned to the operating divisions, acting as an interface between division management and corporate ADP. The Task Force Leaders play a key role in specifying the information to be made available to operating management.

A major management information system study was completed several years ago – no new company-wide study is planned.

Source: The Diebold Research Program

A MAJOR AEROSPACE COMPANY

Applications Level:
- Integrated Management Information System
- Significant Amount of Management Reporting
- Some Management Reporting
- Operations (Production, Inventory, etc.)
- Accounting, Statistical Reporting

CORPORATE ORGANIZATION

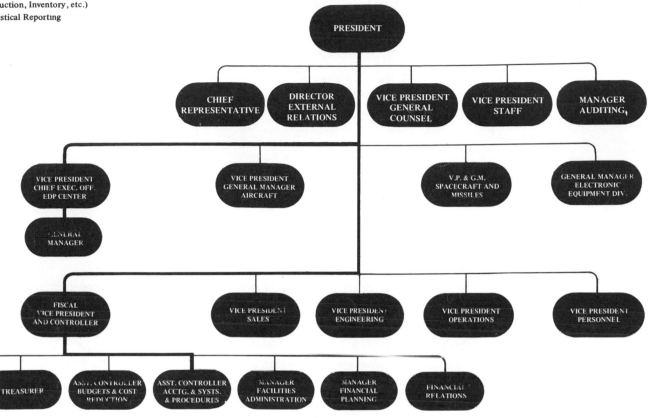

ADP ORGANIZATION

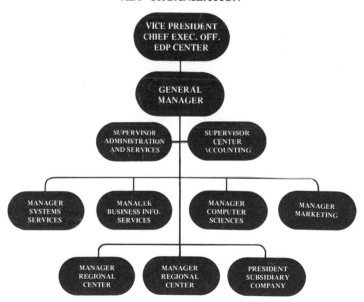

ADP Reporting Level:

ADP Service Centers report through a Vice President of Data Processing to the President. The corporate systems design function reports to the Assistant Controller under the Vice President of Finance.

Centralization/Decentralization of ADP Activities:

All data processing is performed at the Service Centers, which serve outside customers as well. The Corporate Assistant Controller is responsible for the coordination and standard-ization of company-wide information systems. His group acts as interface between management and the Service Centers.

Definition of Information Needs:

In each major division there is a systems group which works with the division to determine its information requirements. This group reports on a staff basis to the corporate Systems Department, which evaluates and approves management information requests and transmits them to the Service Center for their approval, programming and processing.

A long-range planning study is being conducted to develop information systems for the future, under the direction of a systems analyst. Management is not yet convinced that this is the correct approach to perform long-range planning functions.

Source: The Diebold Research Program

105

Information systems have become part of direct line operations; they have ceased to be administrative adjuncts. Pricing, product development, marketing strategy, financial planning, and day-to-day operations are becoming directly interrelated with the computer system. Information systems capability is used as a direct marketing and selling aid.

Scarce capabilities in this area must be directed to the true payoff areas — those related to the heart of the business and its profits. The capabilities for this are increasingly available; top management must provide the guidance.

The increased scope and capability of future systems requires a new kind of participation by top management. Information technology has become too vital a part of a company's activities to be left to the technicians. Management's involvement must be of the following kinds:

Management must set the goals and objectives of the information systems program. This includes making sure that attention is given to the real payout areas, and that the program concerns itself with the heart rather than the periphery of a company's activities. A single simulation program to assist in pricing decisions may be of more value than many man years of effort devoted to automating an administrative function.

Management must manage the program as it manages other major elements of its business. New techniques and standards are being developed that take some of the mystery out of the information activity. Management must see that these are soundly applied.

New systems developments provide opportunities for improved organizational approaches throughout the enterprise. The number of organizational levels can be compressed, through increases in the feasible span of control and through improved communications. This can result in improved operations and significant cost savings. For example, a major insurance company now organized into one headquarters, twenty-two regions, seventy-one districts, and 850 agencies, plans to serve and control the same number of agents with six regions and sixty-three districts.

A major food manfacturer and processor has already reduced its regional distribution centers from over fifty to four, and plans shortly to move to one. Lower costs and significantly improved customer service have been the result.

The determination of the proper organizational level for divisions will be largely independent of the source or location of information. This does not necessarily mean centralization will dominate; it does mean that the location of decision points can be decided on the basis of policy rather than geographical constraints.

The foregoing, then, represent the emerging organizational and management concepts as applied to the control of the computer. Important in this picture are the stress John Diebold places upon the top-level reporting of the individual with the top ADP responsibility, the disappearance of traditional departmental separation, and the increased use of advanced decision-making techniques. Common data bases and management-science techniques will not only permit, they will require management of the computer activity that is attuned to the problems of the organization as a whole, not merely segments.

Developing management capable of making creative use of new technologies has been one of John Diebold's major concerns, and one to which he believes businessmen should devote more time and attention. Here he meets with students of the Institut Europeen d'Administration des Affaires, Fontainebleau, France, at the conclusion of one of his frequent lectures at the school.

The machines of automation are only symbols of fundamental developments that are taking place in the way we organize our world. The training of management personnel must reflect this fact. But such education programs as have accompanied automation hardly even begin to reflect it because businessmen who understand this themselves are as rare as whooping cranes.

"Education for Data Processing – The Real Challenge to Management,"
Great Issues Lecture, Dartmouth College, Hanover, New Hampshire,
November 11, 1957

On the whole, the manager's job will become more difficult rather than easier, for he will need technical skills as well as experience in line functions, an ability to respond to change when everything moves at a faster pace, plus all the traditional entrepreneurial judgment and drive that makes a company dynamic.

"The Computer's Changing Role,"
Management Today,
January, 1969

Developing Managers

The development of managerial skills must take into account the new concepts and techniques of decision-making and the new dimensions provided by modern information technology.

*John Diebold's voice was perhaps the earliest, and certainly the most consistent and insistent, to stress that the computer and related information technology represent more than a powerful technical aid in the administration of a business enterprise. His theme, constantly reiterated over the years, has been that they have opened up an entirely new world of management, calling not only for old skills sharpened, but for **new** skills appropriate to **new ways** of managing. . .and that top management has largely been blind to these new dimensions of its own craft.*

In the earliest days of automation, when the new technology was almost solely thought of in terms of factory operations, he was among the first to see and publicize the computer's implications for management decision-making. This was in keeping with his early urging that management take advantage of the mathematical decisional techniques being developed as part of the "new management sciences." While he realized that most members of management could not be expected to be conversant with the mathematics involved, he called upon them to utilize the services of the engineers and scientists in their own organizations who were. The computer would now, he pointed out, make it possible to deal with large masses of economic and marketing data hitherto impracticable to manipulate:

Even though many of the engineers and scientists employed by industry are perfectly capable of handling the mathematics of differentials and prediction, management on the whole is not. The advantages of a mathematical analysis of business problems are often not perceived. If it is suggested to management, the arguments are raised that the firm has no one capable of doing such an analysis, and that there are insufficient data, or that overly long procedures and too much paperwork are needed to arrive at what should be common-sense decisions.

Yet the common-sense courses of action often have a surprising way of not turning out, upon analysis, to be the best. But the arguments about involved solutions to even simple problems have much validity. It is here that the use of computers will make the application of operations research techniques far more practical for many businesses than is the case today.

> "Automation: The Advent of the Automatic Factory,"
> *Princeton, New Jersey: Van Nostrand Company, Inc.,* **1952.**

THE NEW BREED OF MANAGERS

How will the manager change, as a result of the demands made upon him by the world of automation? Will the same kind of man, John Diebold asks, who has risen to the top by making the right decisions more often than the wrong one, when never having all the data necessary for making any decision, be the same kind who rises to the top when he can have data to his heart's content — and when the premium is on his ability to ask for the right kind of data critical to the decision at hand? And as to his substantive knowledge, will the world of such complexity, scale, and rapid change as the one he so often described require us to return to the universal man of the Renaissance for managers? Questions such as these were speculated upon by John Diebold in the address he gave upon the occasion of his receiving an Honorary Doctor of Science Degree at Clarkson College of Technology:

Many questions come to mind when we look even a brief decade ahead, much less to the world in which today's students will have achieved their prime.

What human qualities will be needed? How can one keep abreast of the changes? Will only mathematicians, physicists or other scientists have a future in management?

Let me begin by dispensing with the last, for it is both important and typical of the problems facing those concerned with management education in a world of automation:

Scientists will still need to be scientists and managers will still be managers. However, tomorrow, as today, some trained in science will make their principal contribution in the field of management, some in the management of science and some in the management of business.

Certainly, business managers of tomorrow will be better grounded in mathematics and the fundamentals of science than are today's managers — as tomorrow's average citizen will be better grounded in these disciplines, for they will be more clearly understood to be fundamental to our world.

But the practice of management is a distinct profession. While the manager will need to understand more than superficially the nature of science and technology in order to make proper enterprise and management decisions, while he will need to know more than he does today about values and outlook of scientists, as he will be managing more of them, while he will need to be able to exercise judgment in evaluating the business consequences of alternative technological developments, he will be trained as a manager. That is something quite distinct from training as a scientist. While he will use more of the "management sciences," the emphasis will be on the "management."

The discipline of management, though, will be more nearly stripped of the underbrush that today obscures the heart of the process. Tomorrow there will be less time consumed by the methological problems of operating — more of the routine will be on magnetic tape. It will be less easy to avoid the hard realities of decision-making and particularly those of identifying problems and posing questions. *The process of making decisions itself can obscure the hard work of posing the proper decision to be made.* The latter also will continue to be the work of managers.

"The Impact of Science and Technology on the
Development of Managers,"
*address upon receipt of an Honorary Doctor of
Science Degree at a Special Convocation, Clarkson
College of Technology, Potsdam, New York,*
October 12, 1965

111

Substantive Knowledge

Knowledge of the processes of making decisions — through logic, through mathematics, through management science techniques — is unquestionably going to become more important than it is today, and anathema as it is to many, we had better accept this fact, for it is a fact.

Another area of substantive knowledge is that which changes continually — the substantive knowledge of particular technologies, product and service areas, business markets, economic opportunities, etc. There was a period — some of us were born in it — when one could get along quite well throughout one's whole life by mastering this kind of substantive knowledge thoroughly in school. That day is no longer with us.

Finally, there will be required a knowledge of people, and how they behave. Their motivations, their response, and in the most human terms their desires, wants, goals and objectives, are going to be the heart of the whole process. The manager who is intellectually more at home with machines than with people is going to be a less important part of tomorrow's world than he or the superficial writers who talk of human computers can even begin to understand. For when all is said and done, it is the human desires that shape the opportunities which spawn enterprise.

> **"The Impact of Science and Technology on the Development of Managers,"**
> *address upon receipt of an Honorary Doctor of Science Degree at a Special Convocation, Clarkson College of Technology, Potsdam, New York,*
> **October 12, 1965.**

Entrepreneurial Understanding

With the growth in the scope of enterprise and increased sophistication of management, we have come to rely in this country, and to an increasing extent abroad, on professional managers. This has been one of the great developments of our times. In the process, though, something has been virtually lost. It is business. For as enterprises have been increasing in scale, fewer and fewer of the managers have been at the same time businessmen. This is an evolution that has received all too little attention. Suffice it to say that the entrepreneurial flair — the flame that burns in the small businessman as well as in the great creators of major industries — tends to be extinguished among the men who fit many of the other requirements that large-scale management systems impose.

The problem of preserving entrepreneurial flair in an environment of many large scale enterprises is one of the more pressing and less considered questions in management education. The premium to a good answer keeps increasing.

Let me clearly state my respect for the educational system of our country. But to continue properly to serve our society, it must change as our society changes — and the change must be in the form of the institution as well as in the content of the curriculum. Learning how to learn, understanding human needs and human behavior, learning a basis for judgment when alternative scientific and technical schemes are the determinants for enterprise success – these are the imperatives for management education in the age of automation.

"The Impact of Science and Technology on the Development of Managers,"
address upon receipt of an Honorary Doctor of Science Degree at a Special Convocation, Clarkson College of Technology, Potsdam, New York,
October 12, 1965.

The Magnitude of the Job

While John Diebold consistently sounded the call for rethinking the job of manager and the kind of training industry and the educational institutions would have to provide, he never minimized the magnitude of the training and education the programs called for:

The job of manager will require an increasing ability to think and to judge; an increased education in the largest sense of the term. The role of management will widen, not narrow, as a result of automation, and it would be a grave error to assume that the task is simply to train management in technical skills.

Management must learn new skills, it is true, but these skills are uniquely managerial and call for a very serious effort to define the qualities that are needed for successful management in an age of automation, and then to learn how we can both acquire and teach these skills. This, to my mind, is the fundamental challenge of automation to the manager.

"Automation as a Challenge to Management,"
International Social Science Bulletin,
June, 1957.

There is virtually no realization of the magnitude of the task of using these wonderful new machines properly, and little understanding at all of how to use them to solve management problems. Consequently, there is an urgent need for basic education in training of the men and women in business, not just in how to work the machines, but in the far more difficult task of how to employ them properly and profitably.

The need to make these changes presents business management with the most colossal job of education we have ever faced. The need is here today. We have no choice but to meet it, and to do so at once. The men and women already in business are the ones who must bring about these changes. They must be adequately trained for the task. And for the present, at least, this gigantic

113

training effort must be performed by business itself. There is no other institution able to do the job.

"Education for Data Processing – The Real Challenge to Management,"
Great Issues Lecture, Dartmouth College, Hanover, New Hampshire,
November 11, 1957.

THE LARGER ASPECTS OF MANAGERIAL DEVELOPMENT

*During the early years of the "computer age," because of the strangeness of the new machines and the problems inherent in getting the early systems "on the air," emphasis perforce had to be on problems of "nuts-and-bolts" application – reorganization of files and data-handling sequences, installation and operation of equipment, training of programmers and operators, policing of data preparation throughout the organization to make it suitable for computer input. In these very years, when John Diebold and the consulting firm he had organized were themselves heavily enmeshed in client problems of equipment choice and operator training, he was already sounding warnings against becoming so preoccupied with the technical aspects of data processing that the larger aspects of the **managerial** potentials of the new technology and the associated **management** training and development would be short cut, if they were recognized at all.*

At the start and for quite a few more years, the practical solution to this problem is going to have to come from business itself. There is no hope, in the immediate future, that the buck can be passed along to the colleges and high schools. In time, if business understands what its needs truly are and makes these needs known, the educational system will begin to produce young men and women trained not just to use automation equipment but to understand the *potentials* of automation.

But as things stand, the great bulk of the people who must accomplish the crucial task of administering the conversion to automation, and those who are going to be living and working in a world at least partly automated, are men and women who have already completed their formal education and are now working in business and industry. The responsibility for training these people is largely that of private business.

Current attempts at training in data processing depend largely on the courses in how to use the machines that equipment manufacturers give to their customers' personnel and on a few similar university extension programs. Such training is almost always tied to the machines of automation, and it is hardly adequate even to develop a understanding of the machines. It rarely begins to indicate the problem of how to apply them. Moreover, these schools are tied not only to machines, which is bad enough, but to the machines of one particular manufacturer. Attending only one of these schools is something like expecting to learn about political science by spending a few weeks in the local Republican or Democratic headquarters.

What is needed is training that is more basic, broader in scope, more intensive, given in greater depth. The success of a computer installation depends only partly on adequate technical training in programming for those who will actually convert a given business task to machine instructions. Even this is a training problem that, in itself, requires many months of on-the-job instruction beyond the scant month or two in a manufacturer's school, if a prudent businessman is to feel confident that the success or failure of the entire program is not just a gamble.

"Education for Data Processing – The Real Challenge to Management,"
Great Issues Lecture, Dartmouth College, Hanover, New Hampshire,
November 11, 1957.

. . .and "Cross-Fertilization"

And there was an additional insight that John Diebold had at the very start – the need for associated training in depth required for people within the organization who are not directly involved in any way with the computer or its operation:

For example, the sales manager must understand a good deal about what a computer can do if he is even to begin to take advantage of its powerful potential for producing new kinds of market and distribution analysis. It is the sales manager, not the head of the data processing center, who knows what sales information is critical. The computer man can only present what he thinks the sales manager needs. This is equally true of production control, of cost and financial accounting – indeed, of virtually all areas of business management.

Few business men have even begun to think about these problems in nearly specific enough terms. But it is business that will have to find the immediate solution through in-company training programs and extensive allocations of time and funds for training.

"Education for Data Processing – The Real Challenge to Management,"
Great Issues Lecture, Dartmouth College, Hanover, New Hampshire,
November 11, 1957.

It is vital to the success of any systems design that all affected managerial personnel (and oftentimes wage earners as well) be as well informed as possible on the ends sought, the means used, and the management directives to the systems analyst. It is also most helpful, where possible, to have these affected personnel acquainted with "how" the systems analysts will arrive at a new system as well as "why" they do so.

"The Next Vital Step to Management Control Systems,"
keynote address before the International Meeting of the Data Processing Management Association, San Francisco, California.
November 20, 1964.

And, of course, as he also pointed out, this need for cross-fertilization works both ways — the systems and computer personnel must themselves be kept from becoming parochialized and compartmentalized specialists:

We need to assure that the data processing manager is aware of considerations of top management policy, so that he can achieve a new organizational role as a contributing member of management itself.

This problem is of special importance as long as there is no formal training inherent in our educational system specifically designed to prepare systems analysts and to insure a position for the data processing manager among top management. Every effort must be made by responsible management to insure that the members of the corporate systems group are continuously exposed to all available writings, seminars, courses and other activities in order to allow the improvement of staff members — without which systems improvement is impossible. The solution of this problem again is an integral part of systems analysis because successful implementation of the system is premised upon it.

"The Next Vital Step to Management Control Systems,"
keynote address before the International Meeting of the Data Processing Management Association, San Francisco, California.
November 20, 1964.

Again, the "Technician Syndrome"

Along with the foregoing concepts have been John Diebold's continuing plea for top-management involvement in the basic planning for the full-potential use of information technology in its operations. To this end as alluded to in Chapter 6, he has cautioned against the "technician syndrome" in deciding the type and scope of the management information system to be developed. The same caveat applies to managerial development.

In the stereotyped idea concerning automation — because automation is highly technical, it must be left to the technicians — we meet a not uncommon condition of our age: the overwhelmingly high regard for the technician. It has been pointed out time and again that ours is an age of specialization, and a narrow "professionalism" has extended from the sciences, and in some cases from the liberal arts, into business.

The machinery of automation is, indeed, extremely complex. The science of communication and control, on which it is based, is one of the most advanced branches of technology, and the computer is the most advanced piece of equipment yet built in this field. But nobody is asking the businessman to build a computer or to repair one if it breaks down. These are jobs that only technicians can do. Management has a unique function, and one that is, in its way, as complex and difficult, and perhaps more so.

> **"Automation as a Challenge to Management,"**
> *International Social Science Bulletin,*
> **June, 1957.**

It is not enough to realize that an automation program is best run by choosing a man who understands your business, rather than by an engineer who understands automation equipment. It is of crucial importance to choose the very best man you can find to head your program. My experience has been that most top management is appalled to learn that it will not only have to put a key person in charge of automation, but that he will have to spend as much as a year simply studying the problems and learning how to solve them. "Why, I can't spare my best man," executives have said to me. "I have to keep the business running, don't I?" Nevertheless, it is false economy to do anything else.

The question is often posed: should we train engineers to be managers or managers to be engineers? Such a question, even when the technical complexities of automation are acknowledged, ignores the real role of management. Automation intensifies the traditional problems management has to face, the economics of a venture, and the equally commanding problem of industrial relations.

On the other hand, as I have pointed out, automation also provides the tools for reaching detailed and far-projecting decisions. The most critical problems facing management are not the technical problems, but the traditional managerial problems thrown into a new relief.

> **"Automation and the Manager,"**
> *address before the XIth International Management Congress of the Comite International de l'Organisation Scientifique (CIOS), Paris, France,*
> **June 26, 1957.**

The ADP Organization —
A Resource for Top-Management Talent

As part of the whole program of management development, John Diebold has strongly advocated the formulation of more rewarding career-paths for ADP personnel — not only in terms of increased status of the ADP activity within the corporate hierarchy, but also in terms of "graduating" from ADP into top policy-deciding positions in management. This will have the two-fold result of improving the caliber of ADP management, and also gradually developing a top-management structure grounded in the theory and application of information technology.

Involved is the matter of developing career paths for creative and professional personnel in general, not merely ADP. Accordingly, the discussion of such career paths, using Diebold Research Group findings with respect to ADP personnel as an illustrative example, is reserved for the following chapter.

THE ROLE OF HIGHER EDUCATION

The role of the universities and the business schools in the new technology was early discerned by John Diebold — but here he found himself, for a long time, a lone voice in calling for a broad-gauged approach that considered the total needs of the new breed of manager called for — not merely exposure to a collection of new technical skills, but education that stressed the relationship between the various management disciplines and specialities, and how information technology could be used to weld them into an integrated whole.

Our business schools are training young people to go into business and this is going right on along conventional lines. Many universities and business schools in the States have tacked on a full course on computers or have half a dozen computer courses on the end of the curricula, but as yet there is no relationship between the course in marketing or the course in industrial management and the course in digital computers. These courses are added because every one feels there will be revolutionary changes in marketing and in industrial management, but there is very little communication between these. We have a great process in the States yet to go through in the problem of changes in business education, and this is, in the end, going to determine how well we actually do use this equipment.

"Electronic Data Processing: A Progress Report,"
address before the Office Management Association, Nottingham, England,
November, 1958.

Business education must change vastly in the next decade. Not only does the business administrator have new tools, such as the computer, with which to work, and a changed organizational environment within which to operate, as a result of automation; he is also faced with a considerable change in the role of the administrator. Insufficient attention is being given to this problem today. While it is fashionable to add courses in computers, little if anything is being done in the required area of fundamental change in approach.

> **"The Basic Economic Consequences of Automation for the State of New York,"**
> *Governor's Conference on Automation, Cooperstown, New York,*
> **June 1-3, 1960.**

The issue of education has taken on major proportions with respect to business needs. New applied sciences have developed in the last few years which have centered about the concepts of automation; these sciences have synthesized the worlds of mathematics, electronics, and business. As business grows more sophisticated in its applications of automation, the demand for management personnel trained in these sciences will grow. Now is the time when these people should be trained. I feel quite strongly that this task — of training management personnel who can make the fullest use of automation concepts and techniques — is not being carried out. With all the profusion of data processing courses and surveys of automation attached to business school curricula, we have few examples of institutions of higher learning in business which fully integrate the concepts of automation into the entire course of study. One of the bottlenecks, then, in making the fullest use of automation may very well be the lack of adequately trained management manpower.

> **Testimony before the Subcommittee on Automation and Energy Resources,**
> *Joint Economic Committee, U.S. Congress, Washington, D.C.,*
> **August, 1960.**

What must happen is a fairly basic change in the business curriculum; there must be a more formal method by which people can develop within this system . . . There is no central core of fundamental relationships — only individual facets. And here is exactly where we are hampered. We add courses in operations research, we add courses in programming, we add courses in other areas, which may be perfectly fine in themselves, but there is very little relationship among them. We can't go on each year adding another four or five courses; that's a smorgasbord approach to education.

> **"A Review of Computer and Data Processing Problems for Management,"**
> *keynote address before the Administrative Management Institute, New York, N.Y.,*
> **May 16, 1962.**

119

TOMORROW'S MANAGER

It can be seen that tomorrow's manager — and "tomorrow" was never closer! — will be faced with formidable problems in a complex world. It will no longer be possible for men and women to rise to top management with a background of first-hand knowledge and experience with every significant working aspect of an enterprise, since all enterprises will continue to undergo rapid and pervading change.

Yet an ability to make judgments in many fields will be a prime requisite of tomorrow's top manager, and this ability will have to be acquired through the processes of education. The educated businessman will certainly be much more than a technician — but he will have to have a realistic understanding of the problems, approaches, and opportunities in many technical fields. In John Diebold's words, he cannot be a "single man for a single task" — he must be a "man for all seasons" in terms of breadth of basic knowledge and diverse disciplines. He must remain a generalist who has developed a flair for the team approach in getting optimum results from specialists.

It is said that "the hour will bring forth the man." And yet we cannot take the chance that this is an automatic process of nature. Therefore we can hardly dispute John Diebold's thesis that management of today has no greater responsibility than seeing to it that tomorrow's hour will indeed bring forth the needed men.

The Diebold Group conducts weekly internal Professional Development seminars at which staff experts exchange information and opinions on developments in computer and communications technology. Here John Diebold is meeting with selected members of his own professional staff.

Too often management unconsciously assumes that spending a given percentage on research, or creating fine working conditions, will produce results. But the perquisites of genius follow – not precede – the essence of genius. Too often this fact is lost sight of. The fine equipment, campus-like plants, and company-paid university courses are but empty trappings if the human quality is not already present.

"Technology's Challenge to Management,"
address before the Plenary Session, European Conference of The High Authority of the European Coal and Steel Community. The Commission of the European Economic Community. The Commission of the European Atomic Energy Community, Brussels, Belgium,
December 6, 1960.

Our whole approach to labor-management relations has been an admirable concern with 'justice.' This has led us to the concept which today in effect guarantees equal treatment and expectation for average performance. This is appropriate to a blue collar world; it is totally inappropriate to knowledge industries where creativity of the worker can determine the success or failure of the enterprise . . . To put to work the energy and talents of creative people is a tough and increasingly central problem for management in the future.

"New Rules and Opportunities for Business – As We Enter the Post-Industrial Era,"
keynote address before the Third Tri-Annual International Productivity Congress, Vienna, Austria,
October 28, 1970.

Managing Creativity

The management of creative personnel has become a central function of business responsibility.

*John Diebold clearly foresaw that the overwhelming importance of technology in large-scale enterprise, and the entry of science into the executive suite itself, would create a new kind of organization and personnel problem for management – the recruitment, management, and **retention** of creative, professional personnel. As he pointed out in an early address before an international management group:*

The problems in this area are substantial and numerous. One is that the product, an idea, is so difficult to schedule; another, that scientists tend to direct their prime loyalty to their professions, rather than their employers; a third is the magnitude of the task of integrating what must remain an individualized effort; and a fourth, the lack of standards to measure performance.

123

There is also a communication impediment growing out of the diversity of background and aggravated by the growing interdependence of science and management. In this connection, studies in human relations have done much to give us insight into the human requirements of effective organization. But this falls short of what is needed . . . Few managements yet understand the essence of the task. The rewards of those that do will be great.

> **"Technology's Challenge to Management,"**
> *address before the Plenary Session, European Conference of The High Authority of the European Coal and Steel Community. The Commission of the European Economic Community. The Commission of the European Atomic Energy Community, Brussels, Belgium,*
> **December 6, 1960.**

In the same address he pointed out that the new emphasis on creative personnel would run into special difficulties because the kind of climate called for would actually mean running counter to the whole trend of management-labor relations:

The results of labor-management relations to date might be summarized as the guarantee of equal treatment and the expectation of average performance. These concepts are already recognized as archaic in dealing with creative personnel. What must be encouraged is *exceptional* performance, and what will be needed is *individualized* treatment.

> **"Technology's Challenge to Management,"**
> *address before the Plenary Session, European Conference of The High Authority of the European Coal and Steel Community. The Commission of the European Economic Community. The Commission of the European Atomic Energy Community, Brussels, Belgium,*
> **December 6, 1960.**

Of course, problems of dealing with and managing creative personnel in the R&D area have existed for a long time, and organizational devices such as project management, control techniques such as PERT and CPM, and personnel procedures in recruitment, freedom in working conditions, and other non-financial perquisites, as well as increased monetary recognition, have been developed to deal with them. Even here, however, the problems of selection of priorities, project manning and supervision, personnel relations, personnel development, and fiscal control have remained formidable, as the large body of literature on the subject attests.

These problems of dealing with and managing creative people, in John Diebold's view, are greatly compounded with the advance of technology in the area of management itself. As decisions become more and more involved with highly technical questions, top management and line managers in levels below must increasingly rely upon technical specialists for advice. Solutions to problems are not only proposed but are also evaluated by mathematical programmers, operations researchers, and systems analysts. And where corporate staff departments have been established for advance planning and management controls, utilizing the techniques of the "new management sciences," specialists in these fields not only propose solutions to given problems, but also propose the "far-out" problems and projects which should be investigated. However, they must depend on line managers for much of their information, and eventually for support when a decision has to be made.

MANAGEMENT-EMPLOYEE COMMUNICATION

It is for the above reasons that John Diebold sees the problems of management-employee communication, which have always been serious between operating people and technical R&D, as intensified between the operating executives and the creative personnel in the newer areas of management research and control.

What managers often do not realize is that the creative problem-solving ability of a good operations research man is due to his freedom to approach problems without preconceptions about the solution. Basically, this kind of freedom of thought, of such great value in an organization, should be the prerogative of the imaginative systems man as well as the new "management science" specialists. It has not been encouraged in actual practice by line managers, who are often not interested in developing it. Managers are accountable for the performance of their division or department. Their contribution to the company's overall performance is through their division or their department, and they are more interested in immediate results than in the long-range results the free-wheeling management-scientist or "total systems" man envisions.

Improved communication between line and creative staff is important for several reasons. One reason is that the staff people are usually more aware of the *newly possible,* since it is part of their job – and inclination – to keep abreast of developments in their field. When communication between line and staff is open and active, the following benefits accrue:

Staff people will be more keenly aware of the difficulties and special problems of the line managers, well beyond the formal calls for assistance on a particular problem.

Staff people will be able to communicate the possible benefits of technological breakthroughs to line managers.

Line managers, through their staff contacts, can have some influence on the selection of problems to which current technology is to be applied.

Only where the management climate is such that communications between line and creative staff are most open and active can the full potentials of technological change be taken advantage of in *any* area of creative work — whether R&D for products and processes, information technology for management information systems and control, or operations research and related approaches for management decision making.

> **"Business, Computers and the Turn Toward Technology."**
> *address before the Economic Club of Chicago, Chicago, Illinois,*
> **February 24, 1966.**

Today an immediate line-operations and creative-staff communications problem rears its head when a management information system is being set up, since managers tend to have a different notion about what kind of information is needed and what reports should be produced than do the staff operations researchers and systems analysts. Typical is the following example from a Diebold Research Program report. It is, of course, cited here not as an experience peculiar to computer-based operations, but as illustrative of the communications problem which John Diebold stresses as endemic in any creative-staff vs. operating management situation:

A case in point is a company that packages products for nationwide distribution where the managers of the several packaging plants have welcomed the idea of a management information system and are anxious to cooperate in setting up a system that will provide up-to-date profit and loss statements for their plants. These statements, they believe, will help them adjust plant output to maximize profits.

However, the manager of the operations research department wants to go one step further. He wants the management information system to produce information about what each plant *should* produce in order to maximize *company* profits rather than individual plant profits. *The plant managers draw the line here,* stiffly resisting the idea that the computer is going to tell them how to run their plants, particularly since their promotions depend on the profits their plants make, not the overall company profits . . . The result is that for a while the system will produce both kinds of reports. The operations research manager is fairly confident that company loyalties are strong—the company has a very low turnover—and that, as has happened in the past, his ideas will gradually be accepted by the line managers.

Operations research, however, requires the greatest possible integration. The operations research manager in this company (who happens to report to the comptroller) has spoken out in favor of integration and has succeeded in achieving it in many instances. To a large extent this has been made possible by the fact that his superiors, although they have a diametrically opposite organizational philosophy, have not pulled rank or put pressures on him through budgets, promotions, and other levers to get in line.

"ADP for Management Decision Making,"
Diebold Research Program Report,
April, 1968.

TURNOVER

That problems of dealing with creative personnel are far from generally solved is indicated by the adverse turnover figures encountered in R&D and other technical and professional personnel in all industries. In computer-related technology turnover among professionals has been especially severe — so that once more findings with respect to that field provide management insights applicable in any field of endeavor:

Turnover rates among computer specialists are far higher than in any other occupation, partly because of the great demand for their skills, partly because of a high incidence of employee dissatisfaction. The cost of losing a key employee to other computer users and to software houses must be measured not only by the expense of replacement and retraining, but also by the expense and disruptions in systems development.

Part of the solution to the turnover problem lies in recognizing that the motivations and aspirations of college-educated professionals are different from those of persons without degrees. Programs of monetary and nonmonetary compensation must be open-ended and flexible enough to accommodate wide differences if they are to be successful in improving employee retention. (See Figure 9-A)

"Turnover Among ADP Personnel,"
Diebold Research Program Report,
August, 1968.

*With the extreme mobility of the professional population, whose productivity is so crucial to business but who are apparently less and less anchored by traditional loyalties, the problem of finding and **retaining** qualified creative personnel is obviously one of deep concern. But John Diebold emphasizes that the problem centers around the creative **key** personnel, and is not necessarily reflected in bare turnover statistics. In a recent interview he quoted the head of one large firm as having stated the problem succinctly.*

"What I fear is a *low* turnover rate, with all the losses being in key personnel. Such a situation is likely to create more serious problems for us than a high turnover of lower level personnel. I can hire a dozen technical assistants with a call to an employment agency, but if one of my good senior researchers leaves, it could take months to replace him, and meanwhile his project stands idle."

Figure 9-A

AVERAGE ANNUAL TURNOVER OF DATA PROCESSING AND LINE PERSONNEL

POSITION	0-20%	20-40%	40-60%	60-80%	80-100%
SYSTEMS ANALYST WITH COLLEGE DEGREE	45	51	3	1	1
SYSTEMS ANALYST WITHOUT COLLEGE DEGREE	75	22	2	1	-
PROGRAMMER WITH COLLEGE DEGREE	50	46	3	2	-
PROGRAMMER WITHOUT COLLEGE DEGREE	77	21	2	1	-
LINE PERSONNEL WITH COLLEGE DEGREE	98	2	-	-	-
LINE PERSONNEL WITHOUT COLLEGE DEGREE	96	3	-	-	-

Distribution of average annual turnover as a percentage of the total number employed in the corresponding group (e.g., systems analysts) at the respondent company. (Rounding accounts for departure of some crosswise totals from 100 per cent.)

Source: The Diebold Research Program

As John Diebold sees it, the solution to the creation of a viable and constructive relationship between the new breed of creative personnel and the rest of the organization, and one that will go a long way to solving the problem of retention, lies in the intelligent application of the insights of the behavioral sciences—the creation of an organizational climate that induces recognition and acceptance rather than antagonism and resistance.

RECOGNITION

Recognition of the efforts of individual creative employees, he says, is one of the most important factors in a satisfactory work environment, and stresses the value of clearly defined career paths such as discussed later in this chapter.

He also reiterates that recognition is established through an effective communications path between management and professional staff members. This makes it easier for the creative employee to identify with his firm's objectives. "The manager of any professional department — whether it's ADP, R&D, or in fact any area of management which seeks to capitalize on the creative talents of its members — must also develop the ability to listen himself and be accessible to his staff. Perhaps most important is the encouragement of free discussion and even criticism at regular meetings of the staff."

Of course, the need for recognition is found in all occupations. However, he says, "it seems to be more acute among creative personnel, who seem to require special doses of reassurance."

RECRUITMENT

A creative person's dissatisfaction with his job situation may also, John Diebold points out, be tied in with misrepresentations made in the initial recruitment. He cites two comments in point — one from a top management man, and one from a disappointed and frustrated employee:

"In some corporations dissatisfaction because of lack of recognition follows the discovery that some of the promises made or implied at the time of hiring are not being kept by the corporation. Recruiters are very much like political campaigners: they will say anything to sign up a qualified applicant. Their responsibility is personnel, and they rarely have any direct knowledge of the data processing environment. When an applicant comes for an interview he is often so starry-eyed and full of enthusiasm to go to work for us, because of what the recruiters have told him, that we hesitate to mention some of the negatives for fear he will change his mind."

"They never made use of what I know, and before I get rusty I want to work for a company that does not discourage my initiative and that offers a chance for wider responsibility. Do you know what I've been doing for the past two years? I've been doing weekly up-dating of the change journal part of an information retrieval program. That's all I ever worked on. My boss told me I did the job better than anybody ever had and he wouldn't consider transferring me to another project."

"Turnover Among ADP Personnel,"
Diebold Research Program Report,
August, 1968.

With respect to recruiting, it must be recognized that there has long been a highly competitive seller's market for creative personnel in all technologies (at least until very recent cutbacks in space and military programs). This has led to a mad scramble in the job market, which has been especially severe in computer-related technology. John Diebold has long sounded caveats in this regard — and his comments originally made in relation to computer-based situations have general management applicability:

A large group of job hoppers has come into existence. This group would be considered "floaters" in any other field, giving themselves impressive job titles — rarely true job descriptions — and going through several employers in a few years. These floaters are disruptive in any organization. Introduced into a company structure — often over the cries of good personnel people — on the grounds of a need for specialists, they mean trouble. The consequences are, of course, none other than you would expect to find after violating any other sound personnel policy.

> **"Pitfalls to Business Data Processing,"**
> *address before the University of California Conference on Automation, San Francisco, California,*
> **January 9, 1957.**

There has been a great difficulty in trying to keep tabs on what these men actually did because many of them will spend two years in one company, two years in another, a year in another, and at the end have tripled their salaries, but never have stayed anywhere long enough to run the programs they have been writing. It is thus very hard in many of these cases to tell whether the man is good, or whether he has simply worked in a number of places where he has had a reasonable amount of experience.

> **"A Review of Recent Experience of U.S. Applications,"**
> *address before a conference of the British Institute of Management on 'Computers: Top Management Appraisal', London, England,*
> **October 21, 1958.**

COMPENSATION

In all of the foregoing we have said little about money — always a disrupting factor in any seller's market, whether for supplies or for people. With respect to creative people in all technologies, John Diebold has always called for a continuing attention to (a) the need to recognize the requirement for high compensation in the starting grades, but also (b) the need to guard against distortions that work to the disadvantage of those who stay in the creative areas rather than switching over to the management side, where there are no dollar ceilings.

The increasing dearth of young engineers has raised the starting salaries enormously, but often at the expense of later salary increases. Salaries of the older engineers, although they have been increased, have not risen proportionately.

Although most engineers prefer to remain unattached to labor unions — while reaping the benefits of union-won increases — they are going to require a clearer definition of their status in the organization. Management would do well to give serious attention to the question before it becomes acute.

It is the opportunity for higher income that lures many engineers into the management area, where basic design abilities are not fully utilized. A top-notch Ph.D. can be hired for $12,000. He is not unaware that he is often working with management personnel earning two or three times more.

"Automation: The Advent of the Automatic Factory,"
Princeton, New Jersey: Van Nostrand Company, Inc.,
1952.

However, while certainly not advocating a pinch-penny approach to compensation, John Diebold does point out that the behavioral-science aspects mentioned above may in many cases be of even greater significance than monetary rewards — assuming that these meet reasonable minimal standards. Again his case example drawn from information technology has universal application:

One of the most positive approaches was developed by the information processing department of a $45-million-a-year Connecticut instrument manufacturer. This department operates effectively on the teamwork principle, at salaries that are significantly below the average of those paid in the region for similar work.

Three times a week the entire staff meets as a group for luncheon in a private dining room in the plant. The room — which they call the data processing lounge — is for their exclusive use and contains a small reference library (contributed by individual members of the group for the most part), a rack of professional journals, a bulletin board, a blackboard, and some audiovisual equipment. Chairmanship of the luncheon program rotates among both senior and junior members of the department. At each session problems of mutual interest are discussed. From time to time staff members from other departments are invited as guest speakers or to discuss interdepartmental matters.

Visitors to the firm often find themselves drafted to present an informal talk to the group or to participate in a "brain-picking" session. A professor of business administration at Harvard makes it a point to attend one of these luncheons every few months. "The discussions are always stimulating, and the fellowship is congenial," he declares. "I don't think they have lost an employee in the three years I have been going there."

"Turnover Among ADP Personnel,"
Diebold Research Program Report,
August, 1968.

131

Money is never unimportant. But creativity, it seems clear, responds to more than money, and may not respond at all to money alone.

CAREER PATHS FOR CREATIVE PERSONNEL

As part of his philosophy of management development, John Diebold has always advocated the formulation of more rewarding career paths for creative personnel — not only in terms of increased status within the professional activity involved, but also in terms of "graduating" from technical specialization into top policy-deciding positions in management. This will have the two-fold result, he points out, of improving the caliber of management within the specific technical or professional function, and also developing a top-management structure grounded in the theory and application of advancing technology.

Again, the following observation, while using ADP career path as its illustration, has wide management application:

Most companies do not have a career-path program [for creative ADP personnel] which is an organized plan for advancement. These companies, which in effect have negative career paths, either do not think in terms of advancement, or they do not want such a program because it requires a large commitment to a line activity . . . In such corporations, a senior programmer, for example, may find that although his increased technical competence brings him more money, he has reached the ceiling and there is no place to go. If he wishes to stay in programming, he can move on to a company where sophisticated technical capabilities are more important than to his present firm. Or, if he wishes to move into middle management, he can look for the rare company that really has a career-path program. However, many programmers and systems analysts will tolerate low salaries and uninteresting work for a reasonable time if they see opportunities for improving their positions in the future. In this respect they are quite similar to people in other occupations.

Planning a career program can start at any time in the occupational life of a data processing professional, and without regard to his experience, education, seniority, or present job classification. The plan can be made by finding his present position on a chart, such as the one shown in Figure 9-B, whenever it is desirable to encourage him to work toward promotion within the data processing facility, or to middle management positions in line functions.

Professional Options . . . and a Chance to Enter Management Ranks

In some cases, data processing experience will qualify a programmer or systems analyst for responsibility in a corporate department with which he has been working for several years, even though he has had minimum supervisory or management training.

Figure 9-B

CAREER PATH DEVELOPMENT IN AN ADP DEPARTMENT

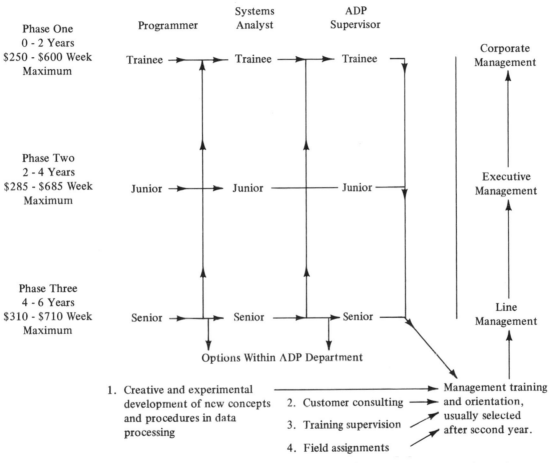

Source: **The Diebold Research Program**

The chart indicates that career development may proceed along several lines, with a variety of options for advancement in both data processing and line positions. The direction a person takes will depend on his own qualifications and ambitions, as well as on corporate requirements and policies. It is usually enough that a person be given the opportunity to advance. Those who are incapable and who leave because they think they have been bypassed unjustly are usually those the company should be least interested in.

The chart also suggests that management positions must follow a change in training and orientation. This requirement is extremely important and should not be overlooked in a frenzied attempt to

133

keep a man who is anxious to leave. A successful career path requires long-term planning, commitment, and training by both the firm and the employee.

"Turnover Among ADP Personnel,"
Diebold Research Program Report,
August, 1968.

DIRECTION AND MANAGEMENT

With all of his emphasis on concepts of communication and freedom of thought and action for creative personnel, John Diebold has by no means been an advocate of fiscal and operational laissez faire as regards the direction and management of their efforts. He made this clear in his early discussions of the danger of loose management control of the then very new computer technology — and again his caveat is directly applicable to the management of any creative activity:

Whole areas of work may be going on with very loose management controls. There are many cases where after six months, or even a year and a half, it will be found that two or three people working in a group have produced no usable work. This is because they have all been working at cross purposes and without tight control over them. In America many [big computer operations] are running on a budget, but the budgets may be 100 percent more than what should be allocated to the operation. There's an enormous amount of padding in some of the very large-scale installations. There has been very little interest in management, but this is just starting to be changed over.

"A Review of Recent Experience of U.S. Applications,"
address before a conference of the British Institute of Management on 'Computers: Top Management Appraisal,' London, England,
October 21, 1958.

The heart of the problem, as John Diebold sees it, is that the top executive who is responsible for the development of directions and goals of a creative activity must be one who has developed a flair for motivating and working with creative people, but who at the same time has a very clear understanding of the objectives of the organization and the competitive milieu in which it operates. And he must see to it that the person in direct charge of the activity itself, is similarly one who can work with creative people but at the same time be alive to the need for budgetary and other administrative controls. Only in this way will the creative work mesh realistically with the needs of a profit-oriented enterprise.

Such men will be in increasing demand, since, in our age of technology, enterprise of every sort will depend more and more upon creative personnel for survival and growth.

PART IV

Examples of Five New Business and Service Opportunities Created by Technological Change and by Enterprise-Oriented Managers

Photograph by Burt Glinn

Instantaneous electronic transfer of money and credit presents business with a dual impact – on the one hand altering the earning streams of financial institutions, on the other opening opportunities for new types of business services. John Diebold here examines a credit checking system which will be important in future retail as well as banking and other business transactions.

Automation will make it possible to render new, more comprehensive, and more economical services. It will, in fact, strengthen and further the trend toward acceleration of the service industries.

"Automation – The New Technology,"
Harvard Business Review,
November-December, 1953.

The current system of money-and-credit transfer could not support the needed expansion of national economic activity. To project a doubling of gross national product by 1983 on the basis of current means of financial transactions is like expecting the 1968 volume of telephone calls to be made through the 1948 telephone system, with its reliance on operators, limited local dialing, mechanical switching, and so on.

"When Money Grows in Computers,"
Columbia Journal of World Business,
November-December, 1967.

The "Cashless Society"

Electronic money and credit transactions change the ground rules and earnings streams of businesses and individuals – and in the process open new business opportunities.

One of John Diebold's most basic and most often reiterated themes has been that new technology, first applied in a given business as a convenience – a simple labor-saving time-saving improvement – soon proliferates into extensions and collateral activities far beyond the scope of the original applications. Before long, imaginative entrepreneurs will combine the new devices and techniques with simultaneously emerging innovations in other areas, extending the original idea into new and greatly enlarged application areas and often originating totally new kinds of businesses. These in turn may drastically change the habits and preferences of users of the new products and services with secondary and tertiary effects on all of the other products and services they consume.

An earlier chapter pointed out that the automobile was more than a transportation improvement over the horse. It totally changed the patterns of where people live, the recreation they seek, the way they allocate their expenditures, and the like — with secondary and tertiary effects on housing, schools, clothing, entertainment, and all the rest.

Looming over the horizon now, as a direct outgrowth of the new information technology, is a development which John Diebold believes will have a similarly drastic impact on our daily lives — namely, the way in which individuals and businesses will carry out their money transactions. Its effect will be felt in so simple a transaction as the purchase of a tube of toothpaste all the way to the most complicated and far-flung settling of business accounts.

Popularly dubbed the "cashless society," its beginnings are witnessed in the continually increasing use of credit cards of all sorts, and its logical extensions (which John Diebold sees as inevitable) are made possible by already available computer-communication systems. Over the next ten to fifteen years it will vitally affect the way the whole banking industry will do business — an industry which has always been quick to adopt the most advanced business machines and electronic data processing equipment. And it will create opportunities for exciting new customer services — which, if the banking industry does not capitalize upon, competing entrepreneurs will.

The following colloquy between John Diebold and an interviewer from U.S. News & World Report is illuminating:

Q. We hear a lot about the coming "checkless-cashless" society. What's there to it?

A. It simply means that credit will be transferred at the instant you make a purchase. For all but minor cash transactions, you'll have a money card. When you go into a store, you'll give a salesclerk the card which will have your account number on it. She will pop it into a special transmittal device connected with the bank. The transmitter will automatically dial the number of your personal account, check the amount of credit available to you, debit your account, credit the store's account, and that's it. No checks have passed, no cash has changed hands.

Q. What would that do to banking?

A. The impact on banks' earnings is going to be important. Banks today deal with something called "float" — the amount of money represented by checks that are in circulation but haven't been presented for payment. This float runs into the hundreds of millions of dollars. Banks can invest that money, and it provides earnings for them. If you eliminate the float, you've cut down an important source of profit for banks. Banks undoubtedly will have to offer many new services to customers, find new sources of profit. I'm sure they will offer overdrafts very widely.

Q. What do you mean by that?

A. If you don't have enough money in your account when you buy something with your money card, the bank will automatically advance you credit, and charge you a fee for that service. Every customer will have a credit ceiling, up to which the bank will advance him funds.

Q. Isn't this all a dream?

A. Actually, it's on the way now. The Bank of Delaware has a money-card system in operation, and many banks already are providing their own credit cards and offering to lend up to $1,000 or more on the strength of that card.

Bankers we've talked with expect that the transition to paperless credit will come about in a series of steps. We did a survey on this subject to which 2,636 bankers and financial people responded. Among those who replied, more than half thought the single biggest obstacle to a money-card system is psychological — not the cost factor, or technical obstacles. Almost all said that banks are likely to participate in a money-card system.

"What Comes Next in the Computer Age,"
Interview with John Diebold, U.S. News & World Report,
June 26, 1967.

THE CONSUMER SYSTEM

The "cashless-society" (the popularized term is essentially a misnomer, since, as Diebold Group reports have pointed out, a substantial number of transactions will continue to be made as they are today, with currency, checks, and other traditional means) has caught the imagination of the popular press, and discussions of it are usually associated with its effect on the general consumer of the future, who will hardly need to carry more than a few dollars in his pocket, will rarely have to write a check, and will perhaps never undergo the chore of totalling check book stubs. As exciting and novel as the impact on consumers will be the effect on interbusiness transactions.

For consumers the "cashless society" will mean the carrying of one or two cards with which to make cash payments or obtain credit at the time and place of purchase, or from any other location, over the telephone. One card could serve both the money and credit transfer functions, or there could be two cards — one for money and the other for credit. In order to prevent fraud, various types of identification procedures will be available, including photographs on the cards, signature comparison, and voice identification.

Consumers will be able to transfer money from their own to others' accounts. Or they could ask for credit through the system. Both the money transfer and the amounts and terms of credit received will depend on the money in the consumers' accounts and on their credit ratings, as recorded within the system. In addition, for a number of purchases, transactions similar to current credit card usage will take place. That is, at the discretion of the retailer, accounts receivable records will be established in the system and the consumers will be billed from that account at regular intervals. It is possible that consumers eligible for this type of transaction will have some kind of designation on their cards, indicating a general, good credit rating, just as today such a rating is implicit in a person's possession of a retail or travel and entertainment credit card. Figure 10-A shows how the consumer part of an electronic money and credit transfer system is likely to operate.

> **"When Money Grows in Computers,"**
> *Columbia Journal of World Business,*
> **November-December, 1967.**

INTERBUSINESS TRANSACTION SYSTEMS

Electronic interbusiness transactions will form the other part of a future system. This will be very simply an extension of current accounting procedures which already are being handled increasingly by computers within companies or by computer service bureaus. It is likely that certain service companies, such as computer manufacturing subsidiaries, accounting firms, communications companies, banks, or others will provide the means by which payments and credit arrangements among enterprises doing business with each other will be automatically made and recorded, without the use of papers for billing, payment, and confirmation as currently required. Business accounts in banks will be debited and credited on a regular and predictable basis. Figure 10-B shows how the interbusiness part of an electronic money and credit transfer system is likely to operate.

> **"When Money Grows in Computers,"**
> *Columbia Journal of World Business,*
> **November-December, 1967.**

The banking industry, already highly mechanized in its "back office" operations, was early conditioned to computerization. Banks were among the first to install large-scale computer systems, and, with the advent of time-sharing, to get "on-line" to large

Figure 10-A.

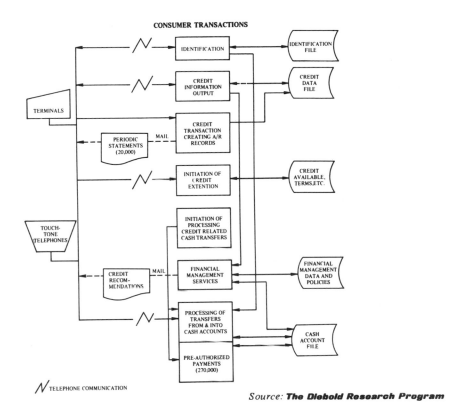

Source: The Diebold Research Program

central computers. The industry also pioneered in source-data automation in the development of magnetic-ink encoded checks (via MICR — magnetic ink character recognition), and — at least within its own industry — an interbusiness computerization through standardization of type-fonts for coding checks to facilitate clearing through the Federal Reserve System. The Diebold Group was early engaged in these developments:

For example, we are currently installing a system that will connect 46 savings banks to the largest banking computer center in the world. At all these banks all the teller withdrawal windows will be connected via input units and direct lines to a computer working in real time. Though this installation will be closer to a conventional computer system than other examples that could be cited, the system gets close to the heart of the business. Operational systems rank as a perfectly colossal development.

"John Diebold's Vista of Automation,"
Business,
December, 1963.

141

Figure 10-B.

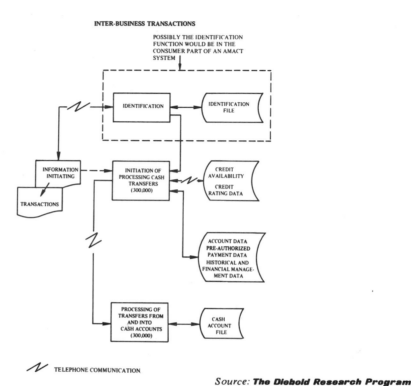

Source: **The Diebold Research Program**

However, what we are here concerned with goes far beyond automation of traditional types of operations. To grasp the opportunity presented by the new technology, the banking industry must, to use a favorite Diebold expression, "rethink" its entire operations and objectives without being hampered by preoccupation with the way business was always transacted, or – indeed with what types of business were transacted. This is reminiscent of his very early advocacy (still, after all these years, largely unheeded) of totally rethinking the operations of a related financial complex, the New York Stock Exchange.

He was a prophet long before his time, as indicated by an account in The New York Times as recently as March 30, 1969. In that issue, the paper ran a feature story on the "back office" glut and confusion in Wall Street. The thrust of the article was that the "paperwork mess" was due to the failure of the brokerage houses and the exchanges to avail themselves of modern information-handling technology. It raised the question of whether the nation's securities industries would wither away through abandonment or death due to asphyxiation by paper.

The Times story contained the following interesting commentary on the New York Stock Exchange:

Characterized as the nerve center of American industry, the exchange is really a glaring anachronism. On the floor of the exchange as in the ancient market places, the traders stand at their posts and offer wares — not stone jugs, but stocks and bonds. Hundreds of men swarm over the paper-strewn floor. Messengers dart to and fro with scribbled bits of paper. The glitter of a few modern devices such as the high-speed ticker tape (which records what has happened but does not participate in the action) is so blinding that we never question the basic process.

How can the exchange be automatized? A faster ticker tape? Walkie-talkie radios from office to floor broker? Conveyor belts for handling papers? These all sound workable, but they amount to no more than adding gadgets to the existing process. These gadgets may be useful in saving manpower, but they represent no basic improvement in the process itself. What is called for is something completely different from the exchange floor as it exists today.

The basic function of the exchange floor is to provide a means for interchange of information concerning the sale, and purchase of stocks and bonds. Computers are designed primarily to receive, manipulate, and communicate information. They provide a means for eliminating the exchange floor altogether.

The Times writer, William D. Smith, reported as follows:

A reading of this comment to several brokers elicited the response, "Well, hindsight is easy," or words to that effect.

It's hardly hindsight, however, for that description of the exchange was written in 1952 by John Diebold, a young management consultant who had just graduated from the Harvard Business School.

Unlike the Stock Exchange, the banking industry has at least shown some imagination in rethinking its operation to the extent of supplementing and expanding traditional services — many of them the result of additional operating flexibility provided by computerization. One example, of course, directly related to the computer, is the employment of excess computer capacity in the form of automatic data processing service centers.

Among these developments, of course, are the major effort of the Bank of America in the credit card field, the interest shown by the commercial banks in the credit information field in California and the Northeast, and the proliferation of services, ranging from automatic overdrafts to travel planning, offered by a number of banks.

Close to 1,000 United States banks are now reportedly in the credit card field, many admittedly with highly mixed results in terms of profits and doubtful prospects for long-term viability. A large number of others are instituting automatic overdraft privileges and/or check cashing guarantees, largely as an alternative to – not an integral part of – credit card operations. At least one of the very major banks is looking once again at the possibility of entering the travelers check market – a business with a glorious past but a rather uncertain domestic future.

> "The Development of an Automated Money and
> Credit Transfer (AMACT) System,"
> *Diebold Research Program Report,*
> **March, 1968.**

Despite such evidences of imaginative enterprise, there are still some significant reservations about the truly basic innovation of the fully automated money and credit transfer (AMACT) concepts. Two important conclusions in this regard are drawn by Diebold Group researchers:

One is that a small but important minority of bankers doesn't think it is going to come about – or not soon, anyway. The other is that a large part of the great majority of bankers expecting it neither can agree on how it will develop nor appear willing to plan for it.

The first of these conclusions is borne out by the survey, *The Impact of Electronics on Money and Credit,* undertaken in 1966 by The Diebold Research Program. A 29-question survey was sent to some 10,000 individuals in the United States, including more than 4,000 presidents and other top executives in banking. Twenty seven percent of the respondents do not believe that an AMACT system will develop within the next ten to 15 years. Even among the 100 leading banks, this view prevails among 20 percent.

The second conclusion finds support not only in the survey but in the apparently chaotic reactions of a large number of bankers in the credit card and related areas of credit and money transfer. Some 95 percent of the bank respondents to the survey, expecting an AMACT system, believe that banks will play a major role in such a system. But there is wide disagreement among them as to how it will evolve – through the further development of credit cards, the expansion of automatic overdraft privileges, the automation of interbusiness transactions, or other means – and as to who, if anyone, will be the operating partners of other principal beneficiaries of the system.

On the other hand 44 percent of the responses from the 100 largest commercial banks indicate the belief that a "money card" will be in widespread use within ten years, and a total of 79 percent believe that this will occur within 15 years. Of special interest is that 84 percent of the responses received from top officials of ten key commercial banks indicating the belief that a "money card" system will be in widespread use within 15 years. (These ten banks are among the 20 largest in the nation.)

While 69 percent of the responses from the 100 largest commercial banks indicate the belief that banks will overcome obstacles to cooperation and assume leadership for the future system, only 48 percent of the responses from all banks indicate this. And from the ten key commercial banks the response was only 57 percent.

Several conclusions can be stated. *First,* the commercial banks have an interest in and have the potential to operate all of the services an AMACT system can provide. But not all banks know or want this. *Second,* while a large number of banks can be expected to play major operational roles — regionally and nationally — in the system, they are likely to meet with considerable difficulties in enlisting the needed, basic cooperation of some of their fellow banks.

The Technologies

As in the case of the Stock Exchange, there is no technological barrier to the realization of the fully automated system that would perform all of the functions envisioned in Figures 10-A and 10-B. John Diebold has categorized the applicable technologies needed in the future systems as follows:

1. Terminal Equipment

Terminals will consist of devices placed in banks, homes, and service establishments to permit communications with the central processors and files. The terminals will be of the building block type (modules) which may be assembled to meet the specific requirements of the home or business establishment in which they are located. They may include a touchtone type input, a card reader and an audio-response unit, as well as several lights indicating system conditions and replies.

2. Communications

Communications may well be provided through a type of Wide Area Telephone Service (WATS). This is a service which permits a customer, by use of an access line, to make calls within a specified zone for a flat monthly charge.

3. Central Processing Units and Mass Storage Files

The computing power of currently available third generation central processors, and the capacities of currently available random-access or disk type memories are fully adequate to the demands of a future system. For example, the Burroughs 5500, RCA Spectra 70/55, IBM System 360/50, or CDC

3600 computers, could serve consumer transactions in any specific region or metropolitan area of two million inhabitants. Also on a regional basis, computers, such as the Digital Equipment Corporation's PDP-6, the CDC 3300, and the Scientific Data Systems Sigma 7, could serve interbusiness transactions.

4. Programming and Systems Analysis, Design, and Installations

These techniques, as developed today, are perfectly adequate to the needs of an automated money and credit transfer system. However, they are costly and subject to great variations depending on the skills of the personnel involved and the diversity and sophistication of the system required. This last element — the variables of system complexity — could well be attributed, at least partly, to marketing costs. The specific services provided, including various safety factors and amounts of information made available to users, will depend to a large extent on user demands, as well as on regulatory and insurance requirements.

5. Voice Recognition

The one technology which is not available in commercially marketable form at this time is represented by voice recognition units. These probably are fundamental to the security of procedures which electronically debit and credit cash accounts, as well as to the privacy and safety of individuals desiring to make medium sized and large purchases on credit. It is expected that voice recognition units will be commercially available by the mid 1970s. They will consist of devices which generate voice spectrograms as the result of voice inputs. These spectrograms will then be converted into digital formats for comparison with the digitalized voice patterns in the identification files of individuals.

"When Money Grows in Computers,"
Columbia Journal of World Business,
November-December, 1967.

6. Security and Privacy

A major requisite of the system envisioned is the prevention of losses through error and fraud, and the prevention of information leakage to unauthorized hands.

Security against error is a hardware and software problem. Currently available computer and communications equipment — except at present in the area of voice identification — can provide a high degree of protection against technological and human failure through built-in controls and redundancies. Fundamentally, decisions on how much to spend for high quality equipment, including controls and redundancy, and on high quality software are managerial in nature. The specifications regarding tolerances will probably change in the light of experience, as the system develops over time.

As to privacy and security against fraud: In order for consumers and business users to authorize an AMACT system to furnish credit information or to transfer funds from their accounts and perform other transactions, they will have to identify themselves. The most basic identification element for consumers and business users is the card or cards they carry. These cards, either at once or upon further identification, will open the holder's account or credit information files for action after insertion in a terminal device or touchtone telephone to the appropriate regions and banks.

To obtain greater security, the account or credit information files could require the card holders to transmit a further set of numbers, not visible on the cards, before becoming open to action. Additional methods of identification, plus variations and combinations of them, are feasible: voice, signature, and picture. (Fingerprint identification is discounted because cost and psychological factors make its use over the next 15 years highly unlikely.)

> **"The Development of an Automated Money and Credit Transfer (AMACT) System,"**
> *Diebold Research Program Report,*
> **March, 1968.**

Other services and safeguards will be built into the systems. For example, the buyer of a television set could delay payment to the retailer until delivery and inspection of the purchase. In this case, the consumer's account would have a record of a pending obligation and the retailer's account would have a record of a pending receivable, but the actual transfer of money would be delayed according to the terms of the purchase. In other words, neither individual consumers nor businesses will fall into the clutches of a relentless, inhuman system automatically disposing of their money regardless of human or machine error and the individual's right to change his mind up to a point.

> **"When Money Grows in Computers,"**
> *Columbia Journal of World Business,*
> **November-December, 1967.**

Figure 10-C designed as a "time tunnel schema" to illustrate the possible evolution of an electronic money and credit transfer system from 1958 through 1983 and beyond. The time periods during which specific steps leading to an electronic or automated system first had — or should begin to have — a significant impact are indicated. Also presented are the approximate points in time when these various steps should begin to interact. By 1983 their interaction is expected to be complete enough to form a total, automated system which can process some two-thirds of the gross volume of money and credit transactions projected for that time.

In order to serve the planning interests of the reader, three general aspects of the diagram should be noted:

1. All time periods are indicated by concentric circles. The size of the "fingers" of the star reading back to the pre-1958 period are intended to convey roughly the significance of the

Figure 10-C

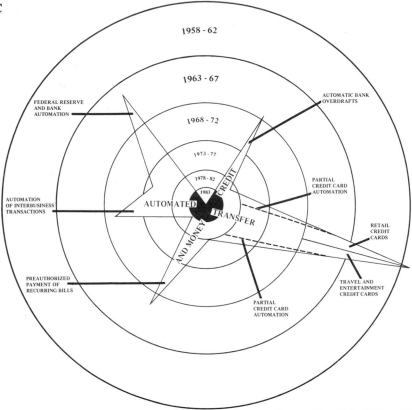

Source: **The Diebold Research Program**

various steps leading to an automated system, relative to the gross volume of projected money and credit transactions.

2. The exhibit depicts a *convergence* of forces and conveys the idea that, as automation is applied with increasing intensity, the time and cost of each transaction will decrease. In other words, as the various steps interact more closely, both external and internal economies will result and this fact is expressed visually in the diagram.

3. A composite picture of development in the United States as a whole is presented. There is no intention to illustrate either the timing or the sequence of the evolution in any particular region. Some major differences among regions are expected.

> "The Development of an Automated Money and Credit Transfer (AMACT) System,"
> *Diebold Research Program Report,*
> **March, 1968.**

ECONOMIC IMPERATIVES

In all of the discussions and publications on AMACT, there seems to hover a general presumption that industry as a whole has a large element of choice in whether a system of the sort described shall be implemented. However, John Diebold has repeatedly stressed that this "choice" may be largely illusory. The basic economic imperatives were clearly set forth in the following passage, from which the quotation on the opening page of this chapter was taken:

It is generally accepted that national economic activity must be at least double over the next fifteen years in order to meet the expected demands of a growing population for greater quantities of higher-quality goods and services. According to detailed projections developed by my firm the number of financial transactions and the volume of data exchanged and recorded in connection with them will have to increase two to five times over current levels – depending on the specific type of operation – in order to support the required expansion of economic activity . . . . . . However, there is one fundamental difficulty with the projected increases: They cannot and will not take place, *unless the very nature of the transactions and the data themselves are basically and radically changed.*

The current system of money-and-credit transfer could not support the needed expansion of national economic activity. To project a doubling of gross national product by 1983 on the basis of current means of financial transactions is similar to expecting the 1968 volume of telephone calls to be made through the 1948 telephone system, with its reliance on operators, limited local dialing, no long-distance dialing, mechanical switching, and so on. Purely physical problems, as well as the resulting dollar costs, would be prohibitive.

"When Money Grows in Computers,"
Columbia Journal of World Business,
November-December, 1967.

Future Technologies and Cost Estimates

The traditional pattern of the past will be repeated: Changes in technology and cost reductions achieved when developments are put on the scale of widespread application will make the seemingly impossible possible. The Diebold Research Program makes the following projections:

A 50 percent reduction for *terminals* by the mid-70s is a conservative projection. Central processor costs are projected to be about 40 percent of today's, based largely on the economies of microelectronics.

In *communications,* reductions are expected to be in the 30 percent to 50 percent range. This will not be due to any significant breakthrough in data transmission but, rather, to a general improvement in the operating efficiency of the common carriers.

While *programming* costs will decrease, along with hardware costs, the drop will not be as dramatic. Relative to hardware, they should actually become greater.

Storage and *mass memory* costs are expected to drop sharply as the result of increased packing densities, the economies of a larger market, and more efficient production techniques. Costs in most cases should be cut at least in half and, in some cases, more by the mid-70s.

"The Development of an Automated Money and Credit Transfer (AMACT) System," *Diebold Research Program Report,* **March, 1968.**

Profits and Entrepreneurial Opportunities

The potential profits for operators and users of AMACT will come from the savings generated and from the additional services that can be supplied. These services appear to reside in the conveniences and other values of automated consumer credit transactions and money transfers, automated interbusiness transactions, and financial management. Consumers will have to carry little currency, and will have to do less bookkeeping. Many of them will obtain credit on more reasonable terms. Retailers may improve their customer relationships. Business and individuals will benefit from smaller liquidity requirements and the optimization of their financial resources.

New services resulting from the automated transactions will be applicable to both consumer and interbusiness transactions. Specifically, says the Diebold report:

1. The provision of high security identification through voice spectrograms, as well as of the lower security identification inherent in the cards distributed to system users. The latter service, of course, offers the various combinations of signature, picture, and primary identification methods discussed above.

2. Greatly improved provision of credit information.

3. Automated designation of alternate sources and terms of credit, on the basis of internal credit information.

4. The initiation and processing of credit transactions, including the debiting and crediting of accounts, the setting up of repayment schedules, and the maintenance of the resulting records.

5. The extension of credit including automatic overdrafts.

6. The initiation and processing of money transfers, including preauthorized payments.

7. The provision of personal financial management services.

Any of these services could and may be operated by commercial banks in a number of regions. Financial management services are here conceived of primarily as consumer-oriented, but could be offered to business accounts as well. It appears to be fairly evident that significant profits are to be made in this area. If one imagines a five percent annual service charge for providing financial management services to demand and time deposit accounts of $100 billion or $200 billion, it may be helpful in getting some perspective on the general magnitude of the potential.

All of the services indicated can be performed best and with the greatest cost effectiveness under the conditions provided by a completely automated system — an **AMACT** system as postulated. Some of the services, such as high security identification and the designation of alternate credit sources and terms, either could not be performed or would make little sense outside of the context of an **AMACT** system. Several of them are closely interdependent. Finally, one or more of the services will be specifically demanded by each of the potential users and operators of the future system of financial transactions.

Defining a business in fundamental terms of markets, unique resources, and managerial capabilities rather than historical product positions has been an important and continuing factor in John Diebold's career. Because of his own rapid transportation needs (here he is seen using a private plane) he has been particularly alert to business opportunities in transportation.

11

It will be possible effectively to control a railroad system so that it will be more responsive to customer as well as national needs . . . But the commercially relevant definition of the railroad's proper and changing role in the space age vis-a-vis other forms of transportation is the prerequisite of such an effective control capability.

"Management and Railroad Cybernetics,"
address before the Plenary Session, International Railway Union, Symposium on Cybernetics, Paris, France,
November 4, 1963.

The railroad industry can remain competitive by accepting the challenge of the new technologies. If it is not to be left behind by the preservation of existing uneconomical systems and services, it must conceive new systems and organize effectively to meet the social problems with which the new technologies have presented it.

"Business Decisions and Technological Change,"
New York, Praeger Publishers, Inc.,
1970.

A Case Of Business Definition: Transportation

Changes in transportation open new profit opportunities — when the enterprise *defines* its business to allow it.

Few industries so aptly demonstrate as do the railroads the two basic tenets of John Diebold's business philosophy — namely the continuing interaction of technological innovation and social change, and the consequent continuing need for a business and an industry to rethink its role and its opportunities in the changing environment.

In the United States, the railroads transformed a whole way of life built around the canal system which they rapidly obsoleted. They consolidated the winning of the West by opening up the continent to waves of population and industrialization. And with the dramatic hammering home of the golden spike in Promontory, Utah on May 10, 1869, linking the Union Pacific and Central Pacific, they forged the East and the West into one nation. As John Diebold has said:

We too easily forget just how great were the innovations of the 19th century which produced today's form of railroad. It has been said of that period that the true history of countries such as the United States was the history of transportation, in which the names of the presidents of railroads are more important than the names of the heads of state.

"Management and Railroad Cybernetics,"
address before the Plenary Session, International Railway Union, Symposium on Cybernetics, Paris, France,
November 4, 1963.

And yet, after emerging as the dominant form of land transportation in the 19th century, and as a continuing economic (and political) force that dictated the location, development, and profitability of whole industries and dominated the economy of whole regions, the railroads themselves in more recent times entered a period of steady decline. New technologies whose threat railroad managements did not perceive early enough captured customer loyalties and revenues, and changing social forces to which the industry would not or could not adjust led to a shrinkage of market, uneasy and costly labor relations, and a political and social climate that imposed burdensome regulatory and tax restraints.

Thus railroads were considered the "sick man" of industry for a period of thirty years, and their steady decline was not halted until the early 1960s, when an aggressive attitude on the part of railroad management – in adjusting to economic and political forces, and above all in actively stimulating technological innovation – succeeded in reversing the trend.

RELATED AWARENESS OF THE SIGNIFICANCE OF
TECHNOLOGICAL AND SOCIAL CHANGE – An Example in Point . . .

In this connection, the report of a Diebold Research Program study on railroad operations makes the the following observations:

Although the railroads realized that they had lost a large share of short-haul passenger business to the automobile by the time of the stock market crash in 1929, they were less aware of the significance of the decline in freight movement. The depression put more pressure on the railroads because the effective demand for long-haul service decreased with the overall decline in economic activity. Depression era measures by the Government to provide publicly financed employment spurred highway development. This, in turn, increased the movement away from the rails at a time when the railroads desperately needed the revenue to cover their very heavy fixed charges.

The decade of the '30s was also the period in which air traffic began its growth. Although it did not seem to be significant to the rails at first, the continued expansion of air service in the period after World War II brought with it an almost complete collapse of long-distance rail passenger service. While this revolution in passenger service was under way, the nation also became actively engaged in a campaign to revitalize as much waterway service as Congress could be persuaded to finance. Consequently, a rapid rise of bulk freight movements on rivers and inland waterways removed important amounts of bulk-tonnage from the nation's railways . . . Additionally, since World War II another bulk-tonnage mover appeared to take important traffic away from the railroads – the oil products pipeline, made feasible by newer techniques.

Thus the decline of the importance of railroad transportation was due in part to the great advancement in the technology of other modes: motor, water, air and pipeline . . . Larger and more efficient equipment made its appearance each year, and these non-rail carriers, not burdened by fixed investment in ways and structures, were able rapidly to replace old facilities with new and better ones. As these modes developed, they were in a position to offer a service-price combination to various important segments of traffic that the railroads were unable to match. Government regulation and support to the development of the other modes also contributed to their success.

> **"Impact of Information Technology on Railroad Operations,"**
> *Diebold Research Program Report,*
> **July, 1965.**

The Turning Point

For an industry considered "sick" for thirty years, railroads today show considerable vitality. The turning point, following a general post-war downward trend, was 1961, when, as Diebold Research Program studies show, the carriers began reaping the rewards of a $20 billion post-war modernization program which wrought a true technological revolution in American transportation. By 1963, John Diebold was able to tell an international gathering:

The diversity of papers presented at this meeting reflects the wide technological stirring within the world railroad industry, particularly since the end of World War II – all leading to major, significant increases in productivity. Thus, in many countries, there has been extensive modernization of plant and equipment; diesel-electrification has importantly supplanted the steam locomotive as railroad motive power.

Rolling stock has increased capacity, stronger and lighter weight construction, vastly improved running gear, axle, and journal performance. Widespread emphasis has been placed on special-purpose freight cars, on larger tare-weight-to-loaded weight ratios.

155

Maintenance of way has become importantly mechanized, in the main performed by small crews with highly efficient, multi-purpose power machinery.

Signalling and communication developments have extensively introduced radio and extended the use of telegraph, and, in switching and car communication, have introduced microwave and centralized traffic control, and have resulted in the introduction of important automated freight yards.

Finally, large electronic computers have begun, albeit slowly, to extend to management areas beyond accounting, payrolls, inventory, and ordering procedures.

"Management and Railroad Cybernetics,"
address before the Plenary Session, International Railway Union, Symposium on Cybernetics, Paris, France,
November 4, 1963.

In the above, John Diebold underscored the new dimension added to the technology of improved rolling stock, materials handling, and maintenance of way: the dimension of **information technology.** *This illustrates, he points out, how the imaginative use of these new capabilities and systems makes it possible for management (and this of course applies to any industry, not railroads alone) to automate the more routine and time consuming management processes that have traditionally been considered as requiring relatively high-level attention. Consequently, top levels of management are freed to concentrate on matters of total function, customer needs, innovations in service, and new entrepreneurial opportunities.*

Aside from these imaginative applications of the new technology, he could, with respect to the railroads specifically, cite obvious and immediate cost-benefit implications:

1. *Effective car utilization,* resulting from an automatic, accurate, and current freight car inventory. Apart from required maintenance periods — scheduled automatically by the system — cars will be used for the major portion of the twenty-four hours of each day of the year, thus appreciably lowering the high inventory of car units. (In the United States, for example, the more than 1.5 million car units are each estimated to be used on an average only slightly more than two hours a day and cover 40 miles daily.)

2. *A substantial increase in freight tons carried per train.* The national averages range now (1963) 40 miles between less than 200 tons per train mile to more than 1,200 tons per train.

3. *Reliable service,* an assurance of consistency of total transit time. No longer will there be long waits in yards to assemble "economic trains," delays in intermediate yards for the reclassification of trains or any of the long delays inherent in freight terminals.

4. *An appreciable increase in productivity.* The national averages of the number of railroad employees per million traffic units —i.e., passenger-miles and freight-ton miles, range (1963) between one and 15 employees per million traffic units.

5. *Proper pricing of customer charges* (tariffs and rates), made possible by data accumulation of precise costs and cost components of freight and passenger operations.

"Management and Railroad Cybernetics,"
address before the Plenary Session, International Railway Union, Symposium on Cybernetics, Paris, France,
November 4, 1963.

Reinvigorated Marketing

A commendable concomitant of the modernization of the physical plant, the application of computer technology to data processing, the streamlining of labor usage, and the merging of separate roads into regional systems, has been a more imaginative and aggressive marketing activity and enlarged customer services. These may be highlighted by the following exerpts from The Diebold Research Program report referred to earlier:

One typical advance in methods of hauling freight is the success attained by the industry's TOFC (truck on flatcar) service, more popularly known as "piggy-backing." First and fastest growing of the new postwar services, piggy-backing represents (1965) more than a 100 percent increase since 1959, and more than five times the 1959 volume in 1966. Industry officials note that piggy-back traffic could double again within five years.

Impressive, from a revenue standpoint, has been the development in recent years of bi-level and tri-level auto rack cars, capable of carrying as many as 12 standard or 15 compact automobiles, enabling the railroads substantially to reduce their costs and their rates (one estimate is a savings of $75 per car to the shipper). Such units have helped to bring back rail loadings of new motor vehicles from truck competition.

Another technological advance is containerization, which adapts wheel-less cargo containers for ready movement by train, truck, ship or plane. Less than one percent of rail piggy-back loads was carried in such "packages" in 1958; in 1965 they account for some 10 percent.

157

Still another new concept, the unitized train, is making possible dramatic rate reductions. The unit train shuttles cargo of a single commodity from origin to destination with little or no switching, uncoupling, or terminal handling. Coal handled by unit train to electric power-generating plants in one case has been credited with forcing a competitive coal slurry pipe line to cease operations. Unitized trains are being employed increasingly in the shipment of grain and ore, and will be applied to other commodities in the future.

> **"Impact of Information Technology on Railroad Operations,"**
> *Diebold Research Program Report,*
> **July, 1965.**

A CLASSIC EXAMPLE OF "RETHINKING" AN INDUSTRY'S ROLE

*However, impressive as the foregoing technological and marketing innovations are, John Diebold, as ever, stresses the need for a total **rethinking** of the problem as a whole, both with respect to public policy, in a public-service enterprise such as railroads, and also with respect to opportunities open to the individual components of an industry.*

The Systems Concept

*The first of these, of course, embraces all modes of transportation, not only the railroads, and here he stresses the capability now provided by information technology to apply the **systems concept** to every segment of transportation and to transportation as a whole, to guide public policy in effecting optimum integration and control.*

Specifically as regards the railroads, he has spelled it out as follows:

Today, we have already moved into the era in which many railroad systems must be substantially larger than they are at present to be effective. This will become even more apparent tomorrow as we begin to apply cybernetics (information technology and automatic control through feedback). This is an imperative of both national economic growth and increased railroad productivity — for there is a pressing need today for coordination of investment policy (on the basis of reliable and comparative cost figures), a pressing need for coordination of tariffs and rates, a pressing need for a railroad network integrated by an overall system of information and control.

The movement toward railroad integration within the European Economic Community and, in a sense, the railroad merger movement in this country are a start in this direction. The efforts being made by the International Railway Union for a common European solution to the problem of automatic coupling; the cooperative interchange of rolling stock among Class I, line-haul railroads of the United States, Canada and Mexico; the electrification program of most European trunk lines in relation to trans-European passenger services; and the planned establishment of a joint fleet of railroad cars by the Soviet Union and countries of Eastern Europe controlled by a central office in Prague — all are straws in this same wind.

"Management and Railroad Cybernetics,"
address before the Plenary Session, International Railway Union, Symposium on Cybernetics, Paris, France,
November 4, 1963.

Fundamental to the proper use of information and communications technologies is an initial conception of the scale and scope of the system. In countries such as the United States, served by a number of interconnecting railroads, or in areas such as Western Europe, it would seem necessary, when first planning the application of these new technologies, to conceive of the system as the full complex of connecting railroads serving the public and treating this as what must be subjected to integrated control. In other words, the constraints of history must not be permitted artificially to limit service to the public in planning the use of technology. There is little justification for the duplication, cost, and loss of control resulting from separate systems for the handling of freight, and for passenger and car accounting, by the interconnecting roads.

"Impact of Information Technology on Railroad Operations,"
Diebold Research Program Report,
July, 1965.

New railroad *systems* are today necessary, based upon management understanding of both the specific conditions which can enable railroads to capitalize on their special assets as well as the proper relationship of railroad transportation vis-a-vis other forms of transportation. Railroad management must project and persuade Government and the public to be permitted to stop doing those things for which they are ill-suited to do, and, as technology permits, do those things for which they are suited.

Such new railroad *systems* will be grounded on the recognition that there is no national or economic justification for many railroads serving a country or countries, interconnected with common transactions, and still have each system repeat and repeat again the handling and processing of information for the same purposes, with resultant increased costs and decreased service.

In truth, we are speaking of a process which has already begun, painfully slow and unevenly as between countries — a process pointing to a coordinated development of all types of transport as components of a single, unified transport system. It is within this inevitable development that railroad management is confronted with the problem of conceiving and implementing new railroad systems.

"Management and Railroad Cybernetics,"
address before the Plenary Session, International Railway Union, Symposium on Cybernetics, Paris, France,
November 4, 1963.

"PERCEIVED USER NEEDS"

John Diebold has always emphasized the importance of "perceived user needs" in thinking through the role of any enterprise. He has frequently taken occasion to point to technologically based improvements in customer service by the railroads as an outstanding case example of what can be done in this regard. None of the recent financial ills besetting the nation's largest system — which have their roots in a multitude of political, labor, regulatory, and other causes — gainsay this assessment; rather, they serve to emphasize that the ultimate salvation of the industry lies along the lines he has advocated.

Studies by The Diebold Research Program indicate significant continuation of current technological innovations, although qualifications expressed in the findings indicate further challenges and potentials. In describing "a railroad operating system for 1975" the following broad outlines are sketched in — restated here as indicative of what technology can offer to improve interface with customers, with obvious implications for any industry:

Recent successful efforts by the industry to reduce "featherbedding" and other labor costs have been noteworthy, although the rise in railroad pay rates has offset this advantage in the past ten years. The capturing of old and new freight markets by new car designs, methods of operations, and train operating speeds is encouraging.

Yet it takes still about 1.5 million freight cars to serve the market (and more in peak seasons). One of the more progressive roads estimates that it takes 18 cars to provide one for loading in an average day. An estimated $4,000 a minute is spent to provide empty cars in the U.S. and Canada.

The railroad industry may be reaching a level of systems improvement where the pay-off from conventional mechanization of the waybill data is less attractive for each dollar invested. Significant time losses in the locations and movements of freight cars still exist in many present and proposed systems . . . Waybill data are still put through numerous handling procedures and processes, many using the same information which already has been processed elsewhere.

A new concept of recording car movement as a primary input to a truly integrated system appears necessary. If such a new method of car movement reporting is linked with or permits a greatly improved method of car, terminal, and train operation, then a major breakthrough in payoff is obvious. Automatic car identification (ACI) offers this possibility if it is coupled with new techniques in both data handling and railroad operation.

> **"Impact of Information Technology on Railroad Operations,"**
> *Diebold Research Program Report,*
> **July, 1965.**

The New Technology: Information System Interface with Customers

Direct contact between the shipper and the rail freight headquarters will characterize 1975 interface with shippers. Large shippers (100 or more car orders per year) will communicate with a railroad by an input/output station at major shipper locations. Most likely, these large shippers will have EDP operations and will prefer to have their orders, diversions, and rate questions recorded on their own computerized system and then transmitted directly to the railroad's central processor. These will include orders for car and special handling, requests for high or wide load, requests for diversions, inquiries for car location, delivery dates, etc., rate contentions, Bill of Lading (serves as order to pick-up car), demurrage (by ACI), and the like.

Acknowledgements and replies to the shipper will be immediate in about 75 percent of these transactions. Small shippers (less than 100 car orders per year) will use common carrier telephone or facsimile for such transactions. By dialing (or keying) the local number for the railroad, an answering device will record the request, store, and forward it to the central shippers service bureau at the railroad's headquarters. Replies to the small shipper by telephone and facsimile will be as fast as the service bureau and will use the same input/output stations (and 75 percent estimated immediate response) as large shippers.

> **"Impact of Information Technology on Railroad Operations,"**
> *Diebold Research Program Report,*
> **July, 1965.**

Customer Savings = Increased Sales

On-line response in many cases to customers' requests for service, plus lower rates made possible by reduced operating costs, will increase the market for freight traffic. Improved turn-around time will make available more cars of each type. This will correct the present practice of offering a late supply of cars or obsolete equipment in an attempt to avoid losing sales.

By eliminating the bill of lading and waybill methods of today, the customer will realize savings in handling such documents in his own operations. Large shippers will reduce their "expediter" work force because of (1) on-line inquiry of car location and status, and (2) fewer requests for tracing cars because of improved communications and faster response and delivery times.

> **"Impact of Information Technology on Railroad Operations,"**
> *Diebold Research Program Report,*
> **July, 1965.**

REDESIGNING PRODUCTS AND PROCESSES

As stated in an earlier chapter, "simply mechanizing past processes or applying advanced technology to products in their existing form does not tap the real potential of the new technology." John Diebold cited the railroads as an outstanding example of this concept in his remarks before the international railroad symposium:

The way in which management uses technology to change operating procedures and methods within the business is important and complex, and can occupy many people for their entire lives. Yet in a way, it is the smallest part of the problem, though it unfortunately too often becomes the center of the entire problem.

More important is the way in which management uses the new technology, not only to change *how* a task is done, but to determine *what the task is* that should be accomplished. Until now, in railroad operation, the application of information technology, computers, and control devices has been directed to the cost of *knowing* (primarily accounting) and to the ways of reducing that cost. In designing railway cybernetic information systems we should be primarily concerned with the costs of *not knowing* — not knowing where cars are, what will cause which delays and for how long, what kind of trouble has started, and where the solutions lie.

Thus, in the utilization of new technology and in the implementation of cybernetic systems on the railroads, management will be confronted with applying technology to the *essence* of the problems of operational costs, car utilization, maintenance ratio and parts utilization and scheduling, rather than with improving techniques to cope with the *results* of such problems. A new order of managerial skills will thus be required.

And a highly important part of management's problem will be knowing what questions to ask. This will involve the ability to see a pattern emerging from changing technology, to be able to introduce *wholly new ways* of performing basic functions.

> **"Management and Railroad Cybernetics,"**
> *address before the Plenary Session, International Railway Union, Symposium on Cybernetics, Paris, France,*
> **November 4, 1963.**

Figure 11-A   **1975 RAILROAD COMPUTER NETWORK**

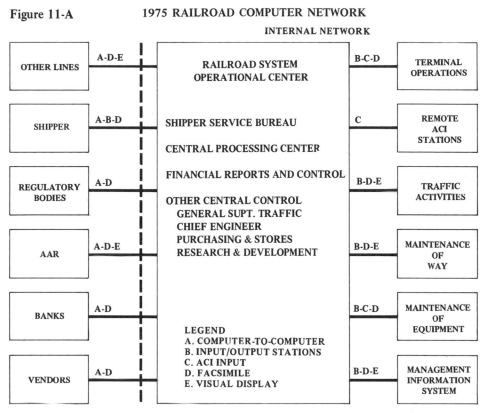

INTERNAL NETWORK

Source: *The Diebold Research Program*

Terminal operations may be cited as only one of the many dramatic improvements that John Diebold's concept of rethinking the application of new technologies can bring to "a railroad operating system for 1975":

Dramatic improvements in car inventory and distribution will be possible. Automatic car identification (ACI) will permit a real-time file on each car on the railroad's system. Present yard checks, trips to the shipper to pick up bills of lading, and numerous other manual and partly mechanized activities will be fully mechanized. The number of empty cars on the system, their location, time required to move an empty car to shipper's siding, etc., will be available from the central processor on an up-to-the-minute basis. In addition, by agreement with other lines, automatic access to connecting lines' empty car files (or a North American pool, possibly) will reduce the non-revenue time per car and provide superior service to shippers. (See Figure 11-A.)

Two-way radios, visual displays, and small computers and printers on switch engines will receive orders from the terminal. Remote control will permit improvements in "through terminal" time.

163

Central processors will have access not only to advance information on car destinations, handling, etc., but also to on-line inputs of movement through the yard. Blocking and classifying of trains will be optimized and be carried out in fully automated classification yards.

Train make-up will benefit by the real-time data which will be available. More economical trains will result, and motive power assigned with more precision.

> **"Impact of Information Technology on Railroad Operations,"**
> *Diebold Research Program Report,*
> **July, 1965.**

CONSTRAINTS TO IMPLEMENTATION

The Need to "Rethink" the Problems of Public Policy, Labor Relations, and the Transition to New Methods

No enterprise of the magnitude of the railroads can expect to effect a technological revolution without encountering formidable constraints — in the public sector as represented by regulatory agencies, and in the now-powerful "establishment" represented by organized labor.

The Diebold researchers point out that the railroad industry may well find itself constrained in installing the "operating system for 1975" which its Report envisions. Quite aside from normally expected resistances to change will be the special problems of technical implementation and transition. For example, beneficial action by regulatory and rate-making bodies might not be forthcoming:

The cumbersome procedure required by the ICC for safeguarding funds used by railroads for purchase of equipment has impeded technical innovation. Also limiting is the ICC's slowness in revising operating and safety regulations to meet technological improvements.

For example, installation of dragging-equipment detectors, which can transmit car conditions to a central location, is held up by a requirement that such installations be connected to the automatic block signalling system. Labor unions apply pressures to the ICC on such issues and further complicate rule changes.

> **"Impact of Information Technology on Railroad Operations,"**
> *Diebold Research Program Report,*
> **July, 1965.**

Labor, they point out, may also well offer a hard core of resistance to the reduction of a large railroad's employment by about 20 to 25 percent over the next ten years (although John Diebold points out that this reduction would be partially offset by new jobs in EDP and other information-technology areas in railroad operations).

With respect to transition to new methods, The Diebold Research Program studies point out that the wholesale adoption of advanced operating systems will require industry-wide cooperation and support of research to produce economically attractive systems. For example, complete compatibility of the vast North American interchange system and related procedures will be required.

As to technology, John Diebold has stated:

"To upgrade (technologically) over a hundred separate companies is a monumental task; as presently constituted, however, the industry is not organized to accomplish the task effectively." This statement by the Department of Commerce report sums up the ultimate problem in the railroad industry. From a technical standpoint, most of the equipment called for in the proposed 1975 railroad operating system is available today. Only its cost and the management willingness and know-how are holding back its implementation.

Why should railroad management avail itself of technological improvements with their concomitant constraints? Competition has recognized the new geometry of society. Population shifts, living habits and standards, and responding industrial patterns have formed a new mosaic. Rail transport must be more reliable, faster, safer, and priced attractively. The revenue ton-miles carried by this mode have remained constant in the past decade while the continental ton-miles for all modes have increased sharply during the same period.

Only in the past few years has the industry recognized the opportunities which new developments offer them. Imaginative systems planning to incorporate computer-power and communications developments are mushrooming. Unfortunately, a key element is lacking — long-range planning. Few, if any of the emerging computer-based systems are based upon a visualization of what kind of railroad system would best serve the marketplace. Consequently, these expensive steps forward will not enable railroad managements to realize the full potential of the technological advances which they have recognized.

"Management and Railroad Cybernetics,"
address before the Plenary Session, International Railway Union, Symposium on Cybernetics, Paris, France,
November 4, 1963.

ENTREPRENEURIAL OPPORTUNITIES

*A pervading characteristic of John Diebold's business philosophy is that the approach to technological and social change must be more than **accommodating** to change imposed from without, and more also than taking advantage of change by improving existing products and processes. Always to the fore, he insists, must be **entrepreneurial innovation**, so that technology is used not only to lower costs and speed operations, but to open up new avenues for new business.*

Using railroads as an example, he contends that through the cost savings and revenue increases predicated upon the applications of technology here alluded to, they as an industry should find ample funds for more research in such important areas as:

Safer cargo handling methods.

New car designs for new markets.

New concepts in operation — e.g., air cushioned trains, universal containers.

Long-range planning, including diversification moves into areas related to railroad know-how by technology, marketing aspects, or other features.

As one example of a new-business opportunity inherent in the very information technology considered primarily for internal administrative application, he cites the possibility that as a result of designing and installing advanced information systems, railroads would be in an attractive position to lease or sell their own design for the input/output information equipment to shippers. The large central processors would permit the selling of time, on a service bureau basis, to shippers, especially to the small ones who have no central processors.

A CASE-STUDY FOR MANAGEMENT

The foregoing are, as John Diebold sees them, some of the major managerial problem areas which increasingly, and most forcefully, will engage the attention and understanding of railroad management. However, he emphasizes that his intent here has not been to present them in terms of a prescription for a particular industry. Rather, his purpose has been to point to the railroads as a highly visible case example of the kinds of challenges and opportunities which all industry must face in one way or another to achieve the economic benefits that are so tantalizingly near in this new age of technological innovation.

Like the railroads, business in general must have the freedom to deploy the new technologies in the way that will produce profits while at the same time best serving their customers and the public as a whole. To some significant degree — albeit perhaps with not the urgency confronting the railroads — all businesses will have to make a fundamental reappraisal of public, labor, and competitive restraints upon maximum implementation.

These constraints take many forms. Some are intangible, such as conflicts in and resistance to ideas as to what the role of the business should be, and how it should behave. Others are far more tangible, such as discriminatory legislation and new forms of public-interest regulation in our new and justified concern with ecological, civil-rights, and other environmental and social questions. There are also institutional restraints, which many industries, like the railroads, have inherited from the past. John Diebold's basic point, of course, is that the admittedly real constraints should not become ready excuses for doing nothing.

The suggested reappraisal will obviously take a different form in each industry, and in each country, for the constraints will differ in each industry and in each country.

But, says John Diebold, the same freedom for intelligent action must emerge.

Photograph by Marvin Newman

Books, lectures, and blackboards are still used to convey the most *avant garde* concepts — as here typified by John Diebold lecturing to a graduate class in management in Europe. However, programmed learning, computer displays, and other new concepts are altering the educational process, and John Diebold sees these developments as opening markets for new products and services.

12

I am convinced that the fundamental problem automation poses for management is the problem of education. On all levels of working and living we need more education. Beyond retraining those who already have jobs, or to prepare them for more highly skilled work, we must all face the larger problem of how we are to increase our resources of good engineers, scientists, and trained technicians. This problem will grow more acute in the years ahead.

"Automation as a Challenge to Management,"
International Social Science Bulletin,
June, 1957.

The impact of educational technology on business, at least in the United States, is going to be phenomenal. It will change not only the markets business serves, but also the operation of business.

"Education, Technology, and Business,"
address presented at the Alumni Homecoming Day,
Swarthmore College, Swarthmore, Pa.,
October 8, 1966.

Business, in meeting its own educational and training problems, is likely to lead the way in the application of advanced technologies for our educational institutions . . . it can [thus] serve a market of immense potential. In order to do so, business must ask, and seek answers to, the fundamental questions of education.

"Man and the Computer"
New York, Frederick A. Praeger,
1969.

Education as a Market

New technology coupled with new insights into the learning process provides important business opportunities – in both the industrial and the school setting.

The interactive effect of technological change, a phenomenon to which John Diebold continually calls attention, is nowhere better illustrated than in the dynamic interaction of technology with education and training, both in industry and in the schools and colleges. The innovations involved in solving a specific problem or making a specific contribution themselves generate new problems requiring further innovation.

Thus, as he points out, education makes technological advances possible, but this very achievement places academic education under new stresses that require institutional and methodological changes — a problem to which the educational system's response is the greater use of technology itself in its own teaching and learning processes.

Similarly in business, he adds, while modern technology has reduced labor requirements for given levels of output, it has in turn created a need for additional manpower with new skills, many of which must be taught in industrial training programs. Corporations that have benefited from technology have found it necessary to retrain their employees, in part to fill newly created positions and in part because the very nature of the jobs for which they were trained has changed radically. Industry is keenly aware that modern technology has profoundly altered the scope and direction of its own training programs.

THE EDUCATION MARKET AS A CASE-STUDY
Building Business Out of Advanced Technology

Total expenditures in this country for education at all levels — operating and capital outlays — are at a level of some $50 billion annually, not counting industrial training. If we add $25 billion accounted for by private expenditure for training and education by business and industry, we arrive at $75 billion — an outlay that competes only with the Department of Defense for the biggest slice of our national budget.

The great bulk of this is for salaries of teachers, trainers, and administrative staff, and for items such as supplies, school lunches, and the like which have formed traditional education markets for private industry. Even so, John Diebold has estimated that in a recent year the market for textbooks, audio-visual aids, materials, and certain technologies and services was already well above the $1.5 billion annually, and growing.

*However, over and above these latter items, it is John Diebold's view that a very significant entrepreneurial opportunity exists for private enterprise to provide "full service" education in many areas, **including** course preparation and teaching. As one example of this he points to the full-fledged "seminar industry" pioneered by the American Management Association and now offered by numerous competing organizations (i.e., for-profit enterprises, not merely professional societies and trade* *associations. Additionally, home study organizations ("correspondence schools") and privately operated trade schools in the automotive, electronics, printing, computer, and other industries have long established the concept of education as a for-profit, entrepreneurial opportunity. In any event, he sees the education market in connection with our present discussion not so much in terms of its dollar size (great as that is) but rather as a case example representing the exciting opportunities as well as the kind of problems that confront business when it undertakes to capitalize on the newer technologies. The potentials in education exist, he says, not merely in supplying more of the traditional products and services associated with that market, and not necessarily in supplying new equipment — but rather in realizing that major institutional changes will inevitably take place as new technologies are developed and applied. These will be conceptual breakthroughs that open up whole new vistas — programmed learning is one example. It is these implications of technological changes that management must be aware of if it is indeed going to develop education into the huge market that its future could portend.*

The market will not develop automatically. It will require farsighted thinking and "re-thinking" on the part of those with enough imagination to read the opportunities in what the new technologies are making possible. In the Swarthmore address cited above, John Diebold indicated some of the opportunities, the ferment, and the caveats in this burgeoning field:

Over the past few years, education has seen a confrontation between unsophisticated buyers and sophisticated machinery. The first attempts, through programmed learning and the so-called teaching machines, on the whole have not proven successful. What, if anything, does this tell us about computer-assisted instruction?

While there have been some companies impatient to sell advanced technologies for education, some consumers have been equally impatient to possess these technologies just because they are available or appear prestigious. Now, however, the balance of forces may be changing. The number of school districts has declined rapidly from 47,000 in 1958 to about 21,000 today, and as the resulting individual units become larger, their purchasing practices appear to be growing more sophisticated. The right questions are beginning to be asked. An increasing number of districts are cooperating with universities, foundations, business enterprises, and federal agencies in experimental programs to test new educational methods and technologies, as well as new forms of community relations to the educational process.

> **"Education, Technology, and Business,"**
> *address presented at the Alumni Homecoming Day,*
> *Swarthmore College, Swarthmore, Pa.,*
> **October 8, 1966.**

The educational market too often has been perceived only in gross terms. Its components, its current and future needs, and the resultant requirements for serving it have been analyzed without due attention either to the obstacles to specific changes or to the pressures that can help to turn the need for change into an effective demand for change. Many of the individual business moves to capitalize on the market were poorly planned — that is, staffed with the wrong people, financially unsophisticated, and dependent on technologies developed for related but actually quite different purposes. Yet the general direction of the response has indeed taken account of the need for interdisciplinary and cooperative approaches.

What has happened has been a great casting about for mergers, acquisitions, and other joint arrangements among electronic manufacturers, publishers, manufacturers of educational materials, and mass communications media, (previously cited).

These new ventures were usually based on the expectation that the electronics manufacturers would supply the ready-made technology that would be combined with the in-house educational know-how of publishers, communications media, and producers of educational materials. The results then would be packaged for sale to the educational market. Unfortunately the know-how, where it actually existed, could rarely, if ever, be combined with the ready-made technology. The successful combination of old educational experience with a new technology, originally designed mostly for noneducational purposes, actually requires a kind of rethinking and *questioning* that we are only beginning to understand. There are few people capable of it as yet.

In the meantime, however, some of the packages of technology and know-how were being sold to unsophisticated buyers. Before long, it became evident that little of value was to be found in these packages. The investments of the sellers in their development and of the buyers in their purchase were lost . . . Some of the joint ventures persisted and developed new packages from scratch. But it is unclear to what extent the newly developed packages actually resulted from the joint ventures.

> **"Education, Technology, and Business,"**
> *address presented at the Alumni Homecoming Day,*
> *Swarthmore College, Swarthmore, Pa.,*
> **October 8, 1966.**

Entrepreneurial Opportunities in Emerging Technologies

Fully aware of the impressive obstacles that must be overcome — involving resistance within the "educational establishment" itself, social inertia, fiscal problems, lack of full understanding of the basics of the learning process itself, and entrepreneurial mistakes on the part of business itself — John Diebold has long been a protagonist of the possibilities inherent in already available and immediately emerging technology. Thus:

Teaching machines and programmed learning are altering some fundamental concepts of industrial education and training, and of public education. Machine systems can pace the individual student, can analyze his learning difficulties and mistakes as they occur, and can introduce remedial instruction as it is needed. Machine teaching is only in its infancy, but with skillful programming some professors have reduced university courses to one-third and one-quarter of the time formerly required. Significantly, machine-taught students exhibit a higher average retention level, one or two years after completing their courses, than is known to have been achieved before.

> **"Applications of Automation,"**
> *address before the International Chamber of Commerce, Paris, France,*
> **November 21, 1961.**

A review of American technology – developments that have come upon us with increasing speed and consequence – might concern itself with the introduction in our classrooms of teaching machines which permit school children to learn mathematics and languages at twice the speed, and much more thoroughly, than classmates taught by conventional methods.

> **"Technology's Challenge to Management,"**
> *address before the Plenary Session, European Conference of The High Authority of the European Coal and Steel Community, The Commission of the European Economic Community, The Commission of the European Atomic Energy Community, Brussels, Belgium,*
> **December 6, 1960.**

And for business and industrial training, he recently highlighted the opportunities as follows:

You're getting these computer-based teaching systems so that a salesman can learn about a new product without coming back to the home office. He sits down at a console in the field and learns about characteristics of the new product, or goes through a training course without flying back to the home office. Many firms are starting to plan for that sort of thing. IBM is experimenting with a training system for their maintenance people in the field, where, between calls, they use the console and address a computer that may be a thousand miles away. The computer takes them through a whole chain of instruction on the new products they are servicing. Your flexibility in this is going to be as great as the telephone system.

> **"Marketing's Role in Coming Age of Automation,"**
> *Sales Management ,*
> **October 1, 1966.**

THE UNDERLYING TECHNOLOGY

The underlying technology has been ready for some time. Here is how John Diebold outlined applicable developments in a discussion of programmed learning before a professional group in educational and training technology. (Programmed learning, it may be briefly explained, is an instruction technique in which educational and industrial training problems are analyzed into a great many small steps. At each step a question or direction is presented – with or without the use of a mechanical device – and the student is required to make an active response. He is then given an immediate check of his accuracy. This is thus a form of self-instruction in which a student proceeds at his own pace. The approach lends itself very readily to machine use, and in particular makes possible highly effective computer-based systems, the computer being programmed to analyze student responses and call for appropriate next steps):

Today, the machine aspects of programmed instruction are crude and all too often the machines are mere contrivances to aid in the sale of a program. There are, of course, notable exceptions, but the exceptions only strengthen my point, namely, that while today the machine is often peripheral to the process, it will not always be that way.

The nature and the speed of developments in the field of information technology are such that it would be wrong, as so many well trained analysts have done, to write off the machine systems as an unimportant aspect of programmed instruction.

The science and technological development that produced the electronic computer have taken a direction which gives every promise that they will in the course of the next two decades produce entirely new families of machine systems which we may here characterize as educational systems. Among the developments that I consider significant to education are the following:

a. *Voice recognition* on the part of the machine system allowing not only activation of the system by a voiced command, but the interpretation and evaluation of the content of the spoken command.

b. *Animated displays* that permit the individual to see a continually changing graphic display of machine system output; this may be in the form of a graph, a printed text, or a photograph.

c. *Machine intelligence* developments, which have already provided us with examples of intelligent behavior on the part of the machine system in its reaction to human commands.

d. *Real time systems* with large numbers of input/output devices for communicating with the system in an on-line manner.

e. *Huge random access storage* of graphic as well as digital information permitting entirely new orders of magnitude in the library that can be stored within the system.

Such improvements, particularly in the man-machine interface, are making it possible for smooth, easy, and natural communication between the student and the machine system, so that we can begin to think in terms of computer-based systems playing a vital role in the education process.

"Programmed Learning: Its Role in Our World,"
keynote address before the Society for Educational and Training Technology, San Antonio, Texas,
April 1, 1964.

Programmed learning is, of course, only one technique or set of techniques in a whole arsenal of innovation now available to educators and industrial trainers. A growing variety of advanced systems are being considered, experimented with, and evaluated in educational and economic terms. These include such developments as computer-based inquiry services especially geared to educational needs; advanced computer-based instructional systems which help the teacher to individualize the instructional process and provide automatic evaluation of each student's capabilities, progress, and responses; and various forms of computer-assisted instructional systems which put the student into direct dialogue with the computer in which the educational materials are stored.

And not to be overlooked, John Diebold reminds us, is audio-visual instruction as potentially a part of any advanced system. He comments on this in his remarks on the possibilities in integrating the various pertinent technologies:

Audio visual instruction can be individualized, either by providing the student with an audio-visual display responsive to the student's immediate interaction with the system, or by directing the student to a generally available audio-visual program. For example, the "tutorial mode" of computer-based instruction might provide the former, while advanced computer-based instructional systems might help the teacher decide to have the student attend a particular series of television lectures — which might be "instructional television" or even general educational television.

It should be quite evident that elements of all of the advanced systems described here can be combined in numerous ways and that eventually the chance will come to integrate the technologies and concepts still in the laboratory, some of which were treated above. The manner and extent to which the systems are implemented depends on economic factors and educational decisions. An educational system, of course, is composed not only of technologies and materials but also methodologies and, above all, of personnel. An advanced system can be thought of as the most cost-effective mixture of these components, compatible with the economic means available and the social purposes decided upon.

"Man and the Computer,"
New York, Frederick A. Praeger,
1969.

175

THE ENTREPRENEURIAL OPPORTUNITY

John Diebold considers the educational system as a "display-case" example — one that has been long delayed in a technological age — of the tremendous increase in productivity which occurs with the application of technology to areas which have had little innovation in basic methodology. A computer-based system, he points out, can perform most of the **routine** *functions of the teacher, allowing one teacher effectively to supervise the learning process of a much greater number of pupils. His analogy with one of the earliest forms of automation brings this to life:*

The Northrup loom achieved great gains in labor productivity in weaving by changing bobbins automatically. This allowed an operator to tend more looms. The Northrup loom could not be used with finer quality thread because of the inability of the automatic mechanism to allow for breakdowns, but it was a satisfactory and more efficient technology for coarser fabrics. The teaching machine, like the Northrup loom, allows the teacher to supervise the "production" process of learning and works well with standardized material but cannot be used with delicate, specialized work.

Computer-based instructional systems are just beginning to be used on an experimental basis. This technique appears to hold great promise as a means of dealing with the knowledge explosion, the teacher shortage, and the difficulties involved in providing all students with a uniformly adequate education. This appears to be one of the areas in which technology will contribute in an extremely valuable way to solving a problem it has itself — at least in part — caused.

> **"Impacts on Urban Governmental Functions of Developments in Science and Technology,"**
> *Monograph No. 7, Governing Urban Society, American Academy of Political and Social Science,*
> **May, 1967.**

Developments in time-sharing techniques should make such systems feasible for even the smallest schools or groups, and developments in communications will make it possible to link such systems over ever increasing distances.

Time-sharing will be of special importance because of its cost-reducing potential in computer usage. Even current technology allows a single central processor to give almost instantaneous access to large numbers of users with different programs. Since each user actually requires only a fraction of a second of a computer's processing time for each inquiry, others can be served before there is any noticeable time lag in the response from the machine to the first user. Thus, costly computer time is shared by many. The advantages of this are obvious for educational systems in which hundreds or thousands of students, perhaps each with an individually tailored program, simultaneously receive computer-assisted instruction. Major further advances in the multi-processing and multi-programming capabilities of computers are expected over the next few years. Finally, communications improvements are expected to make the time-sharing concept even more flexible in application because relatively idle machines would stand ready to take on users from various places if the local equipment should suddenly become overloaded.

"Education, Technology, and Business,"
address presented at the Alumni Homecoming Day,
Swarthmore College, Swarthmore, Pa.,
October 8, 1966.

Academic Potentials: Sources of Funds

Despite the many billions of dollars spent on institutional (i.e., non-business) education, as represented by the $50 billion figure previously mentioned, John Diebold's position is that with most of the money going for current needs rather than for capital expenditures and research, there has actually been little or no growth in educational productivity over the past two decades . . . and that this situation will continue until major breakthroughs are achieved.

He is convinced that the application of advanced technologies can help our schools get ahead in this race. But where will the initial and on-going capital investments in research, programming, and hardware come from? He offers some suggestions:

Sources of funds might be sought in various areas. Perhaps they reside in specific Federal programs, such as Assistance for Educationally Deprived Children, for which nearly $1 billion was appropriated in 1966, and educational research, for which some $70 million was expended in 1965. But the former is a stopgap program of sorts, and the latter is very small. Other specific Federal programs are small also, for example, $15 million for educational television facilities in 1966.

In 1968, it was estimated that business has invested some $75 million in the development of computer-assisted instruction. Additional millions are being spent on the development of simpler technologies and methods. And a beginning has been made on laboratory experimentation with biochemical processes. Also, there is increasing academic talk about – if not yet much investment in – the investigation of basic learning processes.

In 1965, foundations spent an estimated $14 million. The Foundation Library Center believes actual expenditures may be slightly larger, but they are not much, as yet. A total of estimates from various sources indicates that funds expended on educational research are only a fraction of one percent of all expenditures for education. This compares, for example, with the five percent that many corporations spend on research and development in other areas.

"Man and the Computer,"
New York, Frederick A. Praeger,
1969.

The Near-Term Potential Market

While the broad outlines of the potential educational market show tremendous and pressing needs and opportunities in academic education, the nearer-term opportunities, says Diebold, lie in the private sector comprising employee education, training, and retraining programs. In the business and industrial field the pressures are no less, but greater flexibility for action exists, and advantages can more readily be quantified in terms of cost effectiveness. For example, as shown by Diebold Group studies, per-pupil costs are acceptable that are a whole order of magnitude greater than those which are traditionally found in academic education:

In a 1966 survey of one of the major corporations in the United States, 16,000 of its employees (18 percent of the employees in the divisions covered by the survey and 13 percent of the total work force) were engaged in 415 training programs. The programs were in ten categories: management, sales and marketing, finance, science and engineering, systems and automatic data processing, clerical activities, production, safety and maintenance, orientation, and other. Forty-four percent of the courses used training aids other than blackboards, the most prevalent being audio-visual devices. Total educational cost per student-hour was $9.20 — as compared to some 38 cents per student-hour in public elementary and secondary schools; 41 percent of this cost was attributable to training equipment, training materials, and instructors' salaries — with 30 percent of this, or about $1.12 per student-hour, spent on equipment and materials.

In spite of the high costs per student-hour, 65 percent of the managerial respondents to the survey indicated that training programs in science and engineering and safety maintenance could be made more effective through the use of additional training aids. In these programs, such aids were already being utilized more intensively than in most other programs. The threat of job obsolescence was reported to be the most significant stimulus to the establishment of training courses for skilled and semiskilled employees.

It is significant that one major corporation has been willing to spend nearly three times as much for equipment and materials alone per student-hour than the total cost of a student-hour in our public elementary and secondary school systems — although, of course, the total of 24.3 hours per year each employee was engaged in training progrms is only about 2.4 percent of the hours the average student spends in school each year.

"Man and the Computer,"
New York, Frederick A. Praeger,
1969.

The potential market is for total advanced systems — not just technological hardware and materials, but programs, methods, and other software, as well as the training of teachers and administrators to use these items and services. This should involve several billion dollars annually on a national scale within a time frame that is realistic for business planning — ten to fifteen years. However, probably more useful for business efforts would seem to be an evaluation of what individual school districts or groups of them are willing and able to do, in order to direct marketing efforts to such districts.

There are certain interim measures, however, of the national market, divided into products and services on the one hand and user groups on the other. These can be useful for decision-making by business. Now, and probably for some years to come, certain materials (textbooks, programmed instruction texts, audio-visual hardware and software and teaching machines) can be sold in predictable quantities. In addition, CAI systems can be marketed to a limited extent, as can certain services related to the materials. The Diebold Group, Inc., projects that this real market will grow from $1.4 billion in 1965 to $2.7 billion in 1975. It should be emphasized, however, that this is only part of the potential market for total advanced systems. The real market is likely to be considerably larger but is subject to numerous variables. However, it is really this potential market that is of primary concern to the developing business response in education. The extent to which the potential is realized depends on the quality of the business response, which is probably the single most important variable.

"Man and the Computer,"
New York, Frederick A. Praeger,
1969.

SOCIAL AND POLITICAL IMPLICATIONS

The social implications of advancing technology, of which John Diebold keeps reminding business management, are especially acute in the educational field. On the national educational scene, he has alluded to some of these:

We are dealing with human experimentation. The way we teach, the instruments and systems we apply, the age at which we launch our children into the formal educational complex will all have a profound effect not only on what our children learn but also on their psychological make-up. It is no longer a question of pure method, of John Dewey versus the German pedagogues or of the permissive school versus the disciplinarian. These are gentle issues of the past.

The fundamental questions we face are not questions for tomorrow, after the technologies and systems have been installed. They are questions for today. They involve every child in Headstart, every student learning the "new math," every industrial trainee for a new or changing job. Unless an adequate beginning can be made in answering them, the available measures of educational demand and of financing are of little use.

Industry also faces another new training requirement, for demographic, social, and labor market considerations indicate that nonwhites will constitute a larger part of the work force in the 1970s than they have in the 1960s. This particularly bears on the training requirements of industry, because many of these new entrants to the labor force have been denied an adequate education until now, and will need some general preparatory training before they are taught new job skills. Considering the impact of technology and the changing composition of the labor force, one fact is clear: If industry is going to meet its training requirements effectively, it will have to employ the techniques of *individualized instruction* on a *mass scale* provided by programmed instruction, CAI, audio visuals, and all the rest.

Compounding the problem is a profound social effect of our rapidly changing technology: A typical member of the work force will hold twelve different jobs in his working life, and four workers out of five will change their major occupation at least once. Workers who have no more than a high school education tend to hold a series of jobs that are essentially unrelated. The education and training of these workers will be a continuing requirement of industry because the skills they learn in one job are not likely to be transferable to their next job. The computer, which is responsible for many of the new training requirements industry faces, may well be the tool that will enable industry to meet its training requirements.

> **"Education, Technology, and Business."**
> *address presented at the Alumni Homecoming Day,*
> *Swarthmore College, Swarthmore, Pa.,*
> **October 8, 1966.**

Internationally, John Diebold was among the first to see the broad social and political implication of developments in technology applied to education as a means of forcibly bringing underdeveloped countries into the twentieth century:

Nations being thrust into a basic reconstruction of their society have many needs. They must try to affect changes in one generation which have taken advanced countries many generations to achieve.

The most obvious need in a country striving for rapid advances in agriculture and industry is for machinery and equipment. This is perhaps the need most easily met. However, a gift of equipment to people with no skills to use it is quite futile, unless accompanied with help in training people in the required skills.

Fortunately, it is now possible to accelerate the training process by the use of new techniques known as programmed instruction. It has been demonstrated, for example, that people with no knowledge of electronics can quickly be taught to assemble complex equipment with a very high degree of accuracy. On one assembly line where this technique was employed, the reject rate was decreased by a large percentage. This result was achieved by analyzing the assembly procedure into an ordered set of simple steps. At each step a picture of the result was shown, together with an oral instruction, given through earphones. This approach has an important advantage for emerging nations, in that it minimizes the need for general education as a preparation for specific training problems.

The inevitable expansion of governmental responsibilities and activities in emerging nations will require expanded staffs of government employees trained for a variety of tasks. For example, the efficient operation of many government services requires the compilation of much data. The data must be gathered and reported in a standard manner. The personnel required for such activities are generally widely scattered throughout the country.

Here programmed instruction offers the greatest potential. It is the best way to train large numbers of scattered people in standard procedures which demand a minimum level of performance. It has been used successfully in training agents of a major insurance company whose employees are scattered all over the United States. This new technique will be perhaps the most important single weapon in solving problems of mass education. Trained teachers will always be needed, but their talents will be extended to hundreds of thousands of people.

> **"The Applicability of Programmed Learning Techniques to Developing Countries,"**
> *Floor Statement by John Diebold as a member of the U.S. Delegation to U.N. Conference on Science and Technology for Less Developed Areas, Geneva, Switzerland,*
> **February 8, 1963.**

IN SUMMARY . . .

The paramount force of our "age of change," John Diebold constantly reminds us, is the interaction among previously independent disciplines and social entities. Thus he sees the role of private enterprise in education as a case study of the future. It involves a fusion of private and national interests, he says, that we are already beginning to see in areas of endeavor as widely separated as the development of oceanic resources and supersonic air travel, and in concern over the effects of atmospheric pollution on the oceans' organisms.

Still more conspicuous today are the interrelationships between industry's interests in skilled manpower and sophisticated consumers for new products, and the national interest in an educated citizenry. And these interests, he points out, are translated into industry's stake in the markets for advanced educational systems, as well as the nation's stake in the usefulness of these systems.

His major thesis is worth reiterating: In order to make use of the newer technologies, institutional structures such as education will have to change, discarding traditional habits and procedures. We cannot expect the types of new systems here discussed to be bought like textbooks. Business, he argues, must look for more than improved opportunity to sell supplies and equipment. It must look for, and in fact help create, true breakthroughs in the education process itself. And business can prepare the way by first introducing such changes, not in the market represented by the traditional education "establishment," but in the educational market of business itself — its own proliferating training and education needs.

Computer and communication systems have created a new industry – computer-based information services, which will soon reach an annual volume of several billion dollars. They are used by a wide variety of professionals – engineers, financial analysts, physicians, economists. John Diebold here discusses the extension of cathode-ray-tube terminals to one such service

13

The technology of computers and the rapid communications and information processing equipment which this technology makes possible will permit far more extensive analysis of our national economy and business methods, through up-to-the minute market surveys and extensive research on distribution and transportation patterns.

"Automation: The Advent of the Automatic Factory,"
Princeton, New Jersey; Van Nostrand, Inc.,
1952.

There must be more analysis of business needs and more imagination concerning practical business applications of computers – other than the sweeping concept of the totally automatic office.

"Automation—The New Technology"
Harvard Business Review
November-December, 1953.

A new industry is the one now being called the inquiry industry – it is in some ways the publishing field of the future. This development is one which allows the sale of proprietary data over a communication system in answer to a query placed by the customer from a unit on his desk . . . You key this request into the unit on your desk, see the answer on a screen virtually as you ask the question, and then go on to ask another question and so on through a train of questions. When you get what you want, you can even make a copy of it if you so desire.

"Business, Computers, and the Turn Toward Technology,"
address before the Economic Club of Chicago, Chicago, Illinois,
February 24, 1966.

Computer-Based Information Services as a New Business

Communications and computers are creating a brand new $6 billion industry — providing businessmen and scientists, engineers, and other professionals with information.

From the beginning of the application of computers to business data processing, John Diebold sounded the theme of looking upon them as more than simply new, much faster, and more versatile business machines that would merely "put wheels under" existing information processing. He did indeed call for their use in that context — but, as indicated in earlier chapters, he wanted them used in the bold and new dimension of completely integrated "total management information systems."

*However, from the very first, he went much farther than that. He saw automation in general not merely as a means of improving **internal** operations, but as an exciting **entrepreneurial opportunity** — a catalyst and implementor of entirely new kinds of service businesses. Thus as early as 1953 he wrote:*

The technology of feedback will by no means be used exclusively to replace labor or to improve present operations. It will make its greatest contribution to our society by enabling us to do more and different things and to satisfy human wants in new and better ways. Management will have more facts and consequently a better basis for making decisions. Similarly, other areas of human enterprise too will benefit. While mathematicians, economists, military theorists, and meterologists are already using computers, still wider uses will become possible when smaller and cheaper computers become available; and new devices will be developed for use in medicine, retailing, and many other lines.

When applied in these ways, automation, rather than replacing human labor, will make it possible to render new, more comprehensive, and more economical services. It will, in fact, strengthen and further the already established trend toward accentuation of the service industries, with higher employment in that area and higher consumption generally.

> **"Automation—the New Technology,"**
> *Harvard Business Review,*
> **November-December, 1953.**

Even during the years when he and his firm were heavily engaged in the pioneering work of computerizing administrative operations, he stressed the possibilities in special services efficiently performed by special-purpose computers, providing information based on the performing of limited calculations and simple repetitive operations. Many of these have since been put into practice.

One can envisage a hotel reservation service embracing an information storage and retrieval system working in real time over large geographic areas. You would have thousands of input-output units in airports and railway terminals and travel agencies and the offices of large companies. With these units you could then make reservations for specific rooms in specific hotels for specific days for a period ahead. Here would emerge a service business selling proprietary information. It would sell the information that a certain room is available and make a booking.

We have been doing a good deal of planning work for some businesses of this kind in the States, and the investment level is high. A system of this kind in the States would run to 120 million dollars.

However, once you have the system and build it and are offering the service, you are unlikely to have competition, and you can have a protected profit position. There are many business opportunities for this kind of service.

"John Diebold's Vista of Automation,"
Business,
December, 1963.

"TIME-SHARING" AND "REAL TIME" OPEN NEW VISTAS

The possibliities for new types of businesses such as John Diebold has been espousing became more visible with the advent of the remotely accessible third-generation "time-sharing" computers into general application, together with greatly increased capacities of direct-access memories. The seven emerging changes in information technology as he foresaw them in 1965 are recapitulated below as a succinct statement of the technological underpinning of entirely new kinds of computer-based inquiry services, apart from the sale of time-shared computer use for problem-solving or data processing. See Figure 13-A for characteristics of on-line information service organizations.

1. Future information systems will be more versatile and will more nearly parallel the real flow of information within an organization.

2. Information systems will tend increasingly to be "real time"; that is, they will reflect important and routine events as they occur.

3. Systems flexibility for new applications will be vastly increased, and costs greatly reduced, through a broad range of new peripheral equipment developments.

4. Significant cost reductions and vastly expanded use of random-access files and memory will permit the drawing together on an integrated basis of the data needed to manage and operate the company, and provide instantaneous and flexible access to it.

5. A totally new data storage and processing capability — graphic storage and processing — will become economical and commonly available.

6. Information storage and retrieval of technical, management, and general data will become an increasingly important aspect of information systems.

7. There will be significant improvements in the means of communicating with the system — the so-called man-machine interface.

"What's Ahead in Information Technology,"
Harvard Business Review,
September-October, 1965.

Figure 13-A. ON-LINE INFORMATION SERVICE ORGANIZATION CHARACTERISTICS

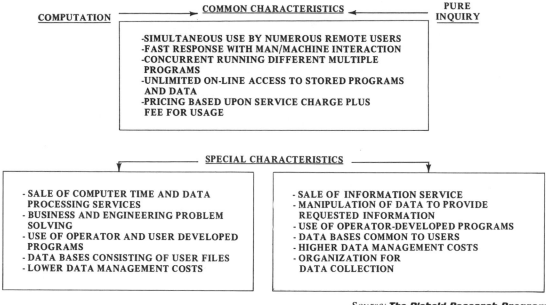

Source: The Diebold Research Program

NEW: THE COMPUTER-BASED INFORMATION SERVICES

The above developments, of course, have greatly extended the scope and economic application of the traditional data-processing service center — the "data processing utility" which John Diebold described in the following terms:

A large central processor handles information at a very low unit cost just as a large central generator produces electricity for many customers at a low unit cost. It is cheaper for many people to make use of this central utility, than it is for each individual to have his own generator. The same economic reasoning applies to the "data processing utility," where many people can use the machine simultaneously. It will be the technology of real-time processing, time-sharing, and communications which allows this to happen. Small and medium-sized business — and, for some purposes, large businesses — will just plug in for data processing as they now do for electricity.

> **"Business, Computers and the Turn Toward Technology,"**
> *address before the Economic Club of Chicago, Chicago, Illinois,*
> **February 24, 1966.**

*However, it is computer-based **information services**, making use of readily accessed comprehensive data bases tied into communication lines, that John Diebold sees as the exciting and entirely **new** entrepreneurial opportunity:*

It is not merely a more inclusive name for computer time sharing, conventional service bureaus, or so-called "real time" computer systems. Moreover, we are not referring to digital data communications as such, nor to information storage and retrieval as such. The new computer-based information service involves the effective combination of appropriate aspects of *all* of these developments into profitable, commercial enterprises, for the express purpose of providing information custom-tailored to specific groups of users.

"Needed: A Yardstick for Computers,"
an interview with John Diebold, Dun's Review,
August 1968.

Diebold research studies have projected the potential for this new industry to reach $6 billion by the mid-70s — from an estimated annual volume of $50 million in 1968. (See Figure 13-B.)

It has already gone a long way toward that rate of activity since the following observations and predictions were made by John Diebold only a few short years ago:

New services will become available from information service centers. Credit reports; legal, market, and technical information; and a variety of other special services will be available "on call" from regional or national centers. Some companies currently providing such services in published form are planning for service centers, and a legal-information service already is operating in New York.

"What's Ahead in Information Technology,"
Harvard Business Review,
September-October, 1965.

The additional industry to come about is one that is described as the inquiry industry, where you sell data, you distribute information, and you answer questions that people ask. A financial analyst, for example, will have a console in front of him, a terminal unit on his desk, like a telephone. It's going to be a unit that has a keyboard and in some a TV screen and perhaps even a method of making hard copy. Eventually, too, some voice capability so that it can be talked to.

The financial analyst, for example, might say: "I'd like to see the rank by price-earnings ratio, of the stocks of such-and-such industry," and they will appear on the screen. And then he'll say he's interested in a particular company and look at its financial history and go through a whole chain of questions.

The industry providing such service is going to be a multibillion-dollar one before we get far into the seventies, and it doesn't exist today. Some of today's publishers will be a part of it. You see, this is a *completely new growth opportunity.* You can think of it, if you like, as a major growth of the publishing industry, but it's quite a *new kind* of business.

"Marketing's Role in the Coming Age of Automation"
Sales Management,
October 1, 1966.

Figure 13-B.

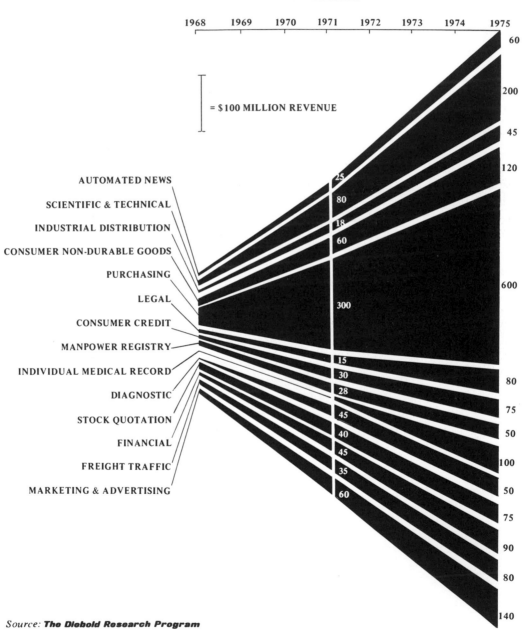

GROWTH OF
INFORMATION SERVICE MARKETS

Source: *The Diebold Research Program*

An example of the service I have been talking about is in employment. You use a simple telex if you are a subscriber to the service. Say you are looking for a very special kind of aeronautical engineer. You put your request into the telex, addressing the computer which is in Buffalo, N.Y., while you are in Los Angeles. You say: I want an aeronautical engineer with vertical take-off experience, who speaks Japanese. The computer types back in a brief second or two. It says there are no aeronautical engineers available who speak Japanese.

So you say, "Let us take off the Japanese language constraint." The computer comes back and says: "There are 73. Do you want an abstract of the resumes?" You say you do. It then types out one- or two-sentence abstracts of the resumes, and you tell the machine, "This one and this one and this one are interesting to me." At this stage it prints out the full several-page resume and the service company puts it into the mail for you that evening.

This is one of many, many such businesses of this kind that are already in existence. It is a wholly new kind of industry, this inquiry business. It has a long way to go. It is still in its infancy.

Extemporaneous address before the XIVth Conference of the Comite International de l'Organisation Scientifique (CIOS), Rotterdam, Holland, **September 21, 1966.**

THE INFORMATION SERVICES IN ACTION

Probably no organization has made a more exhaustive study of the probable user needs, technological base, market characteristics, and new-business potentials of the type of information services we have been discussing, than has The Diebold Group. The discussion that follows is based on Diebold data files, findings of analysts working on Diebold Research Program studies pertinent to this field, and on interviews with John Diebold, reviews of his addresses before professional societies, and transcripts of his remarks before staff and Diebold Research Program sponsor groups:

The essence of a computer-based information service is the provision of information and related computational service to remote users on an as-needed basis. It has become a commercially attractive activity because of the capability of modern computers to serve a large number of remote users concurrently, coupled with the availability of low-cost mass-storage memories and the improvements in the cost and technology of data communication. Early examples of such inquiry services include:

Stock quotation inquiry services, where the subscriber uses a TV-like terminal with a keyboard. He indicates the stock in which he is interested, and the last trading price appears on the screen.

Services for automated statute research, storing on magnetic tape complete texts of all statutes for covered states. It can cite any laws pertaining to specific subjects as requests, and on demand print out complete texts of any statutes or sections cited.

Personnel services, in which employers communicate their needs to a remote computer via teleprinters, and the computer searches its file of candidates to find those that best match the requirements.

From remarks by John Diebold at a meeting of
Diebold Research Program sponsors,
October 3, 1969.

Possible Markets

In the market of the size and scope here visualized there will obviously be many segments and offshoots, not all of which can be definitively indicated at this time. However, The Diebold Research Program foresees at least the following market segments open to computer-based inquiry services in the mid-70s:

Consumer goods sales and "pipeline" inventory data (largely non-durables, branded merchandise)
Distribution information
Credit information
Financial information and financial analysis service
Legal information
Manpower registry
Marketing and Advertising information
Medical—individual medical record centers, and diagnostic information and services
News Services
Purchasing information
Scientific and technical information and references
Stock quotations
Traffic information
Computation services as required by the above.

Most of the above categories, of course, comprise separate business opportunities. And even in specific categories such as purchasing information service or scientific and technical reference services, it is envisioned that different companies will provide special kinds of the services indicated for separate customer groups, or industries, or geographic areas. Additionally, a service "package" developed for a specific clientele may combine several of the categories. Marketing and Advertising, for example, might in some businesses be organized around inquiry services combined with industrial distribution information and consumer credit information, as well as special types of computation services in connection with market analysis and evaluation. Other business will be built around an individual information service, as for example stock quotations. At this writing the whole concept is quite fluid, with many marketing, technical, competitive, and organizational factors involved.

"Management Implications of the New Technology,"
Diebold Research Program Report,
July, 1965.

Operation

The technological base has already been indicated. The distinctive feature is the central data bank to which all or selected users of the service have access, and which can be updated either by the operator of the information service or (in some cases) by authorized users. The data base, The Diebold Group points out, is simply a body of indexed and coded and readily accessed information in the memory of the computer system. It can consist of internal company data (such as customers' names and address lists) or a common body of knowledge (such as data on companies listed on the New York Stock Exchange), or extensive economic and market data, credit information, and the like compiled by the operator of the service. Operations may cover a broad spectrum of complexity:

The service may consist largely of providing computing capability (thus merging into on-line data processing centers) where, say an engineer performs stress analyses on a design, using a terminal with direct access to a computer. The service may offer the use of many proprietary programs applicable to specific types of analyses.

On-line sale of information only, utilizing information obtained by the operator of the service and stored in the computer system memory, is exemplified by stock quotation services. There is an immediate response to a broker's query as to the last transaction price for a given stock.

Information sold in a more complex form may involve some computation or processing in response to a query. In a manpower registry service, for example, an inquiry may request a listing of all filed resumes that meet specific listed criteria. The response involves searching the file on the basis of each criterion to provide the final listing.

Review of Developments in Information Processing,"
Diebold Research Program Report,
October, 1963.

As John Diebold points out, nearly all inquiry services will involve some computation. Even where computation services are the prime offering, access to a data base will be involved, consisting either of the subscriber's data, or of data common to a number of subscribers. The more sophisticated types of computer-based information services, he adds, will involve interaction between the user and the system. For example, a subscriber to a financial analysis service may ask for the names and financial statistics on any companies of a given type. Having received this information, he may request the computer system to perform calculations based on the data (ratios, trend fittings, and the like). In the course of this processing he may query the system for additional information (on other companies, further data on companies already given him, or general industry and economic data), and so on.

*The important point he makes is that while computation services may be involved, these are as adjuncts to a new kind of business — the information business — and are not to be confused with the traditional type of computer-center services, even though the latter may now offer computer time-sharing and on-line real-time access. The essence of the new concept is that it fulfills a totally **different** kind of customer need.*

Government Involvement

Because of close linkage with communications common carriers, the general public and governmental sensitivity to matters of "privacy," and antitrust aspects involved (where information is gathered from and-or distributed to competing companies), the entrepreneur here must assume that varying degrees of governmental control may be expected. Rates for communication services will of course continue to be regulated, as will be the kind of activities in which existing public utilities will be permitted to engage. Many of the types of information conceivably supplied will be of direct interest to Government regulatory agencies, and the extent to which information supplied to them may be resold as-is or recombined and sold may be subject to restriction. Additionally, the Government may preempt fields in which private enterprise cannot profitably provide service.

Regulatory agencies will be involved in many sensitive areas. For example, the SEC will be interested in financial information services both as a possible subscriber, and in terms of possible regulation of the type and form of information disseminated. Other departments and agencies will be interested in health-information services. Antitrust personnel will be concerned with any services that pool information affecting competition. As technical and scientific information services develop, there may also be some national security questions involved in dissemination. And, of course, there is the possibility that the FCC will choose to regulate on-line information services as public utilities, and that it will obtain support for this concept.

The Government may be expected to continue encouragement of data banks and information services that are obviously in the public interest — health, scientific and technical information, and educational services.

Except for a limited number of activities – such as the Defense Documentation Center – the posture of the Federal Government has been to encourage the development of computer-based information services rather than to enter the field directly, although the states can be expected to increase their creation and operation of data banks and information networks in connection with police activities, vital statistics, and other activities. The much discussed National Data Center is primarily for operation of Government departments. On the whole, if private enterprise moves with reasonable speed in the development of information services, governmental competition, at least at the Federal level, is unlikely to be a major factor.

"Impacts on Urban Governmental Functions of Developments in Science and Technology,"
The Annals of the American Academy of Political and Social Science,
May, 1967.

INFORMATION-SERVICE EXAMPLES

Referring to the categories of services previously listed, we summarize here the kinds of services John Diebold and his associates envision:

Consumer Goods Sales

Consumer non-durable goods activity, monitored now by periodically auditing selected retailers, could be made a much more valuable marketing information resource. Even if it is assumed that current services always provide statistically valid samples, the retail audits still suffer from significant delays before results are available at marketing and sales decision levels. With existing technology, a system could easily report the daily or weekly movement of high-turnover products such as toiletries and branded foods from warehouses to retail outlet and (albeit not daily) from retailers' shelves to consumers. A service of this sort utilizing manual techniques has been available for some time in the food and drug fields, but vast segments of the market remain untapped.

As a byproduct of its detailed sales and inventory data, such a service could provide various ratios, evaluations, statistical analyses, test-market studies, and the like for subscribers. A lucrative satellite service would be processing data for the warehouses and wholesalers involved.

Distribution Information

Distribution information is available promptly only to a few large manufacturers of industrial products and consumer durable goods – and then only from captive or exclusive distributors. For most such companies – producers of commercial hardware, auto parts, appliances, medical equipment, and the like – facts on what is happening in the distribution pipeline are hard to come by and chronically dated. Statistics gathered by industry associations have limited tactical value, and internal sales data usually lag events significantly. This situation presents an attractive opportunity for a service applying available technology to provide on-going information on the movement of these goods out of distributors' warehouses. Again, as a byproduct, valuable special statistical and data processing services could be rendered.

Credit Information

Consumer credit is currently extended or denied on the basis of a patchwork of information that is not always complete, recent, or reliable. The total data base is dispersed among numerous credit bureaus and grantors, and much of it is obsolete. A computer-based service could provide comprehensive, reliable, and prompt information, scaling the credit quality of individuals or applying evaluation criteria supplied by specific subscribers. It could also process actual credit transactions, accumulating valuable data on creditor performance.

Financial Information

The rendering of financial-analysis services has already attracted a number of entrepreneurs. Excluding conventional print services, Diebold Research Program studies indicate that this is about a $3 million market today — only about a sixth of the size of the market for "instant" stock quotations. However, the technology is undergoing active development, and as systems achieve greater flexibility with more comprehensive data bases, the demand is expected to burgeon. Potential subscribers are brokerage firms, bank trust departments, funds, investment advisors, insurance companies, and publications in the field.

Financial information such as operating results, value and performance ratios, dividend history, and past stock prices, is quite widely available; but capturing it in an effective proprietary data bank calls for substantial investment. Speedy response to requests is not particularly important, and a given subscriber terminal would probably have infrequent (but daily) use. On the other hand, a "dialogue" capability would be desirable, so that an analyst could call for further analyses, comparisons, and the like as already noted.

Legal Information

The great volume and variety of documents to be dealt with, the stubborn developmental problems to be solved, and the inherent conservatism of the potential subscribers have combined to hold down the pace of market penetration achieved by the limited-service pioneers already in the field. Still, there are about 290,000 practicing lawyers in the country now, with a net increase of 4,000 a year, and every one of them — as well as every law library and school — needs legal reference.

Today, these reference needs are met by various indexing and abstracting services, plus an enormous amount of search time expended by law clerks and attorneys. An exhaustively indexed, automated system could go well beyond freeing this time for more productive use. The speed, thoroughness, and convenience it promises would make for superior preparation of cases.

Manpower Registry

Manpower information service probably will not involve computation, unless a service organized for this market decides to offer a commercially usable index derived from its primary activities. Basically what is involved is efficient storage and retrieval.

The ideal alternative to the present inefficient, and usually local, job-candidate matching process is a comprehensive nation-wide system. The relatively simple matching tasks are routine for computers, so services may proliferate rapidly. Limited interconnections of local and regional services should be possible at a relatively early date.

Marketing and Advertising Services

Several interesting possibilities are already feasible from a technical and data-base standpoint. One is an on-going report of consumer dynamics—attitudes, purchasing patterns, brand switching, price sensitivity, and the like. Consumer panels, which could provide the input data, already exist, but feedback to marketers is significantly slow. A computerized data base, by contrast, augmented by secondary market statistics, could provide *immediate* insights, tailored to each subscriber's requirements.

Another possibility is computerized industrial market research. Dun & Bradstreet already offers such a service on an off-line basis, supplying data to subscribers in machine-readable form. However, an on-line operation could readily be wired into place. Sales information from a subscriber could be combined with an extensive proprietary data base and the results of limited research, to provide a variety of useful analyses. For example, sales data could quickly be compared with prospect lists to reveal marketing strengths and weaknesses and to identify specific prospects. One can foresee the day when a subscriber could ask the system, via a terminal on his desk, "Is the Akron plant of Friesen Furniture a good prospect for our pallets?" Advertising agencies might respond to a centralized facility to which they could turn for information on television spots. Now such information as availability of spots, price and discounts, cost-per-thousand, and viewer characteristics must be gathered from the networks and a host of independent agents, each offering facts on only one station in a market. Armed with a comprehensive data bank, a computer-based service could swiftly generate busy schedules to advertiser specifications, and its inventory of spots would always be current.

Medical Information

This vastly promising market seems destined to go largely untapped, in any comprehensive way, for a number of years to come. Two basic kinds of information needs, requiring quite different technologies, are involved, although they will overlap in certain ways in the future. The first is

197

institutionally oriented processing concerned with administration, purchasing, billing, accounting, and the like. This is basically a data-center operation, rather than an information service, but much more could be done, and should be — and it might be done by the same organization supplying the information needs, and related treatment-oriented services.

The second class of service — treatment oriented — is concerned with efficiently storing and retrieving medical literature, processing data for medical researchers, and monitoring patients. It is envisioned that some day a doctor will be able to query the system by asking, for example, "What drugs work well when the following symptoms are present?" At the present time, however, even central data banks of the medical records of everyone in the community would be a major advance, saving critical time and paving the way for analytical groupings and statistical insights that can only be guessed at today. One bright spot in the current picture is computerized medical laboratory analysis, for which both the technology and a receptive market already exist.

News Services

Highly efficient news wire services have been with us a long time. However, a related field shows high entrepreneurial promise — the handling of public relations releases. It is virtually impossible, (or economically unfeasible) for any business firm today to maintain an adequate media records system which will assure the dissemination of a news release to every editor with an interest in the subject, and to a minimum of others. Media dissemination services which attempt to deal with this problem do exist. However, because they are small organizations and are not using available computer technology, they are only moderately effective.

Purchasing Information

Product and purchasing information for industrial buyers could be captured in a comprehensive, continually-updated data bank, and offered to purchasing agents, industrial engineers, designers, and the like on an as-needed inquiry basis. The indexed data base, drawn largely from manufacturers' literature, would contain information on the performance and specifications of products, delivery times and FOB points, company guarantees and service policy, terms, prices, discounts, and the like.

Farther in the future one might see purchase orders entered through a central computer, with the "fall-out" statistics analyzed on a fee basis for marketing implications.

Scientific and Technical Information

Scientific and technical information has been estimated to double in volume every ten years. This cascade of literature is extremely diverse, not only in subject matter, origin, and language, but also in quality, originality, and utility. The Stanford Research Institute has estimated that scientists and engineers spend some 20 percent of their work searching for information, and technicians about five percent. Many independent efforts at comprehensive storage and retrieval are under way, and a number of limited systems are already being operated by various Government agencies, professional societies, and private organizations. A variety of indexing, abstracting, input, storage, retrieval, and dissemination techniques are being tried, and the formidable problems involved will inevitably be solved.

Stock Quotations

Stock quotation services have already achieved good market penetration, and the technology is fairly well established. These services, providing instant response to queries on the latest price of actively traded securities, are a good example of a "pure" computer-based information service. No computation is involved (although up-to-the-minute facts on price movements as compared to industrial averages might prove useful), and hard copy output is not needed. Speed is pivotal, though, and terminals must accommodate frequent usage. Such terminals are already installed in thousands of brokerage offices.

Traffic Information

Freight traffic generates a prodigious amount of paperwork in this country, and the advantages of computerizing the task of coping with our very complex freight tariff structure have long been recognized. All necessary information is currently available, and a computer system could not only give it greater accessibility, but also provide almost instant solutions to such day-by-day problems as identifying optimum rates and routes for shipments, and auditing freight bills for overcharges. To date, however, work has been severely hampered by the lack of standard formats and commodity descriptions, and by widespread resistance to innovation. Still, several large shippers have already developed partial computer systems.

GETTING INTO THE BUSINESS

A number of approaches are open for entering this new field. Aside from the obvious one of acquiring and developing fledgling enterprises that have already pioneered in given market segments, and, having proved their point, offer prime opportunities through the infusion of substantial capital, The Diebold Group has indicated certain possibilities, although many others will undoubtedly present themselves.
(See Figures 13-C, 13-D and 13-E.)

    Gradual build-up of existing data processing services. This has already been illustrated in the case of hospitals. In a number of instances a group of hospitals had joined in a cooperative data

Figure 13-C.

FORMS OF PARTICIPATION IN THE ON-LINE
INFORMATION SERVICE BUSINESS

OFF-LINE SERVICE CENTER

  PERFORMS "CUSTOM" WORK
  TYPICAL OF EXISTING SERVICE BUREAUS

ON-LINE TIME-SHARED COMPUTATION SERVICES

  HIGH PROFIT POTENTIAL THROUGH
  HIGH EQUIPMENT AND PLANT USAGE
  PACKAGE PROGRAMS AND/OR DATA BASE
  NECESSARY FOR LONG—RUN SUCCESS

OFF-LINE INQUIRY TO DATA BASE

  INQUIRIES VIA MAIL OR TELEPHONE

TYPIFIED BY CREDIT DATA CORPORATION
OPERATIONS

ON-LINE INQUIRY ORIENTED CENTER

  HIGH PROFIT POTENTIAL
  UTILIZES REMOTE TERMINALS AT USER LOCATIONS

"DEDICATED SYSTEM"

  SERVES A PARTICULAR FUNCTION OR INDUSTRY
  SYSTEM OPERATED UNDER CONTRACT FOR A
  SPECIFIC CUSTOMER OR GROUP OF CUSTOMERS

Source: The Diebold Research Program

Figure 13-D. DISTRIBUTION AND ACQUISITION VARIATIONS

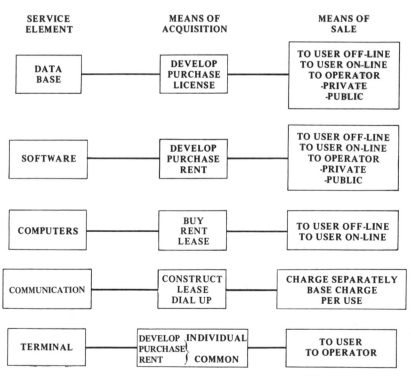

Source: The Diebold Research Program

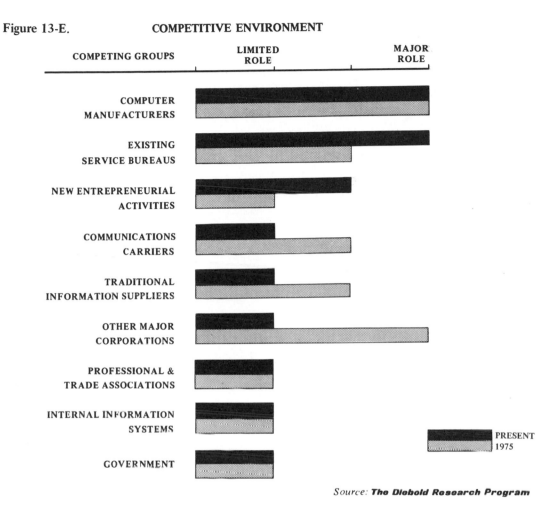

Figure 13-E.   **COMPETITIVE ENVIRONMENT**

Source: *The Diebold Research Program*

processing activity comprising traditional accounting and other administrative chores. These were then gradually built up to include medical records and statistical information – a good example of the point that the new technology, originally applied merely for cost-cutting purposes, opened up originally unperceived entrepreneurial opportunities.

Serving as an "R&D" contractor, in the development of special program packages and methodology, for foundations or other groups ready to provide funds for research into new information-service concepts in areas such as medicine, science, law, and like.

Serving as an operating contractor. Certain professional or governmental groups may wish to control an information-utility in their fields, but would prefer to contract out for the actual operation of the service.

201

Joint ventures with manufacturers. Computer manufacturers have, of course, been in the traditional service-center business from the start — some solely or primarily for customer service, others as profit-center entities. Many of the latter have proven unprofitable adjuncts to the main business of manufacturing computers, and the manufacturers involved are prime prospects for a joint venture, teaming up with an organization (publisher, credit service, marketing research firm, literature-indexing service, etc.) whose prime business already *is* information.

Acting as a distribution channel. This could be for modified or non-modified versions of existing services. Thus an information service concentrating on a specific user group, or serving users in a given geographic area, may arrange for distribution rights for an already developed service. (An example is that of an English company in the financial information business which acquired the rights to Standard & Poor's financial data base on United States companies.)

THE $6 BILLION ENTREPRENEURIAL OPPORTUNITY

The foregoing, in broad outline, constitutes a case example of how an entirely new industry is being created by fast-moving technology. In this case, the opportunity is a $6 billion dollar one created by the business world's insatiable appetite for information. That a full-fledged computer-based information service industry will emerge from its present beginnings John Diebold considers inevitable and imminent.

*The essential point is that this will be a **new** industry, not simply an extension of traditional computer service centers into enlarged data processing and problem-solving services made possible by time-sharing and other computer developments. (This, in any event, will be marginally profitable in John Diebold's view since manufacturers and large-scale computer users not having full use of certain machine capacities will tend to provide the traditional type of services on a marginal cost basis.) Who will profit from the new opportunity will depend upon individual initiative and imagination.*

And, of course, this case example should be viewed not merely as a discussion of a specific industry, but rather as another illustration of John Diebold's reiterated theme: Technological change always represents new entrepreneurial opportunity, and full exploitation should not be hampered by tunnel vision that sees only the chance to cut costs or speed up services which, in terms of customers' real needs, are essentially no different from what has been offered all along.

Photograph by Burt Glinn

John Diebold has from the beginning perceived the new information technology as opening up new markets in the public sector — national, regional, and local. These include, in addition to computer services for administration, provision of sophisticated data collection for policy decisions, and the development of computer-based models to aid in value judgments.

14

Industry will usher in the new world, and industry should greatly benefit from it. Entirely new markets are coming into existence, and alert businessmen are already seizing the opportunities they see before them. Automation offers as great a challenge and reward as any which industry has ever known.

"Automation — Its Impact on Industry,"
address before the 7th Annual Industrial Engineering Institute, University of California, Berkeley and Los Angeles,
January 20-February 1, 1955.

Urban governments offer new markets for business. The most direct is setting up and applying business concepts to the administrative work of government. Next is applying information technology and analyzing and solving various urban problems ranging from pollution control to tax collection . . . But of even greater potential, and up to now hardly tapped, are fields where business can perform functions now performed by urban governments.

"Business Decisions and Technological Change,"
New York, Praeger Publishers, Inc.,
1970.

New Markets in the Public Sector

New profit can derive from the provision of services for government — on the national level, and for local and regional jurisdictions — in education, pollution control, sanitation, health, welfare, crime prevention, and similar areas.

*John Diebold sees the totally new market opened up by the impact of technological change upon education, detailed in Chapter 12, as only a small fraction of the entrepreneurial opportunities which technology has created in the public sector. Indeed, in his view they are more than opportunities — they are imperatives, for they represent tremendously complex and interlocking problems which **must** be solved, problems with which public jurisdictions have in the main been grappling unsuccessfully, and which must thus become the concern of business initiative.*

Examples all about us of the deterioration in public services bear out his thesis. The burgeoning demands created by technology itself — through its stimulation of exploding population, its creation of greater affluence, and its provision of greater leisure — continue to overtax existing public facilities and outrun the resources of public administrative and taxing bodies. We need only contemplate the complete breakdown of the postal service in Chicago of a few years ago, the widely publicized frustrations of unsatisfactory telephone service in New York City and other metropolitan centers in recent years, the continuing threat of brownouts and blackouts due to overloaded power generators in New York and elsewhere, and the stackups at major airports. It is the involvement of the private sector in these problems, stimulated by business opportunity, he contends, which in the last analysis represents society's greatest hope.

A number of years before it became "fashionable" to deplore technology's threats to ecology, he reminded an academic gathering that:

The chemical magic that pours forth from our laboratories and process plants and kills insects, preserves crops from blight, and promotes cleanliness unknown before detergents, turns out to be a not-unalloyed blessing, for hand-in-hand it brings the spectre of Rachel Carson's silent spring.

The harnessed power of the automobile brings the open countryside within an afternoon's reach to those city dwellers who would otherwise never see trees; it brings patients within reach of emergency medical treatment; it changes for the better much of our life; but it too is accompanied by congestion, by the blight of highways, and by unbelievable pollution of the air we breathe.

"The Impact of Science and Technology on the Development of Managers,"
address upon receipt of an Honorary Doctor of Science Degree at a Special Convocation, Clarkson College of Technology, Potsdam, New York, **October 12, 1965.**

THE SCOPE OF THE URBAN PROBLEMS

It is on the local level that the pressures alluded to above are most painfully apparent, since here they impinge directly upon our daily lives. In the urban areas especially, the shift from a predominantly agricultural to an industrial economy, the proliferation of cities into urban sprawls with their decaying "inner cities" and spreading ghettos, and the overcrowding, overuse, and under-maintenance of public facilities of every sort have posed the uneasy question as to whether our huge metropolitan complexes are, indeed, manageable and governable. In his wide-ranging monograph

*published by the American Academy of Political and Social Science, John Diebold
spelled out the scope of the problem:*

Technological change has altered fundamentally the scope and character of our problems; it has created challenges for urban governments in several areas. The demand and need for education at all levels are increasing at an accelerating pace – in terms of both quantity and quality. Population growth, the need to respond to the training and retraining needs of unskilled labor, and the need to provide for the continuing education of even highly skilled persons imposes severe burdens on urban school systems. Urban police as now equipped and organized cannot cope with the increasingly intolerable threat of crime.

Traffic congestion, through the failure of urban areas to make rational plans for public transport and traffic flow, threatens to choke commerce and destroy the advantage of proximity. Pollution of air, water, and the countryside cannot be permitted to continue uncontrolled.

The sociological, cultural, and basic welfare effects of unemployment, a traditional urban problem which has been aggravated by technological change, have overwhelmed the means of urban governments. The health, cultural, and recreational facilities now provided by governments will have to be expanded to meet the public's expanded expectations and hours of leisure. Cities have frequently been unable to provide a climate which attracts and retains commercial activity.

Furthermore, urban tax systems are ill-designed to deal with the accelerated demands created by a technology which is changing the economic structure of cities and their surrounding areas, as well as the populations inhabiting them. City property taxes and indirect taxation by states have been inadequate for financing local government services. Their collection is constrained by limitations of residence which have been effectively erased by the socioeconomic consequences of technological change. People benefiting from the services of the city have been enabled actually to reside outside the city. Corporate headquarters making use of urban facilities no longer contribute their share to city revenues, since communications and transportation technologies have enabled businesses to move taxable production centers to distant areas.

> **"Impacts on Urban Governmental Functions of Developments in Science and Technology."** *Monograph No. 7, Governing Urban Society, American Academy of Political and Social Science,* **May, 1967.**

. . .AND THE CHALLENGE TO PRIVATE BUSINESS

But who would wish to turn back the clock – even if we could? The only possible answer, says John Diebold, is to meet technology's problems with technology's solutions. And the solutions, in his view, will not come from monolithic government, but from prolific private enterprise:

One of the most interesting changes taking place on the business scene is the beginning of private business activities in the performance of services, some of which are traditionally the province of governmental agencies. The impetus for this development is the desire to apply to our critical urban and other domestic problems the techniques of systems analysis, program planning, and budgeting and other managerial approaches that have so well served the military in applying new technologies to solve the problems of the service aspect of the public sector.

Much innovation is possible in this process, and considerable thrashing about is accompanying the current experimentation. Numerous contracts have already been let to aerospace and other "systems" companies in such fields as crime and traffic control, urban renewal, education, and pollution. Proposals are already being put forward to turn the fire department function over to insurance companies and the operation of junior colleges to other businesses, such as those that operate the training centers of the Federal Job Corps. More than one U.S. industrial firm has already established divisions whose "products" are the delivery of complete new cities.

Innovation in the concept of what constitutes a business, as well as the more obvious innovation in products, services, and marketing, may well be, in retrospect, the outstanding characteristic of the 1970s . . . the crucial time for reassessment for most businesses and various governmental entities is now. By the end of the decade of the 1970s, and certainly by 1985, new patterns will have been set. The roles of private and governmental enterprises in the as yet difficult to envisage period of change that follows will have been assigned.

> **"Automation in the Future,"**
> *keynote address before the 37th International Conference of the Financial Executives Institute, New York, New York,*
> **October 25, 1968.**

As is so often the case, the technological underpinnings already exist for the solution of most of the public-sector problems mentioned above. The problems, he points out, are basically not technological, but managerial — comprising imaginative planning and establishment of priorities, marshalling of resources, and effective follow-through. Here the latest in information technology must provide the solution.

*No one doubts, for example, that the problem of air and water pollution will be solved — if for no other reason that it **has** to be solved, for reasons of sheer survival. The **technological directions** are already well formulated in the laboratory and in* *pilot tests. The **implementation** calls first for intelligent choices among alternatives, followed by appropriate legislation, organization, financing, procurement, and deployment of technical work forces.*

As John Diebold sees them, these are managerial processes that must be meshed into other priorities and other demands upon resources and facilities. Thus among the immediate challenges to the private sector is the need to bring to government the best that modern information technology has to offer – in terms of know-how gained in its own operations, in the marketing of the systems and the hardware needed for the task, and above all in the application of the new technology far beyond the mere speeding up of data processing.

Thus the answer to the question raised earlier – as to whether our metropolitan complexes are governable – is, says John Diebold, "yes – if"... if the right sort of rethinking of goals and purposes is done, and if modern information technology is imaginatively applied to the ramified and interlocking problems of metropolitan-area management. If that is done, he insists, technology, which created these problems, will provide means for meeting them.

He sees the solutions as being found along the following lines, stimulated and supported by private enterprise. (In some cases, new operations may be carried on by private organizations under contract arrangements competitively arrived at; in other cases, the public jurisdictions involved may install and operate the new systems with their own staffs, perhaps drawing upon private consulting services for initial know-how; or such consulting services may be retained for development work and installation, with subsequent operation by the jurisdiction's workforce. Many arrangements are possible.):

Systems Analysis through Advanced Data Processing and Communications Technology

Systems analysis, the technique for the scientific application of information made available through advanced data processing and communications technologies, must be brought to bear upon urban management. In addition, it will lend itself to the intelligent establishment and weighting of alternative goals, in terms of the resources to be devoted to their attainment.

By systems analysis, urban governments faced with the problem of performing a multitude of complex, interrelated, and almost equally important functions, within definite budgetary limitations, can examine the interplay and causal relationships among these functions. The data pertaining to a large number of variables can be brought into play in order to determine priorities for action. The logical and necessary sequence of steps for the achievement of community goals can thus be established.

The data base supporting systems analysis implies a lessening of the autonomy of various traditional urban departments. The separate data relevant to welfare programs, education projects, and police protection, for example, are often equally relevant to more than one of these. Therefore, not only in the achievement of overall goals, but in the assembling of data, the close interdependence of various urban functions becomes evident. Actions which do not recognize this interdependence in the most basic areas, such as the building of data bases, are wasteful and even counterproductive.

The widely publicized California experiment, in which the State of California contracted with four aerospace companies to study four major urban problems, is a good example of both the value of systems analysis techniques and the problems involved in their use by civilian agencies.

Sharing Private-Enterprise Facilities

Purchasing from and sharing with private enterprise the information and communications technologies and the systems analysis techniques already developed by business to meet its own managerial and research and development needs could provide a cost-effective approach for many urban governments. Such an approach could make use of various alternatives or combinations of alternatives.

For example, major firms with advanced computer and communications facilities and systems capabilities could be asked to undertake on contract the data gathering and analytical functions necessary for the decision-making of urban governments. In this way, the functions of urban governments could concentrate upon the making of political and value judgments and upon the furnishing of human service to human beings.

Alternatively, the urban governments may decide to retain a top-level staff of systems analysts and data-processing managers but purchase hardware, software packages, and services from private enterprise.

Another route, especially for the largest cities, may be the development of total systems capabilities from the most elementary programming through systems design and systems analysis. In that event it may be possible to recoup part of the costs by sharing with, or selling to, private enterprise the techniques and technologies owned by the city.

In all of these alternatives, recognition must be given to the need for strict legal restraints. Private enterprise must be limited in the way it may use data to which it has access through its work for the city. It is interesting that the nature of the technology itself greatly eases the problem of misuse of information — misuse which threatens privacy or provides unfair competitive advantages. The programs making information available can be so constructed as to answer only specified questions. These answers, in turn, could be limited to receipt by a selected number of politically responsible officials. Thus, for example, the names of individuals with police records or with poor tax and employment histories must never appear before the eyes of unauthorized individuals. This in fact constitutes a great improvement over current procedures.

> **"Impacts on Urban Governmental Functions of Developments in Science and Technology."**
> *Monograph No. 7, Governing Urban Society, American Academy of Political and Social Science,*
> **May, 1967.**

Use of the New Technology in Decision-Making

With today's computers and related communications technology, together with the analysis and decision-making techniques of the "new management sciences," informed decisions can now be made which could not have been possible for government policy-makers only a few years ago. Applications cited by John Diebold include:

Econometric or sociometric models. These make possible a detailed examination of the interaction of economic and social variables. The public-policy maker can use them to explore the statistical relationships between the national rate of growth and local unemployment or between juvenile delinquency and school performance.

Input-output models of a region's economy. These can be used to explore the implications of changes in certain industrial sectors of the economy for the industrial base of the region.

Simulation models. These can be constructed to estimate optimal traffic flow patterns, cash flows, or electric power requirements, and planning can proceed accordingly.

> **"Impacts on Urban Governmental Functions of Developments in Science and Technology."**
> *Monograph No. 7, Governing Urban Society, American Academy of Political and Social Science,*
> **May, 1967.**

However, present applications, he says, have not kept pace with the potentials, and urban managements are grossly underutilizing information technology. With a few outstanding exceptions, they have by and large converted old data collection and control systems to computerized operation rather than designing new systems. Thus:

According to William H. Mitchel, Director of Municipal Management Information Systems Research Project at the School of Public Administration of the University of California, local governments have either not faced the computer issue or have been content to blunder into the acquisition of hardware "with its use dictated by old wives' tales, or their commercial equivalent – the advice of vendor salesmen."

Dr. Nachman Bench, Consultant to the Office of the Mayor of New York City, recently pointed out that although New York has successfully applied electronic data processing to traditional operations at a cost of $9 million per year, the systems were geared to accounting and tax systems rather than management decisions. Decentralized operation by departments led to duplication and underutilization, and the analysis of available information was not supported by the methods of systems analysis and operations research.

> **"Impacts on Urban Governmental Functions of Developments in Science and Technology,"** *Monograph No. 7, Governing Urban Society, American Academy of Political and Social Science,* **May, 1967.**

On the other hand, some governments are beginning to respond to the challenges of modern information technology and systems analysis, and in his American Academy of Political and Social Science paper John Diebold could cite some applications which have been proposed or are already in operation, including the following:

The government of New Haven, in cooperation with IBM, is planning a complete, computerized, central file of all data on individuals in the city. The file is to be electronically cross-indexed to provide any department with rapid access to information it requires – even though the information may have been generated by a different department.

In 1965, the Lockheed Missiles and Space Corporation prepared for the State of California a Statewide Information System to provide for a well-organized system of information collection and distribution for all levels of government in the state.

Since 1962, government agencies in five cities, Denver, Wichita, Tulsa, Fort Worth, and Little Rock, have been engaged in a pilot program, the Metropolitan Data Center Project, supported by the Federal Urban Renewal Administration. The purpose of the project has been the creation of a systems approach to the information needs of various city agencies.

Our own organization is working with the city of Phoenix to devise a police network which will speed communications between the man in the field and the computer. Initially, the system may operate with a key-type input device and a voice response — but the possibility of voice input is also under consideration.

Los Angeles and Toronto are using computers to control traffic lights and traffic flows, and other cities are using computers to simulate optimal traffic flows for control and planning purposes.

New York City maintains a computerized data bank on stolen vehicles and traffic violators. New York police hold random checks of vehicles on limited-access throughfares by sending the license number of passing vehicles to the computer. In return they receive information instantaneously identifying stolen vehicles and "scoff-law" violators.

The Urban Data Center of the University of Cincinnati has had success in gathering and organizing data on land and structure patterns, people and social networks, economic systems, and air, water, and ecological systems. This work is the urban planning effort of the city of Cincinnati, and is also used by nonprofit planning organization, commercial operations, and local utilities. The cities of Detroit, San Francisco, and Los Angeles are also working with urban data bank projects.

> **"Impacts on Urban Governmental Functions of Developments in Science and Technology,"** *Monograph No. 7, Governing Urban Society, American Academy of Political and Social Science,* **May, 1967.**

All of these applications point the way to the potential of information and communications technology in solving problems and indicate the beginnings of flexibility and responsiveness to change on the part of traditional institutions. An obvious example are the developments and potentials in education, described in Chapter 12.

AT THE REGIONAL LEVEL

The implications of systems analysis techniques and information and communications technology for the internal organization of urban governments, discussed in the foregoing, apply also with reference to the relationships between governmental entities in a regional, or larger, area. As John Diebold points out, problems rarely fall neatly within politically bounded areas. For example:

The waste management study performed by the Aerojet General Corporation for the State of California concludes that "wastes cannot be efficiently managed in the geographic plots dictated by the boundaries of political jurisdiction, but the geographic boundries must stem from the analysis of the waste system itself." This is equally true of the other problems facing urban governments. Furthermore, the difficulties of financing urban governmental services through taxation . . . indicate the need for a redefinition of the relationships between urban governments and those of surrounding areas. The need clearly is for the definition of regional goals, and a flexibility that will enable existing jurisdictions to meet them.

The mobility of criminals, for example, and the widening impact of their actions have made it important to recognize the interdependence of police records and files among cities and regions. Thus, New York State has created an integrated system of information on crime which makes a central data bank in Albany accessible to various local forces within the state and even in neighboring states. Cooperative systems in New England, Ohio, and California are further examples of this approach.

> **"Impacts on Urban Governmental Functions of Developments in Science and Technology,"** *Monograph No. 7, Governing Urban Society, American Academy of Political and Social Science,* **May, 1967.**

AT THE NATIONAL LEVEL

On October 12, 1965, President Johnson directed "the introduction of an integrated programming-planning-budgeting system (PPBS) in the executive branch." The system is an advanced management method for measuring the effectiveness of expenditures in reaching program goals, and has been cited by John Diebold as an example of the use of computer technology in conjunction with new management approaches, rather than simply speeding up existing operations.

*However, even though computer and communications technology were applied to administrative purposes in the Federal Government before they were adopted by business, and were developed at an accelerated pace there, he now sees a lag in the various Government agencies with respect to the significant use of the new technology for sophisticated management-information and decision-making applications. In this respect he sees Government going through some of the same phases of organizational impediments and resistance-to-change psychology that slowed up the optimum use of the technology in the private sector — and that in the noncompetitive business environment the delays will probably be aggravated. **But they need not be!** Business, says John Diebold, must capitalize upon its own hard-won experience and seize the opportunity aggressively to "sell" government on the need to use the applicable techniques and services which it is in a position to supply.*

Parallels Between Business and Government Experience

In the context of a discussion of the opportunities for and advantages of using the newest tools of information and communications technology in the conduct of foreign affairs, John Diebold drew the following parallels. Although they are based on an analysis of administrative and management problems in the State Department, they have general applicability:

There are important parallels between business and governmental experiences in the application of information and related technologies.

Perhaps the most fundamental similarity resides in the need for a man at the top to understand the systems approach and to ensure its success. There are other similarities of interest to business management. But since use of the new technologies will also change the substance of the conduct of foreign relations — as it is changing the substance of what business does — there are even more important elements for business planning to consider. It is quite possible, for example, that the entire basis for trade negotiations will be altered by the use of information technology, including simulation and gaming techniques. The nature of treaties will change as the result of information in globally available data banks. Thus, investment policies and the allocation and use of international resources will be based on different criteria.

Just as in business, and probably much more so, fundamental human and political problems will prevent the use of technology from becoming a panacea in foreign-affairs management. In order to minimize these obstacles, training and organizational planning are required. The central question remains: *What do we want from our technology?* If we know, we can get it, in government as in business.

"Business Decisions and Technological Change,"
New York: Praeger Publishers, Inc.,
1970.

In the same publication he sketched a brief review of historical developments on the national level in government during the precomputer and early computer eras, to provide an example approximately analogous to the business problems that are now beginning to be overcome in the private sector through intensive analysis and imagination:

1. As early as 1902, cost-benefit analyses for water-resources programs were called for in the Rivers and Harbors Act. And the Flood Control Act of 1936 stated explicitly that projects should only be begun when estimated benefits exceed costs. In 1943, the Bureau of the Budget began to review all such projects on this basis before they were submitted to Congress. Particular guidelines for these reviews were formalized in 1952 and revised in 1961, 1964, and 1965 — a period that saw the painful development of methods for business computer applications.

Ironically enough, although the most advanced computer and communications technologies were first developed by the Government for use in defense, space, and related programs from which business was only beginning to learn, little use was made of them in other governmental activities, with the notable exceptions of the Internal Revenue Service, the Bureau of the Census, and the FBI and, of course, in payroll and routine accounting.

2. In 1946, the Budget Bureau inaugurated longer-range projections of up to five years for the preparation and examination of agency budget requests. In 1961, these were readied to prepare public projections of alternative dimension of the Federal budget for the years 1965-1970. By 1965, these types of projections were integrated with agency program plans and priorities, more or less containing the elements of the planning, programming, budgeting, and accounting directive (PPBS) called for by the Presidential directive of that year.

3. In 1949, the first Hoover Commission recommended the development of the concept of performance-and-cost-based budgets. The legal framework for this was incorporated in the Budget Accounting and Procedures Act of 1950. A program incorporating the concept actually had begun internally in the Budget Bureau in 1947 and, later, as exercised jointly by the Comptroller-General, the Secretary of the Treasury, and the Director of the Budget, became known as the Joint Financial Management Improvement Program. It evolved into the present plan for the integrating of planning, programming, budgeting, and accounting.

Thus, we can see that there are in the Government a number of procedures with a long tradition predating the availability of technologies suitable for the optimum use of information for management-control and policy-planning purposes. Will tradition delay the development of such optimum use as it earlier did in business? As a whole, the outlook is not encouraging, although significant breakthroughs are now being made after a time lag of more than a decade. The problems of comparing the business experience with the potential of governmental action reside in the differences between competitive and noncompetitive environments, the internal complexities and the vast responsibilities of government. These factors could add even greater delays than those experienced by the private sector. However, it is possible that the 1969 moves by the new Administration could change this prognosis.

"Business Decisions and Technological Change,"
New York: Praeger Publishers, Inc.,
1970.

EVALUATION OF GOALS

An important area not usually thought of in connection with the application of information technology to the public sector is the accurate evaluation of public demands in terms of goals. This involves the collection of information regarding the value placed by citizens on government services and the use of this information as a guide in establishing levels of expenditures.

Perhaps the most difficult problem here, says John Diebold, is the lack of a conceptual framework to compare the benefits of public services with incidence of costs — the very root of the economic rationale for public administration of "collective" goods. People find it difficult, he points out, to compare the utility of an extra dollar's worth of private consumption with the loss of a dollar's worth of public services in the form of parks or snow-removal. However:

The revolution in information technology and market research techniques makes possible some systematic improvements in the knowledge which could be obtained about the people's valuation of the relative importance of public services. No large private corporation today would launch a new product for the consumer without engaging in market research to determine the extent of the available market. Surely it is possible to use similar methods to ascertain preferences and quantitative judgments as to the relative importance of people's demands for public goods.

Several years ago the State of Washington conducted a survey to determine the recreational value of the state's salmon fishery to evaluate proposed expenditures on hatcheries, pollution control, and fish-ladders. A sample questionnaire was distributed to fishermen, asking them to list their expenditures for various items connected with the sport and asking them how much they would be willing to pay for a fishing license if it were required. The information collected helped to establish an estimate of the recreational value of the sport to the state and to the fishermen of the state.

Public planners must, for example, know how much air pollution is costing the people in terms of actual cleaning and redecorating costs. The costs in discomfort could be estimated by asking people how much they would be willing to pay to breathe clean air. Estimates of the public's losses from air pollution in actual costs and in pleasure foregone can be used in the context of a systems analysis approach which depends heavily on quantifiable objectives.

"Impacts on Urban Governmental Functions of Developments in Science and Technology," *Monograph No. 7, Governing Urban Society, American Academy of Political and Social Science,* **May, 1967.**

THE CHALLENGE AND THE OPPORTUNITY

John Diebold's concluding remarks in his Academy of Political and Social Science paper, although specifically directed to his analysis of urban problems, can, with negligible change in wording, serve to sum up the problems and directions for solutions for all levels of government:

The growth in the size and range of functions of governmental units in the United States over the past century has not resulted from some Parkinsonian tendency of bureaucrats to reproduce their numbers at a geometric rate. It has occurred because of the public's recognition that the development of an urban, industrial society poses a need for social control of the environment which is different from the need of an increasing realization that governments could play a valuable role in the positive provision of a sparsely settled, agricultural society. It has come about because of health, transportation, education, leisure-time facilities, and amenities for improving the quality of life as well as the traditional functions of providing for security of person and property and a stable social framework.

The important question facing governments is not *whether* they will provide services at a rising level, but *at what rate* the provision of public services will increase. This is a quantitative decision. It is one which ought to be based on hard facts about people's preferences and the social returns from alternative expenditures. It is also a decision which will depend in large part on the cost-effectiveness of government-administered programs.

Technology has been the cause of many public-sector problems. But governments can use technology to improve services in all traditional areas—and to provide new services.

"Impacts on Urban Governmental Functions of Developments in Science and Technology," *Monograph No. 7, Governing Urban Society, American Academy of Political and Social Science,* **May, 1967.**

Therein lies the entrepreneurial opportunity for private enterprise — and the challenge for all of us professionally concerned in management, in the public and private sectors alike!

PART V

Technology as an Agent of Social Change—Creation of New Business Opportunities

CONTROL CONSOLE
THIS IS AN EXACT DUPLICATE OF THE
N. S. SAVANNAH CONSOLE
WHERE THE OPERATORS CONTROL
THE NUCLEAR POWER PLANT

Photograph by Marvin Newman

Response of organized labor to technological change importantly influences the rate of innovation. John Diebold maintains that business must be active, not defensive, in this regard. Here he inspects the mock-up of a highly automated atomic ship, product of an industry long characterized by lack of labor-management agreement on technological innovation and change.

Fundamental to the successful integration of automation into our mechanized society is the recognition by all parties concerned—unions, management, and Government—that they have a common interest. No one, least of all the American businessman, wants to see increased unemployment. All of us stand to gain by automation as long as we stand together.

"Automation – Its Application and Uses,"
address before the National Conference on Automation, CIO Committee on Economic Policy, Washington, D.C.,
April 14, 1955.

One of the principal strengths of our private enterprise system is its flexibility in permitting change to occur. Government's role is important, and it must provide a favorable climate for change by cooperating with the parties when assistance is needed. In the final analysis, however, the parties themselves must make the decisions and work out the detailed problems of adjustment. Simple mechanisms that can be applied with flexibility to individual situations are preferable to legislation, and a responsible private manpower policy is required.

"New Rules and Opportunities for Business – As We Enter the Post-Industrial Era,"
keynote address before the Third Tri-Annual International Productivity Congress, Vienna, Austria,
October 28, 1970.

Labor and Technological Change

Labor-management relations take on a new look in the perspective of the new kinds of talents needed by business, new standards of productivity, and new employee expectations.

Automation, in the popular mind, early became a "scare word" in terms of its widely envisioned effects upon unemployment. What sprang to most people's minds when the word, in all of its Sunday-supplement connotations, came up in conversation was a "pushbutton factory," with only a few engineers and technicians in sight, and with most direct workers displaced into technological unemployment and government dole. However, it is interesting to note that the country's experience in the two decades that have passed since John Diebold first sparked public and professional awareness of automation has confirmed the stance he took from the start—at a time *when the emotional heat engendered by the subject made it most unpopular to do so—and the stance that he has consistently maintained over the years: namely, that automation would **not** cause large-scale unemployment. The chilling picture of a complete takeover by machines and the bleak predictions of labor spokesmen and of voices in Congress and in the press about millions of workers idled have not come to pass.*

Citing this in retrospect is not, of course, to deprecate the concern of labor leaders, sociologists, legislators, and business writers about the threat of mass unemployment. Indeed, it is the voicing of such concern which led to the steps that have already been taken by management, labor, and government to minimize the effects of the inevitable dislocations that did occur. But the fact that the science-fiction nightmare of gleaming and whirring machines and rusty and useless men did not come to pass does bear out the balanced view John Diebold expressed. While fully realizing that individual and often painful readjustments would be called for, he has always emphasized that long-term general benefits were bound to result from technological progress. While he emphasized that the changes would indeed be revolutionary, he also pointed out that they would not materialize overnight. Given proper awareness by management of its social responsibilities, he contended, there would always be sufficient elbowroom (or "elbowtime") for procedural adjustments, employee conditioning, retraining, new placement, and the like. (In factories, experience has shown that it takes on the average two and a half years to get an automated process going; in office automation, even where the "hardware" is commercially available, the change to large-scale computer data processing requires from one to two years merely to prepare for the advent of the machines.)

HUMAN CONSEQUENCES AND MANAGEMENT RESPONSIBILITY

*However, while deprecating the notion of immediate cataclysmic economic effects of automation, John Diebold was realistic enough to recognize that what **could** happen could be serious enough to large numbers of people. He early stressed the importance of making employees aware of the advantages of automation in terms of strengthening the company's competitive position, insuring safer working conditions, and improving overall plant operations, thereby improving the employees' jobs. But at the same time he pointed out that citing long-term benefits to someone whose livelihood is injured or threatened in the short run is cold comfort, and urged that management should face up to its human responsibilities from the very start:*

While it is obvious that in the long run automation will be of tremendous benefit to us all, it is the short run that worries most of us. Despite the fact that in today's Industrial Revolution the new jobs are being created before the old ones are destroyed and that the pressure will be on us simply to hold our own with a smaller percentage of our population in the workforce, there still exists the danger that temporary dislocations of personnel will occur in some cases. We should begin planning for this now.

> **"Automation – Its Applications and Uses,"**
> *address before the National Conference on Automation, CIO Committee on Economic Policy, Washington, D.C.,*
> **April 14, 1955.**

The problem is not how to prevent all displacement, but how to keep it at an absolute minimum and how to insure that as little human suffering as possible follows from it. Some of the responsibility clearly falls on society, which may have to agree to such steps as increasing the length and amount of unemployment benefits. But industry will also have to accept some of it. It should be a regular part of planning for automation to give consideration to such matters as dismissal pay, training allowances, and other measures to cushion the blow to individuals. Management attitude and performance in these areas will unquestionably do much to mitigate labor resistance to automation.

> **"The Economic and Social Effects of Automation,"**
> *address before the 2nd International Congress on Cybernetics, International Cybernetics Association, Namur, Belgium,*
> **September 3-10, 1958.**

Where discharges are unavoidable, an orderly management plan should be adopted which would offer maximum advance notice to affected employees, personal assistance in finding employment elsewhere in the community, and dismissal compensation where necessary and desirable. It is in alleviating the rough spots in what is overall a good and socially desirable movement that progressive management has a great opportunity.

> **"Automation - It's Impact on Human Relations,"**
> *address before the Congress of American Industry, National Association of Manufacturers, New York, New York,*
> **December 3, 1954.**

More is involved than merely the introduction of new machines. The markets and economic positions of industries and, therefore, the total work-force are affected. Technological change is becoming less and less distinguishable from total industrial change in the pattern of accelerating activity.

In other words, technological change, as heretofore defined in labor contracts, may be beginning to lose its meaning. However, the several means applied in labor contracts to meet technological change may be increasing in validity: advance notice; attrition arrangements; early retirement provisions; extended vacations; relocation allowances; retraining programs; severance pay plans; transferability of pension rights, seniority, and other benefits; union-management cooperation in the setting up of special funds and study committees; and worksharing plans. These are the labor-management instruments which are being or could be applied to the problems of total change, caused both directly and indirectly by an advancing technology.

> **Labor Contracts and Technological Change, Part I,**
> *Diebold Research Program Report,*
> **February, 1966.**

MANAGEMENT-EMPLOYEE COMMUNICATION

From the start, and continuously, John Diebold stressed the need to keep lines of communication with employees open and clear—not only to ease transitional problems through worker understanding and acceptance, but also to avoid the kind of active labor antagonism and perhaps even governmental involvement that would jeopardize management's prerogative to make the basic decisions about the use of technology in its operations. Thus:

Point Number One—Management must stop trying to ignore the problem out of existence. It should be clear by now that this approach will not work. By now, labor is fully alert to the fact of automation and will simply not be convinced by statements that it is only another technological phase which can be relied on to pass without any harmful, or even serious, effects.

Point Number Two—Management must take its employees into its confidence in this regard. Labor leader after labor leader has stressed the point that workers have a right to know what is going to happen to them. If justification exists for the introduction of automatic devices on economic grounds or to relieve labor shortages, if they assist in easing the burden of arduous tasks, if they eliminate hazards to health or reduce the causes of accidents, let the workers be told.

A British labor official has pleaded: "If men have to change their occupations, let them know what steps are contemplated to train and equip them for new occupations; let them know that they are appreciated as human beings and not as so many hands to be hired or fired at the whim of management." Unless this is done, he warns, unions will be forced to oppose changes, " if only to insure that they are consulted at their inception to protect the interests of their members."

Management, of course, cannot consult with its employees about the desirability of automating in the first place. That is clearly and exclusively a management decision. But equally it should not make the mistake of one concern where management gave no indication of its intentions to automate until the last moment, and did not even bother to pass along the good news that the new machines, far from putting men out of work, would in fact demand additional workers.

Only after the workers had taken action which, as they thought, would safeguard their interests did management explain. An ounce of consultation may well be worth a pound of explanation after the fact.

"The Economic and Social Effects of Automation,"
address before the 2nd International Congress on Cybernetics, International Cybernetics Association, Namur, Belgium,
September 3-10, 1958.

Above all, the development of precise definitions of management's right to introduce new processes and products will become even more important to assure sufficient flexibility for management in meeting competition and in serving new markets.

Labor Contracts and Technological Change, Part I,
Diebold Research Program Report,
February, 1966.

ENLIGHTENED COLLECTIVE BARGAINING

With varying degrees of success, management and labor have attempted to deal with the problems of technological change and automation in their collective bargaining agreements. In John Diebold's words, unilateral action by either party no longer suffices, and mutual cooperation is required.

*Implementing his deep interest in this subject, the Diebold Research Program has engaged in a continuing study of management-labor agreements. It has produced two definitive reports from which citations have already been given here (**Labor Contracts and Technological Change**, Parts I and II, February, 1966 and May, 1967), based on analysis of hundreds of contracts . Of these, some forty contracts were chosen from which illustrative clauses are reproduced and discussed in Part I. Part II discusses in detail four collective bargaining agreements that have successfully coped with many of the problems raised by technological change. It also discusses many of the relevant sections of the 1966 Report of the National Commission on Technology, Automation, and Economic change, and makes recommendations concerning the future course of technological change vis-a-vis the collective bargaining agreement.*

The four contracts were selected because the approaches taken by the contracting parties were considered by the Diebold researchers as worthy of being taken as models by other companies facing problems arising from automation and the effects of new technology. These case examples concern the contracts negotiated with their respective unions by the Armour Meat Packing Company, the Kaiser Steel Company, the West Coast Longshoremen, and the New York Lithographers.

The following discussion of contract provisions is based on these reports, showing the type of clauses that have been designed to cope with technological change and presenting highlights of the four case-study contracts. The latter are necessarily highly summarized here, but to give an insight into the methodology employed, the Armour case is presented in somewhat greater detail than the others.

It is emphasized that the examples are presented as approaches, and that where specific dollar figures are mentioned in connection with unemployment funds, retirement payments, and the like, they are given as illuminating factual information with respect to the examples themselves and not as generally applicable yardsticks. The reports themselves mention, as indicated in the findings summarized at the conclusion of the excerpted discussion, that while the experiences of the parties were generally favorable at the time of the study, continued success in terms of "cushions" set aside would depend upon continued prosperity. As a matter of fact, the Longshoremen's "automation fund" faced depletion in mid-1970. All of the examples do illustrate the main areas of concern confronting those industries deeply affected by automation and technological change.*

Typical Contract Provisions

Broad Scale Automation Provisions

Contracts with these provisions attempt to provide for all of the anticipated problems arising out of automation and technological change. Usually covered are the following:

1. Advance notice of plant closing and other changes.
2. Automation funds and study committees.

---

*An analysis of the plans, based upon work of The Diebold Research Program and the background research of The Diebold Group, is available in *Labor Management Contracts and Technological Change – Case Studies and Contract Clauses,* edited by Herbert J. Blitz, Frederick A. Praeger, Inc., New York, 1969. This is the first of a series of publications of The Diebold Institute for Public Policy Studies, Inc.

3. Displacement differential payments for workers who, as a result of technological change, must take lower paying jobs or are denied higher paying jobs due them.
4. Early retirement.
5. Employment reserves for technologically displaced workers.
6. Extended vacations and savings plans to expand employment opportunities.
7. Income and work guarantees.
8. Management rights to introduce changes.
9. Promotion of employment opportunities outside the company.
10. Relocation allowances.
11. Separation payments.
12. Sharing of savings from automation.
13. Training and retraining programs.
14. Transfer rights.

The Armour, Kaiser Steel, and the West Coast Longshoremen contracts mentioned above are among the best and the most complete examples of the broad-scale approach.

General Automation Provisions

These differ from broad-scale provisions only in degree, less detailed and specific. Some are:

Management Rights Clauses. These generally give management the exclusive right to determine what automation and technological change can and will be introduced. However, most contracts containing such clauses also contain provisions that tend to reduce this apparent absolute right. Provisions setting forth restrictive work rules, sought and obtained by the union, in many instances effectively control the management rights clause. Management right provisions are also tied in with grievance and arbitration procedures.

Advance Notice. These provisions vary greatly. The union must be given notice, ranging from a few days to six months, or simply stated as "reasonable," of the installation of new machinery, new methodology, or other changes.

Attrition. These clauses attempt to minimize job loss. Generally a specified number of employees who lose their jobs directly or indirectly through automation or technological change are retained in some capacity until they voluntarily leave or retire. These provisions also provide for the use of temporary employees so that if layoffs occur, the temporaries will be discharged first. Early retirement and job transfer may also be considered a form of attrition.

227

Early Retirement. Plans for early retirement vary. Most involve reductions in payments because of the longer period of payout. Some, however, encourage the employee to retire by providing higher payments until he is eligible for full Social Security payments.

Extended Vacations. Extended vacations are a deliberate attempt to spread available work. A carefully coordinated plan will always have someone in a large department or section on extended vacation. As a result, the regular work force is larger. If a department requires 60 workers and three are always on vacation, the regular work force will be 63, not 60.

Relocation Allowances. Here a fixed amount is to be paid for relocation from the old plant to the new one. The amount increeaces with distance, and married employees receive benefits on a different and higher scale.

Retraining. Various provisions for retraining are found in the contracts. Some provide for on-the-job training at reduced rates; others for on-the-job training at regular rates through the payment of something akin to the Kaiser Steel displacement differential. Some provide for training not related to the company's work. Both the Longshoremen's and Lithographer's contracts provide for jointly-administered schools to provide retraining.

Unemployment Pools. Displaced workers' names are placed on a list of workers who have priority in the case of recall or hiring by their company or industry. (The Kaiser pool is an exception. Its displaced workers are retained and are paid while they are in the pool. This is most unusual.)

Work Sharing. When there is danger of layoff, an attempt will be made to keep everyone working through a reduction in hours per employee.

Work Week Maintenance. This provision is the exact opposite of work sharing. Workers are deliberately discharged in order to preserve a full work week for the remaining employees.

Severance Pay Plans and Supplemental Unemployment Benefit Plans. Usually the employee must choose between terminating his employment and receiving severance pay or going on a lay-off status and receiving supplementary unemployment benefits. Severance pay is often geared to technological change to determine eligibility. In some contracts severance pay to those technologically displaced is higher, or comes after fewer years of service, than for workers displaced for other reasons.

Subcontracting Limitations. Technological change in some companies leads to an increase in outside subcontracting. Various provisions have been negotiated to reduce if not stop this practice.

Transfer Rights. Many contracts provide for transfer within the company. Often a choice is offered between transfer and severance pay.

Wage Maintenance. Examples include guaranteeing a full period of work once the worker starts; guaranteeing a full work week; guaranteeing the average wage before the technological change.

Job Maintenance. These provisions stipulate that there will be no job loss due to automation or technological change.

Wages, Incentive Pay, and Job Classifications. Provisions on changes in job classification which result in wage and incentive pay changes usually call for such changes to be submitted by management to the union. The question is then subject to negotiations under various procedures and methods.

ARMOUR & CO.
(Amalgamated Meatcutters and Butcher Workmen and the United Packinghouse Workers of America)

The Armour Automation Committee, established in 1959 by management and labor, has been instrumental in bringing about improved labor relations which create a climate conducive to the introduction of technological change. Between 1959 and 1966, Armour introduced more technological improvements than in its entire prior history. A detailed study of the Armour Plan, and the manner in which the committee dealt with the serious problems raised by mass displacement brought about by plant closings, could profitably be made by any company faced with similar problems. The Diebold Research Program believes that part of the solution to the problem of worker displacement, as it affects both Labor and Management, will be a direct outgrowth of the activities and programs conducted by the Armour Automation Committee.

Armour & Company is the nation's second largest meat packer and its total sales for 1965 were over $2 billion. The company is diversified and engages in the manufacture of foods, soaps, chemicals, machinery, and electronics. In the past sixteen years, twenty-one Armour meat packing and/or slaughtering plants have been closed and the number of production employees has fallen from 25,000 to 12,000.

Unions

The vast majority of Armour production workers are represented by the United Packinghouse Workers of America and the Amalgamated Meat Cutters & Butcher Workmen. The UPWA from its founding in the 1930s has been a militant industrial union; the Amalgamated, established in 1890, is a larger union with a more conservative craft background and history. Approximately three-fourths of the Amalgamated membership are employed as butchers and clerks in retail stores.

Serious post war strikes in 1946 (resulting in government seizure and operation), 1948, 1956 and 1959 plagued the industry. Bargaining is not industry wide. Each company prefers to negotiate its own contract; each contract has somewhat different clauses and provisions. The 1959 Armour negotiations, which led to the Armour Automation Committee and Automation Fund, heralded a new approach to labor relations.

Armour Automation Committee and Plant Closings

The 1959 contract negotiations between the unions and Armour were conducted under unfavorable conditions because of recent closing of six plants and the layoff of 5,000 employees. This was one-fourth of Armour's total unionized labor force. To the credit of both labor and management, the negotiations culminated in a two year pact which established a nine-man tripartite committee comprised of four representatives from Armour, two from the UPWA, two from the Amalgamated, and an impartial chairman. The Committee was authorized to study the problems created by automation and modernization and to make recommendations to the parties directed to the solution of these problems. It was not established to provide direct benefits to the employees. (The Kaiser Plan and West Coast Longshoremen's Plan do provide for direct benefits.) The activities of the Committee were to be financed with an Armour contribution of one cent for each hundredweight of total tonnage shipped, unitl an Automation Fund of $500,000 had been accumulated.

Shortly after its inception the Committee authorized and financed the following studies:

Economic Prospects for the Meat Industry 1960-1975.

Employment and Economic Problems Experienced by Displaced Armour Employees 1959-1960.

Problems of Interplant Transfer.

Analysis of Armour's Severance Pay Provisions.

Problems of Advance Notice.

Problems of Providing Adequate Maintenance Personnel for Automated Equipment.

The 1961 collective bargaining agreement and subsequent agreements contain many provisions directly attributed to these studies and resultant Committee discussions. Their application played an important role in the labor attempts of the Automation Committee to cope with serious displacement problems. The 1961 provisions are summarized as follows:

1. *Advance Notice.* Armour must give 90 days' notice of a department or plant closing and must guarantee 90 days' work or equivalent wages.

2. *Seniority Rights Transfer.* An employee who is under 60 and has the ability to do the job or learn the job in a reasonable time, may displace a junior employee in another plant hired after August 7, 1961. Employees with seniority rights in a closed plant are to be offered jobs in a replacement plant in order of seniority.

3. *Relocation Costs.* Sums, ranging from $40 for a single employee relocating less than 100 miles away to $500 for a married employee relocating 1,000 miles away, may be paid out of the Automation Fund.

4. *Increased Severance Pay.* Employees who are eligible receive one week's pay for each year of service up to 10 years plus 1-3/4 weeks pay for each year between 11 and 20, plus 2 weeks' pay for each year over 20.

5. *Technological Adjustment Pay (TAP).* A worker under 60 is eligible if he has 5 years' seniority and registers for transfer to another department or plant. TAP is at the rate of $65 per week less any unemployment benefits received. It is paid until the employee is transferred to another company job, up to a maximum of 26 weeks for employees of less than 25 years' seniority and 39 weeks for employees with seniority in excess of 25 years.

6. *Early Retirement.* An employee with 20 years of service who is displaced because of a plant or department closing can retire at age 55. He receives 1-1/2 times his regular retirement pay until he is eligible for Social Security at age 62, at which time his pay will revert to the regular retirement pay. The employee can claim TAP or severance pay in lieu of early retirement.

Results

The Armour Automation Committee record shows that it has directly faced the most serious problem that could be caused by technological change, and has taken positive, affirmative action in response to the needs of the displaced worker. Its efforts achieved greater and more meaningful results as its experience increased. Following are examples:

In Oklahoma City, 58 workers, or 14 percent of those displaced, benefited from Committee endeavors. In Fort Worth, 359, or 36 percent, have been helped. In Sioux City, over 600, or more than 50 percent of those affected, came within Committee program and 200 more took advantage of interplant transfers. The Kansas City results are also substantial. More than 1,200, or approximately 60 percent, were aided by the Committee.

Interviews with representatives of both management and labor indicate that the activities of the Armour Automation Committee have resulted in improved labor relations. Between 1959 and the time of the study, only a few walkouts, characterized by management as insignificant, had occurred. In this improved climate, Armour, according to its spokesman, undertook more modernization and introduced more technological improvements between 1959 and 1966 than in its entire prior history.

Both management and labor at Armour believe that the Committee is on the right track. They do, however, believe that the problems of worker displacement are too great for management and/or labor to solve alone. Government assistance is required. However, the assistance envisioned is not a massive Government crash program, or the establishment of another Government agency. The programs administered in Sioux City and Kansas City under the Manpower Development Training Act were well received, and substantially aided the participants. However, there were not enough of these programs and a tremendous amount of time and energy was spent "dealing with Government red tape." (Even though red tape was kept to a minimum at Kansas City, the minimum was considered too much.) The parties believe that joint efforts are needed and they suggest a study to explore the different methods in which these joint efforts may be meaningfully applied.

KAISER STEEL CORPORATION
(United Steelworkers of America)

In 1959 Kaiser Steel and the United Steelworkers established a Long Range Sharing Plan whereby savings generated largely by mechanization and improved technology were shared by management and labor in a 2/3 to 1/3 ratio respectively. An Employee Reserve was also established, which, for all practical purposes, guaranteed that no employee would be displaced by technological change. The plan, with some qualification, has been successful. During the first three years of its operation savings of over 29 million dollars were realized and Kaiser employees received wages in excess of the industry average.

The Employee Reserve has worked exceptionally well. As of March 1966 only 369 employees had been in the reserve and the average stay was about two weeks. Provisions were also made to pay wage differentials if a displaced worker took a lower paying job. The original intent on the part of both management and labor to eliminate incentives, common in the steel industry, was unsuccessful and production lagged. As a result, there has been some re-establishment of incentives at Kaiser.

The Kaiser experience is an example of both management and labor reaping substantial benefits from automation and technological change.

PACIFIC MARITIME ASSOCIATION
(International Longshoremen's and Warehousemen's Union)

The West Coast Longshoremen have taken the initiative in bringing about mechanization, modernization, and the elimination of restrictive work rules on the West Coast docks. In exchange for the right to eliminate many restrictive work rules and to mechanize and modernize, the Pacific Maritime Association paid 29 million dollars to the ILWU between 1959 and 1966. As a direct result of this payment, the net savings to management during this period are estimated to be in the sum of 120 million dollars. Automation and technological change on the West Coast docks occurred without worker displacement.

The 1966 agreement provided for the payment by management of 34.5 million dollars over a period of five years. As a result, the longshoreman could look forward to an income in excess of $10,000 per year, a lump sum retirement payment of $13,000, monthly benefits of $235 per month over and above Social Security payments, and other fringe benefits.

The new contract also called for an increased rate of mechanization. Significantly, the inclusion of this provision was insisted upon by the union.

METROPOLITAN LITHOGRAPHERS ASSOCIATION
(Local 1, Amalgamated Lithographers of America)

Local 1 Amalgamated Lithographers is an outstanding exception to the general rule that organized labor has resisted automation and technological change. For many years this union has realized that if lithography is to compete successfully in the printing industry, it must avail itself of improved technology. The union has taken the initiative and has continually pressed for the introduction of new technology whenever possible. As a result of this attitude, management and labor have prospered. There has been a steady increase in the number of lithographic employees, the number of plants, and the total sale of lithographic printing. At the time of the study the annual sales rate of lithography was increasing at the rate of 8 percent per annum while the annual rate of increase for the rest of the printing industry was only 3 percent.

Significant provisions concerned with technological change are as follows:

New Machines or Processes. New machines and processes are to be operated by union men under a scale of wages and with a complement of men agreed upon by a joint committee of the Association and union, subject to arbitration if there is no agreement. The employer must give written notice to the union and Association upon purchase of new equipment or a reasonable time before installation of a new process.

233

If an employer who is not a member of the Association installs a new machine or process, the Association and union will meet at the request of either party to arrive at a minimum wage and complement of help, which the union will attempt to establish in such shops.

No Transfer of Equipment. The employers agree to make no transfer of equipment to any other plant, which would result in the removal of jobs or work under this contract.

Retraining and Rehabilitation

The parties agree that technological developments will affect lithographic workers. They agree upon the request of either party to consider programs for retraining and rehabilitation.

Findings

In summary, it can be stated that the plans discussed have done a fairly good job, but all of them are greatly dependent on continued economic prosperity. It is doubtful whether any of them would stand against serious economic recession. Technological and economic displacement would occur.

The plans do offer constructive approaches, even if necessarily limited. The techniques and methods, if not the specifics, are transferable to many industries, although it is clear that the collective bargaining agreements alone cannot cope with all of the problems of technological change.

Diebold Research Program studies.

LESSONS THAT HAVE BEEN LEARNED

If we agree that we want to preserve our profit-enterprise system, the private sector, says John Diebold, must meet the complex labor-management issues raised by onrushing technology through fresh insights and effective innovation in management-labor relations. Collective bargaining must continue to play an important role. Based on in-depth studies of labor contracts and technological change by The Diebold Research Program, he is confident that the machinery of collective bargaining can be made to work.

But it is necessary to underscore John Diebold's point that "bargaining" must be construed in its literal sense, implying give-and-take on both sides, for the good of the parties themselves and of their "silent partner," the public. Thus:

Labor and management, working together, must show foresight, forbearance, commonsense, and some degree of mutual trust. Automation, it has been well said, is bound to require a high degree of "social orchestration" in industry. Lip service will not be enough, for it is still true that actions speak louder than words. But if this can be achieved, the price need not be high, and all of society will gain from the new abundance . . .

Another real problem is how the benefits of automation should be divided. This is a problem the whole economy faces, but it must also be decided by the management of each individual firm. Labor's biggest worry, next to mass unemployment, is that it will not get its fair share of the new wealth automation will create. In an automated plant, individual output ceases to have any real meaning, for the machine sets and follows its own pace.

> **"The Economic and Social Effects of Automation,"**
> *address before the 2nd International Congress on Cybernetics, International Cybernetics Association, Namur, Belgium,*
> **September 3-10, 1958.**

The encouragement of innovation in industry must be supported by labor, if we are to achieve its full benefits. Featherbedding in industry has become a valid issue; it is wasteful not only to the individual company in which it occurs, but to the entire economy as well. In many instances, labor has shown that it can facilitate change by sponsoring its own retraining programs and by intelligent collective bargaining. The responsibilities of labor in this area will be much greater in the years to come. It remains to be seen whether present labor-mangement relations, which mainly revolve about periodic collective bargaining sessions, are sufficient to cope with future problems.

> **Testimony before the Subcommittee on Automation and Energy Resources,**
> *Joint Economic Committee, U.S. Congress, Washington, D.C.,*
> **August, 1960.**

Once Government has set a favorable climate, labor and management should join forces to prepare for inevitable changes. Labor unions must drop their blind fear of automation and use their organizations to work out with management plans for orderly stages of automation. Unions must also accept responsibility for helping their own members adjust to changes in jobs.

> **"Facing Up to Automation,"**
> *The Saturday Evening Post,*
> **September 22, 1962.**

THE ROLE OF GOVERNMENT

Research and interviews have shown that private parties generally have greater flexibility in dealing with most labor situations than does a governmental body or agency. However, John Diebold recognized that certain situations are beyond the capabilities of private parties acting alone. In some programs, he acknowledges, Government must assume the major burden and role; in others, a combination of government and private parties is desirable.

In its 1966 report, the President's National Commission on Technology, Automation, and Economic Progress set forth four basic requirements for adjustment to technological change: (1) The displaced worker should be offered an equivalent or a better job. (2) Adequate financial security should be guaranteed while he seeks a job or undergoes retraining. (3) Financial relocation assistance should be made available. And (4) he should be protected against forfeiture of earned security rights (pension, retirement benefits, insurance).

It is worth noting that the four plans discussed earlier go a long way toward meeting these requirements. The Commission suggests, in the interests of better manpower planning, that information be shared through conferences with Federal, state, and local governments, employers, and union about the degree of technological advance in various industries to assist in the preparation for impending change. However, the Armour Automation Committee, after seven years of experience at the time of The Diebold Research Program study, was still unable to predict manpower requirements for Armour and Company. Thus, while the Commission's conference idea is without question a good one, students of management-labor relations fear that the results, in terms of actual accomplishments, may be minimal.

It is of particular interest that the Commission's recommendations do not speak of a massive Federal take-over, or the formation of more Federal agencies. All of its recommendations refrain from doing violence to the basic American concepts of capitalism and free enterprise. The Report makes it abundantly clear that management and labor as private parties should be fully able to cope with most of the problems of automation and technological change. Government, in its view, should step into the picture only when that is the best way to deal with a particular problem.

As stated in one of the lead-in quotations in this chapter, one of the principal strengths of our private-enterprise system is its flexibility in permitting change to occur. Government's role is important, and it must provide a favorable climate for change by cooperating with the parties when assistance is needed. In the final analysis, however, as John Diebold insists, the private-sector parties themselves must make the decisions and work out the detailed problems of adjustment. Simple mechanisms that can be applied with flexibility to individual situations are preferable to legislation, and a responsible private manpower policy is required.

Public Policy and Unemployment

The spectre that, over the years, has hovered over discussions of public policy and influenced the posture of organized labor has, of course, been unemployment. In times of relatively full employment it is difficult to look back and recreate the emotional change in the environment when there was widespread concern over large-scale unemployment. However, in the aftermath of the 1957 recession, extravagant projections were being made of the unemployment that would result from automation. Some congressmen predicted fourteen million unemployed in the following few years, and there were numerous proposals for varying degrees of controls on investment in automating equipment. At the same time there was, as John Diebold kept insisting, a remarkable paucity of hard facts upon which to base coherent policy. The following observations provided cogent insights when John Diebold made them as the first witness at the first Congressional Hearing ever held on automation. His remarks remain highly germane to the issue as it has evolved:

The problem in assessing the economic and social impact of automation is that we do not have the facts. If there is concern over the effects of automation, it seems to me highly desirable that we get these facts in the most expeditious way possible: through a thorough analysis of automation based upon a complete, factual, industry-wide investigation. Such a study would provide, for the first time, a realistic basis for planning on both a national and a private scale. With the broader perspective such a study would provide, industry could plan automation policy with a finer regard for the consequences. National policy concerning education and training problems, retirement benefits, and unemployment compensation must be based on a factual and intimate understanding of the subject.

> **Testimony before the Subcommittee on Economic Stabilization,**
> *Joint Committee on the Economic Report, U.S. Congress, Washington, D.C.,*
> **October 14, 1955.**

The 1955 guaranteed annual wage battle provided a glimpse of organized labor's future attitude toward automation. Widely applauded in principle, automation was used as a marching banner and rallying cry when negotiation time came. With the next change of administration in Washington, labor may try to use automation as a justification for a central Government committee on automation.

A committee like this would initially act as a clearing house for information, but this could prove an easy stepping stone to control of investment decisions regarding automation.

"**Automation 1958: Industry at the Crossroads,**"
Dun's Review,
August, 1958.

I began my original testimony of 1955 by emphasizing the need "to derive some factual information about automation and its impact upon the economy." This need is more urgent than it was before. While I do not feel that automation has been introduced at as high a rate as has been technically possible, its introduction and its impact have far outstripped what little we have learned about it. My original recommendations included "an outline of a factual study of automation." I have submitted a more complete "guide" to such a study, once again, in this statement.

Studies are still vitally necessary. Academic groups and government agencies have effected fine studies in this areas, but they have been limited by serious lack of funds to carry this work further. This would be a proper area for supportable research by all levels of government: Federal, state, and local. Private foundations could also do more to support study in this field. A solid, comprehensive body of facts on the economic and social effects of automation is still nonexistent.

Testimony before the Subcommittee on Automation and Energy Resources,
Joint Economic Committee, U.S. Congress, Washington, D.C.,
August, 1960.

In this connection, John Diebold, in looking ahead to the probable human consequences of automation, was among the first to point out that technology itself is only one factor in the complex causes of such unemployment as we have experienced:

There is insufficient clarity with respect to the fact that the causes of unemployment—as well as the ingredients of full employment—are multiform. Thus, automation is only one important expression of technological change; and technological change (including automation) is only one of the major causes of unemployment. Other major causes, as recognized by Congress itself in the enactment of the Manpower Development and Training Act of 1962, are foreign competition, relocation of industry, shifts in market demands, and other changes in the structure of the economy. Full employment, in turn, is the result of a proper mix of monetary, fiscal, tax, labor, and other related policies, legislative as well as administrative.

Testimony before the Subcommittee on Employment and Manpower,
Committee on Labor and Public Welfare, U.S. Senate, Washington, D.C.,
September 20, 1963.

238

In the last analysis, John Diebold reiterates today, the prime requisites for the success of any policy regarding technological change and its human consequences, be it public or private, are twofold: (1) it must be built on a solid basis of fact rather than conjecture and emotion; and (2) it must be flexible.

Even where all available pertinent facts have been taken into account, a plan that is highly structured and rigid and does not leave room for experimentation and change will soon become ineffectual. The negotiators of collective bargaining agreements and the drafters of legislation, he advises, must keep this in mind.

"Technological change," John Diebold keeps insisting, "is essential to progress. With careful planning, some imagination, and a little luck, the benefits of this progress can be shared by all America."

Photograph by Burt Glinn

New forecasting methods, integrating scientific, technical, and socio-economic developments into business planning, John Diebold points out, call for management teams capable of assessing external environmental forces as well as the internal determinants influencing the firm's growth

Very few analyses of the nature and extent of industrial automation have been made in terms of the realities of either our present technological knowledge and economic environment, or of historical perspective. . . . Its effects are bound to be widespread. Indeed, it is very difficult to consider any one economic or social effect without finding oneself exploring the effects of automation on all phases of our life and society.

"Automation: The Advent of the Automatic Factory,"
Princeton, New Jersey; Van Nostrand Company, Inc.,
1952.

We have the most dynamic and productive economy the world has ever known. To sell short its marvelous capacity for growth and production has been the undoing of more than one pessimistic economist. Our needs increase continually . . . the continual emergence of new needs is a basic cause of the dynamic qualities of our economy.

"Automation – Its Impact on Human Relations,"
address before the Congress of American Industry, National Association of Manufacturers, New York, New York,
December 3, 1954.

Machines change society itself: Change human wants, human aspirations, the whole complexion and nature of society. And this is the deepest meaning . . . because it's out of understanding human needs and changing needs that you create new businesses, new services and new industry.

"Automation in the Future,"
keynote address before the 37th International Conference of the Financial Executives Institute, New York, New York,
October 25, 1968.

Profit from Forecasting

Scientific, technological, and socio-economic forecasting methodologies must be designed for both internal systems and external business planning.

In the areas of what might be termed "traditional" fact-gathering, forecasting, and decision making, the developments in automatic data processing and associated communications and information technology have added new dimensions of sophistication and versatility. And in recent years the new management science disciplines — operations research, advanced statistical manipulation, simulation models, and related mathematical programming — have added impressive new capabilities of analysis, interpretation, and prediction. However, while these uses of the new technology should certainly be incorporated to the greatest possible extent in all business forecasting and strategy formulation (and we shall address ourselves to them later in this chapter), John Diebold has always called attention to a much broader canvass.

SOCIO-ECONOMIC FORECASTING

As he has repeatedly said, it is the influence of advancing technology as a harbinger of **social change** *that gives it its abiding importance. In the context of business forecasting, he insists, it is the entrepreneurial opportunities opened by such social change that must be looked for, and methodologies must be developed for such external business planning, over and above the improvement of systems for gathering and interpreting data and making predictions about traditional markets.*

It is only when there is appropriate insight into **where underlying technology is heading**, *he says, that we can be adequately prepared for its challenges and opportunities. What is therefore called for, he adds, is more attention by business management to imaginative* **socio-economic** *forecasting. The following remarks for a marketing readership, made originally in the context of a discussion of computer technology and marketing, serve admirably to sum up his thesis as applied to technological advance in general:*

The effect of [advancing technology] on people, on society, on living patterns, the effect on the home, on the way we buy and what we buy — all this is going to change totally what we do in business.

It's going to change our lives. It's going to change social structure. It's going to change aspirations. It goes right to the heart of the major determinant of social structure, which is communications . . . Suddenly we're changing that, and it's going to change our living pattern. It's going to change the way a person buys. It's going to change the way a person learns. It's going to change what he does when he gets into an automobile. It's going to change the way a doctor deals with his patients. It's going to change the nature and structure of hospitals.

And all of that is going to add up to a huge change in markets and products. . . The automobile is important because it has done many more things than just change transportation. It changed the way we live, it changed our aspirations, it created whole new industries. The computer is doing it all over again. The social change, the human change – the change in the society – that's the big business in the computer. Yet almost no attention is being given to it.

"Marketing's Role in the Coming Age of Automation,
Sales Management,
October 1, 1966.

The whole broad spectrum of all technology is undergoing explosive change. The accompanying accelerated social changes, if properly anticipated, will indeed present unlimited entrepreneurial opportunity, but they are also fraught with dangerous social and economic consequences, as indicated in preceding chapters. John Diebold's point is that it is meaningless to discuss how the opportunities can be grasped or the dangers averted without taking measures to keep us abreast of the direction in which technology is progressing, and of the fantastic shapes of things already in the laboratories and on the drawing boards. He has been sounding this theme before scientific, academic, and business audiences:

The problem. . . is maintaining a rational basis in looking ahead. The changes, technological and social, are so great and the problems so numerous that to look ahead properly one must balance the difficulty of bringing about even simple change with the inevitability of great change.

But it is not so pedantic nor so difficult either that we should shy away from it. . . My point is that we gain little from a conservative view of innovation – only the avoidance of fads. And we lose much – the ability to lead in our use of the technology, not to be dragged by our heels, letting the rapid changes in technology alter our business and social structure at random.

"Automation as a Historical Development,"
address before the Society for the History of Technology and American Association for the Advancement of Science, New York, New York,
December 29, 1960.

The Frontiers of Technology – Opportunities and Dangers

What has happened is really very simple to understand. Technological advance has become self-generating. To borrow a phrase from the economic terminology for developing countries, technology has reached the "take-off point." No longer must technological progress wait on the next individual scientific discovery. Technology itself is pushing research into new discoveries and new dimensions. . .

243

The direct result of man's increasing control and manipulation of knowledge is man's ability to produce new materials, shape new forms, test hypotheses, monitor events ... resulting in breakthroughs such as the creation of "cyborgs" – people with artificial organs – and the determination of genetic patterns. . . Man has catapulted himself from his earthbound physical and intellectual base to the rim or core of universal creation ... The undirected or misdirected application of technology is threatening not only man's environment, but the quality of future generations ... Clearly these phenomena are accompanied by infinite dangers – but also by infinite opportunities.

> **"Science, Technology and Man's Relation to the Universe,"**
> *address upon receipt of an Honorary Doctor of Laws Degree at the 80th Anniversary Convocation, Rollins College, Winter Park, Florida,*
> **February 22, 1965.**

Last year, an amputee was able to think about raising his artificial arm, and because a computer was connected to the man's nerves, the artifical arm could move when he thought about it. Today, there is a roomful of equipment for accomplishing this, but the history of these developments is that tomorrow the equipment will be carried around in one's pocket. This is remarkable, hopeful, and all rather frightening. It is illustrative of the many fundamental changes that are coming about as this new technology moves into our daily life ... As we move into the frontier areas of medicine, and biology, and of human and animal behavior, we move from the remarkable to the bizarre. Occurrences which we used to read about in scientific fiction and in the comic pages have moved into the news pages of our papers ... We had better think seriously about the potential – and the infinite problems – of such happenings.

> **"Business, Computers and the Turn Toward Technology,"**
> *address before the Economic Club of Chicago, Chicago, Illinois,*
> **February 24, 1966.**

Looking at automation as a historical development not only helps put today's machines in perspective, but makes clear the context in which tomorrow's technology will both evolve and be put to work. The value of such perspective to business and to society simply cannot be overstated. Yet to many – even, I think to most – it still appears an academic exercise. So difficult is it to think of a world which differs in any major way from that in which we live at the moment. . . We still find it virtually impossible to look ahead.

> **"Automation as a Historical Development,"**
> *address before the Society for the History of Technology and the American Association for the Advancement of Science, New York, New York.*
> **December 29, 1960.**

It is understandable that much of John Diebold's urgings for broadbased studies of the direction, pace, and societal effects of technological change have been somewhat in the nature of a voice crying in the wilderness. As indicated in the preceding chapter, the comprehensive programs called for are not the kind that would readily be undertaken by individual enterprise. They would require government or foundation funding, and the process of having the need for them articulated from sufficient quarters to stimulate action is a slow one. We have already seen that from the very earliest days, almost two decades ago when the implications of automation first began to arouse widespread concern, he hammered – with little success in striking a responsive chord – upon the theme that no intelligent forecasting of the effects of the new technology could be done without a strong factual basis.

Individual Technological Forecasting

The implications of many of the technological developments alluded to above clearly raise issues of public policy, and will be discussed in our concluding chapter. In the meantime, however, John Diebold points out that for continued growth if not sheer competitive survival individual enterprises must develop procedures and organization for formalized technological forecasting of their own:

The imperatives of our burgeoning technology obviously call not only for an alertness to technological change in a given industry and its related activity areas, but also for an imaginative insight into the effects of existing and over-the-horizon innovation that may at first glance be considered too far removed to have any discernible impact upon a business. They add up to the need for a new approach – in fact, a new discipline, a new management function – already formalized in a few companies under the term *technological forecasting.*

> **"The Impact of Science and Technology on the Development of Managers,"**
> *address upon receipt of an Honorary Doctor of Science Degree at a Special Convocation, Clarkson College of Technology, Potsdam, New York,*
> October 12, 1965.

It would seem that some sort of formal organizational mechanism is called for to provide the necessary linkage between administrative, marketing, and financial decision makers and the accelerating technological developments of every sort – even those on the most far-out fringes of science – that can have a conceivable impact on the nature and function of the business. This admittedly covers a lot of ground, but only with a recognized function of this sort can a modern corporation, vulnerable as it is to technological changes which may strike at the very underpinnings of its existence, make intelligent, periodic reviews of its research and development policies, or of its programs for acquisition and diversification.

This is something different from an organization for basic research, for it envisions an activity which not only interprets to management what its basic research is doing, but also develops guidelines that form the parameters of the basic research program itself. (It may even recommend that management, by the merger and acquisition process, acquire the requisite scientific and developmental talent and facilities.) Organizationally, the function could consist of a small analysis group (or in a smaller organization, a single knowledgeable staff scientist), whose responsibility it is to keep under constant review the frontier developments of science, and to interpret their possible impact on the firm's technology and markets.

"Major Expansion of Knowledge and Technology," *address presented before the Second Presidents Forum, Blue Cross Association Seminar, Princeton, New Jersey,* **October 11, 1965.**

The term "frontier developments" today opens a very broad door indeed, when one contemplates what has been going on in the frontiers of medicine, biology, sub-atomic particles, space exploration, and all the rest, to say nothing of the experiments and new insights of the behavioral sciences. Obviously, the approach must be an interdisciplinary one, engaging the talents of men and women of diverse training and backgrounds, since the technological developments of this century have left the "universal man," or the "man for all seasons" far behind in the dust of our churning advance.

However, it is assumed that where the realities of budgets put limitations on in-house staff, these would be supplemented by use of outside professionals as required, and by requisite liaison with universities and other focal points of research. ("Think tanks" are now recognized and respected entities in our technical-scientific society, even one that says its function is to "think the unthinkable.") Originally nurtured on Government contracts, many have now achieved the status of private or semi-private "far-out" research groups, and place themselves at the service of private industry.) The Diebold Research Program, for example, jointly sponsored by more than one hundred and sixty major corporations here and abroad, is engaged in a continuing study of the impact of change in information technology on corporate planning decisions.

Above all, says John Diebold, the approach called for is one of perceiving the possible through the eyes of imagination, untrammeled by what has been thought to be impregnably difficult or by scientific theory impossible:

Negative predictions in science are very, very dangerous. Arthur Clark has formulated what he calls, "Clark's Law," — "When a distinguished but elderly scientist states that something is possible, he is almost certainly right. When he states that something is impossible, he's very probably wrong."

"Automation in the Future," *keynote address before the 37th International Conference of the Financial Executives Institute,* *New York, New York,* **October 25, 1968.**

THE NEW CAPABILITIES OF FORECASTING AND DECISION-MAKING

Returning to the traditional areas of fact-gathering, forecasting, and decision-making, and the "multidimensional" impact upon them of the new information technology to which John Diebold has referred, these have been succinctly summarized as follows:

1. The new technology has given the decision maker access to a considerably greater amount of detailed data on the *internal* operations of his own organization. The rapidly improving cost-performance capabilities of bulk storage devices have had a major impact on the volume and type of data that business now considers important for its operations. Similar trends in data capture will result in further increases of this type.

2. The availability of data from *external* sources, including the government and various syndicated services, has enabled the decision maker to widen the horizons of his evaluation process. At the same time, however, the widespread use of information processing has created an environment in which the firm must improve its capability in this direction if it is to survive.

3. The mathematical techniques made practical by the modern computer and the growing availability of data have permitted considerable improvement in the decision maker's ability to forecast future occurrence on the basis of current trends. This, in turn, has improved his decision making capability. It has also permitted him to transfer certain low-level decision making problems, such as inventory control, to straightforward operational procedures.

4. The communications capability of information processing has, at the same time, somewhat reduced the decision maker's dependence on forecasting, at least in the short run. On the one hand, it has permitted him to delay decision making by shortening the time period required for the implementation of operational decisions. For example, the train status information system used by the railroads enables them to reroute trains already traveling in some general direction. Thus they can react to actual market prices at alternate destinations rather than relying solely on short-term forecasts.

5. On the other hand, information processing has permitted the decision maker to react more quickly to a poor decision or to a change in the variables on which he based his original choice. This is actually the underlying premise of certain PERT models. The decision maker can react quickly to schedule slippages by reallocating certain resources.

ADP for Management Decision Making,
Diebold Research Program Report,
April, 1968.

In the next few years, say Diebold researchers, a continuation of these trends can be expected, and at a geometric rate of advance. Data capture devices will continue to improve and become less expensive, and the sources of external data will increase in number and improve in quality. Here, it is pointed out, the computerized information services previously discussed will be an important source of external data to feed into industry's more sophisticated information processing and forecasting systems.

Sources of Information

The most significant occurrence is the appearance of firms offering information in computer readable formats or willing to process such data according to the specifications of the subscriber. This is important because it provides the opportunity to acquire relatively specific data that can then be fitted into the user's information system. [Cf. Chapter 13.]

The Government is currently the best source of information in a wide variety of areas. A good deal of this is available on punched cards or magnetic tape. More is maintained on tape but is not directly available, although the bureaus will process it according to the user's requirements, for a fee.

The Government promises to be an even more important source of data in the future. For example, Senator Edward Kennedy has proposed the establishment of a "computerized information system to provide state and local governments with information on Federal programs." In part, he cited a study by IBM which concluded that at least four kinds of input data would be required:

> "First, socio-economic data involving income distribution, education, law enforcement, health, and welfare, and the like."

> "Second, community resource data involving labor force and employment, industry and trade, transportation, housing and community facilities, financial, etc.

> "Third, program reference data concerning the nature and purpose of assistance programs, conditions of eligibility, information contact, authorizing legislation, and the administering agency.

> "Fourth, program status data involving the nature and extent of usage of various aid programs, the status of obligated funds, the names and numbers of communities involved, and the like."

The actual development of such a system would have enormous potential for private industry. First, it would create a central source for a wide variety of data on consumer and industrial markets.

Secondly, it would provide information on the growing market associated with government development plans. Information such as this, especially after a time lapse to provide the perspective of trend patterns, will furnish a strong factual base for forecasting.

Additionally, the availability and quality of external data will significantly increase as more companies begin to sell information as a by-product of normal business operations. An example is the index developed by the Kroger Company (which is also a neat example of the entrepreneurial opportunities in computer-based information services discussed in Chapter 13).

> The Kroger Company's Product Movement Index (PMI) is a by-product of the supermarket chain's own ordering and replenishment system. Thus, the initial development of this system offered the dual return of improved internal operations and a saleable commodity.

> Another approach is that of an information service which collects product movement data from participating food operators and sells it to food manufacturers. In return for their own data, the participants receive reports showing the movement of their products compared with the balance of the measured market, plus a share in the gross revenues accruing from the sale of the reports to manufacturers.

The dissemination of such internally generated data will certainly increase with the development of sophisticated information systems.

The acquisition of increasing amounts of data and improvements in computer hardware and software will result in a totally new order of magnitude of data analysis. Market researchers experimenting with this approach have suggested that ultimately it may be possible to predict ten or twenty consumer variables from a single data series, and that these data may be as simple and inexpensive to acquire as census data are today. In other words, input data will become more effective, not only because of reductions in acquisition costs, but because far less data will be required once a clearer understanding of various relationships is discovered.

> **"Integrated Management Information Systems and Management Decision-Making,"**
> *Diebold Research Program Report,*
> **June, 1965.**

Predictive Simulations

The availability of more, and more reliable, input data, will enhance the effectiveness of mathematical techniques and the use of marketing simulation models, such as discussed in Chapter 5, for predictive and decision-making purposes. As stated in the earlier chapter, limitations of developmental expense and of the verisimilitude of complex models thus far produced are still serious. However, Diebold Research

Program studies show the direction of the technology as pointing to their increasing applicability in the near future in areas of pricing and bidding, distribution, new-product timing, financial-credit questions, product lines, marketing mix, and the like.

If marketing management accepts the simulation as a reasonable representation of the external environment, it has a valuable tool for setting explicit objectives which can be used to evaluate future performances.

For example, given a particular marketing strategy, expected competitive actions, and known population characteristics, marketing management may use its consumer simulation to establish standards (expectations) through a forecast of relevant market variables including awareness, trial, usage and attitude data. Variations, if statistically significant, form the basis for a "management by exception" system which can be used in controlling the marketing process.

ADP for Management Decision Making,
Diebold Research Program Report,
April, 1968.

A simple method for obtaining a *predictive* model is to use a descriptive model to forecast the future. This can be an effective method for testing the descriptive model's validity. For example, if a firm has developed a mathematical model describing the relationship of the firm's sales to its marketing mix (i.e. price, advertising, and distribution), the model may be used as a predictor by using as inputs proposed levels of price, advertising, and distribution. The model will then predict the sales level associated with the proposed market mix. If the firm's actual sales do not correspond to the model's predictions, then the question of the adequacy of the model's description is raised. On the other hand, if the predicted and actual results are very close, confidence can be expressed in the validity of the model's representation of the process.

Predictive models also can be used to evaluate alternative strategies. For example, the marketing mix model mentioned above might be used to generate sales predictions for different combinations of levels of each of the marketing variables. The marketing managers then might choose the marketing mix which generated the most predicted profit.

ADP for Management Decision Making,
Diebold Research Program Report,
April, 1968.

MODELS OF THE ECONOMY

Leaving aside activities of individual firms, there is considerable ongoing academic research — government and foundation-sponsored — to provide simulations for eco-

nomic policy formulation. Studies by The Diebold Group indicate that econometric models have provided improvements in performance to user organizations, although they include a large number of uncontrollable elements. The existence of a large number of alternative hypotheses to explain the significant variables in econometric models requires significant investment in data collection and validation, and in experimentation. As one report states:

Three major uses can be defined for large-scale econometric models: policy simulations, testing of business-cycle and growth theories, and forecasting.

Although several large econometric models have been successfully implemented, the reliability of the forecasts must be left to question. The models have required a great deal of development time (several years) and as yet no one model is generally accepted. Management involvement is required to identify areas of particular importance with the model so that higher forecast accuracy can be achieved.

A major problem in economic policy evaluation is tracing through the impacts of a particular policy decision at all points in the economic system. If the model has a reasonably accurate set of parameters, it is especially useful in this role.

Knowledge of the cyclical and growth behavior of our economy is also of major importance. Through this knowledge we can more accurately determine that combination of government policies which will yield a desired rate of growth. A more detailed knowledge of how business cycles are actually propagated in our economic system and how these responses are modified in response to changes in government policy, promises to aid in the establishment of improved contracyclical policies.

Finally, the model may prove to be a useful tool for forecasting economic conditions. These models which have been used over a period of time have produced substantially better forecasts than both naive forecasts and most subjective forecasts. Countering these successes, econometricians note the inaccuracies in the model in terms of estimates of the parameters, exclusion of many important factors, and changes in the actual relationships due to changing technologies and tastes.

ADP for Management Decision Making,
Diebold Research Program Report,
April, 1968.

"THE EYES OF IMAGINATION"

The foregoing remarks represent the thrust of computers and information technology in the areas of traditional forecasting and decision-making. The developments discussed represent the new and improved tools of fact-gathering and evaluation to determine what is possible and feasible. However, they remain only tools. The real entrepreneurial spark will only be struck when they are combined with an awareness of the social changes wrought by technology in general. This calls for methodologies of socio-economic and technological forecasting. John Diebold provides a vivid summing up:

I am a businessman. I deal in what is possible, otherwise I go broke. I have studied for and obtained degrees in engineering and economics. This is of some help in evaluating what is possible — what the mathematicians and technicians of my firm tell me, what the learned books and papers say.

We have seen over the past decade the development of technologies and theories which range from cryogenics and molectronics to the simulation of rudimentary mental process . . . Ten years ago artificial intelligence was good business for science fiction publications. My interest was academic. Today I am seeking a methodology for the application of artificial intelligence to management information systems.

"Science, Technology and Man's Relation to the Universe,"
address upon receipt of an Honorary Doctor of Laws Degree at the 80th Anniversary Convocation, Rollins College, Winter Park, Florida,
February 22, 1965.

That is, indeed, perceiving the possible through the eyes of imagination!

Photograph by J. G. Cadou

John Diebold has long called attention to the public policy problems raised by technological change. These, he feels, should be the active concern of the private sector as well as government. As early as 1963 he was, as pictured here, one of the leaders of a large U.S. delegation to a U.N. conference assessing the meaning of scientific and technological change for developing countries.

Our generation has grown up in an age of social awareness. The 1930s and 1940s were a period of reaction and awakening. There was strong resentment of the callousness and indifference to human suffering that marked at least the formal doctrine and rationalizations of former generations. Out of this social awareness has come an acute sense of the responsibility of society to the individual.

"Individuals in a World of Change,"
commencement address at East Contra Costa Junior College and West Contra Costa Junior College, San Pablo, California,
June 20, 1956.

Our obligation is to be sure, when public policy problems are posed by technology, that we, as business leaders, involve ourselves. Our task, as leaders of the private sector, is to lead in the social innovation that matches the technological innovation . . . We must involve ourselves in a major way with the human problems resulting from technological change. Capitalism must be dynamic, not rigid, in its response.

"Automation in the Future,"
keynote address before the 37th International Conference of the Financial Executives Institute, New York, New York,
October 25, 1968.

Business and Public Policy

Business management must play a more active role in public policy issues resulting from and related to technological change.

It was John Diebold's early recognition of the truly revolutionary technological change represented by automation, and, more importantly, his insight into the social changes of which the technological change would be the precursor, that led him from his first discussions of the role of business in public policy issues to take the position which he has steadfastly maintained throughout. This stance, consistent with what we have already noted in connection with his observations on automation's effect on unemployment and labor policy, was in direct variance with early scare stories in the popular press and the dire tenor of much of the testimony at public hearings on the effects of automation.

*Briefly, his thesis as regards public policy (which, let it be noted, he does not equate with "government" policy) has always been (a) that automation and all of the related technology of cybernetics, communication, and information processing are not a Frankenstein monster to be in terror of and to regulate and legislate into submission, but rather a development to be welcomed for the untold benefits it would bring to mankind; (b) that in any event, the multiplying wants of the world's expanding populations would make automation a matter of urgent necessity rather than of gingerly approached choice; (c) that indeed many of the purportedly existing or feared ill effects of automation are in fact symptoms of underlying societal problems which automation is simply uncovering; (d) that while the dislocative effects could not be ignored, they represent a challenge to public policy makers and to the private sector to plan for and to work on **in concert**; and, finally, (e) that the private sector working in a free-enterprise system, not a totalitarian system or private industry under stifling governmental control, will be the agency that will bring to society the full benefits of the new technology — **provided** business management is alive to the social consequences of its actions and assumes the public responsibility which they entail.*

EMERGING SOCIAL CONSCIOUSNESS

*In recent years business leadership has in fact been evidencing a growing social awareness — a recognition that business has societal obligations over and beyond the primary concern of conducting an enterprise at a profit. It is an awareness of an obligation to be concerned about and to participate in solving the human problems of **society as a whole** created by advancing technology, and it is similar to the revolution in business thinking which took place roughly half a century ago when business accepted a similar responsibility with respect to the human problems of its employees.*

In that earlier day we had, indeed, come a long way from the era when, to use John Diebold's stark description, "armies of eight-and ten-year old children walked to work at four o'clock in the morning, across a landscape of hell that the Industrial Revolution had created out of the British Midlands." Tragically, the social and economic upheaval of the Industrial Revolution was to give rise to much human exploitation and misery before the (traditionally lagging) collective conscience of society, reinforcing suasion with legislative strictures, led industry to institute widespread improvements in compensation, hours, and working conditions.

Here again we see the syndrome so often cited by John Diebold: Advancing technology, which created the problem in the first place, also provided the basis for solution through the tremendous increase in the production of physical goods made possible by the new machines. Employers saw that labor, participating in the wealth it produced, would have the purchasing power to create markets for industry's stepped-up output. And although at first reluctant to spend money on adequate lighting, ventilation, sanitation, and the like, they soon came to realize that entirely aside from humanitarian reasons, increased employee efficiency made expenditures for good working conditions good business.

What we are witnessing now, he says, is a parallel upheaval and transition, and if we are to preserve our free enterprise form of society, it behooves the private sector to avoid as many as possible of the mistakes made in the past:

I am myself a capitalist and I hope we will be able to preserve the private enterprise form of society for our children. I believe, however, that it is only going to be possible if we recognize that capitalism must not be viewed as a static form standing rigid against all change. It is only by creating a dynamic form of capitalist government and economy that can continually adjust to the requirements of each new change that we have any hope whatever of preserving free enterprise in our quarter of the world. . .

This is no one-time problem. The easiest thing is to assume that only through central state control can the necessary adjustments be made. Enormous quantities of literature are being produced to this effect in many quarters of the world. It is my view that this would lead us down the wrong path entirely, for I believe most sincerely and strongly in private enterprise.

> **Testimony before the Select House Subcommittee on Labor,**
> *Committee on Education and Labor, U.S. House of Representatives, Washington, D.C.,*
> **August 5, 1963.**

PUBLIC PROBLEMS: WHOSE RESPONSIBILITIES?

While John Diebold has opted strongly for the free-enterprise approach to the public problems raised by technology, he has by no means been inarticulate in reiterating their extent and seriousness — since, to use his phrase, they cannot be "ignored out of existence" but must be resolved by frontal attack. Business, he holds, must, with a new social consciousness, take the initiative in anticipating dislocative effects, and work with involved groups and with public authorities toward their resolution — even if this means a departure from the literal interpretation of "being in business for a profit."

In any event, as he sees it, there can be no real departure from "business for a profit." It is not a question of putting responsibility to the general public "ahead" of responsibility to shareholders, or vice versa. The two responsibilities, he says, are linked, and in the long run it is only possible to meet one's obligations to stockholders by being actively concerned about the public effects of the firm's operations:

If business is merely passive, or if business is resistant, it is going to suffer very badly, because the technology is changing society totally. The social changes are going to make people concerned over whether they will be hurt, and in this day and age they are going to take steps to see that they are not hurt.

"A Review of Computer and Data Processing Problems for Management,"
keynote address before the Administrative Management Institute, New York, New York,
May 16, 1962.

Legal and Economic Questions

Without presuming to offer ready-made answers, John Diebold urges that more "rethinking" must be done about policy implications of developments that will inevitably result from technology already being implemented. These go far beyond matters of labor displacement and unemployment which to date have received the lion's share of public discussion. The consequences of technological changes, he points out, are extremely complicated, and permeate so many human activities — not only directly, but with secondary, tertiary, and further effects on our behavior — that no simple response to them is possible:

Think for a moment of the legal problems arising from this new technology. What do you do about copyrights when you have electronic distribution in publishing? What do you do about the problems of property when you can go from the satellite directly into the home with TV and skip the local TV stations? What about the property values involved? These and other fundamental legal problems are raised. They are only a few of the many kinds of problems facing us.

These are clearly *public* problems. But as businessmen, we should not sit by and let "public" be equated with "government." It is all too easy to equate *public* problems with government action and allow *government* to make the moves and take the steps in handling these problems.

Many of us feel that, to far too great an extent, we as a society have too readily relinquished our responsibilities to government. Public policy used to mean that while government was involved, the private sectors were involved too — trade unions, individuals, and private institutions were all involved. Should we not make it mean that again, and should we not do it by meeting in discussion in this area? If we leave these new questions of public policy and the need for social innovation purely to government, the response will probably not be to our liking, nor is it likely to be one that insures the healthiest growth of our country.

"Business, Computers and the Turn Toward Technology,"
address before the Economic Club of Chicago, Chicago, Illinois,
February 24, 1964.

The heart of the matter is finding ways in which the dynamics of the private sector can be brought to bear on such problems as housing, the distribution of medical services, on widespread and extensive mass transportation, and on education. In other words, on the areas that unquestionably *do* present the serious problems of our day. It seems to me that the alternatives to applying private-sector effort to these problems are just not acceptable.

. . . If we don't harness the dynamics of the private sector, the alternative is to leave it all to government. This, it seems to me, is just not going to achieve the desired results . . . We cannot get the results we need simply by heaping more and more on the government structure — on top of a whole series of bureaucratic organizations which are already overburdened.

"Youth and Business,"
commencement address upon receipt of an Honorary Doctor of Engineering Degree, Newark College of Engineering, Newark, New Jersey,
May 27, 1970.

The issue of government involvement becomes especially acute, John Diebold points out, when we look at some of the problems of scale in the more advanced areas of technology. Thus:

The supersonic transport is posing problems for risk capital that not even an industry can face without governmental participation. This is more characteristic of our times than most businessmen will as yet accept to be true. The fundamental questions it poses with regard to the characteristics of private enterprise in such a world are as basic as any business or economic questions that can be posed today in our country.

Interestingly enough, these questions, like so many others of the most fundamental importance, are being almost totally ignored. This is one of the most interesting, upsetting phenomena of our times, yet it is a condition we can change at will.

The questions of how we preserve entrepreneurial flair and creativity while we increase enormously the scope of enterprise, how we provide risk capital of a scale necessary to cover the risk without eliminating the venture, how we guard against the very real dangers that generations of antitrust people have been concerned with — all these are inherent in the problem of scale.

> **"The Impact of Science and Technology on the Development of Managers,"**
> *address upon receipt of an Honorary Doctor of Science Degree at a Special Convocation, Clarkson College of Technology, Potsdam, New York,*
> **October 12, 1965.**

. . . and Moral Issues

In earlier chapters we indicated the entrepreneurial opportunities represented by change. But many of these changes, John Diebold points out, will raise social and moral questions with no ready black-and-white answers, over and above the kind of legal and economic issues just mentioned. The problem of increasing leisure is an example of an obvious good with some possible not-so-good social side effects:

Leisure is sure to change patterns of consumption. People with more time off will spend more money on sports clothes and equipment, on hobbies, on travel and its adjuncts. The already booming do-it-yourself movement is certain to boom even further.

But additional leisure may also have more subtle and perhaps less favorable effects. Some observers, like Erich Fromm, feel that increasing men's leisure tends only to increase his sense of insecurity. Too much time may isolate him psychologically, create problems which he is unprepared to face, and drive him to socially harmful actions. And David Riesman contends that many Americans look on additional leisure as "a threat, a problem, a burden, or hazard."

The report of one Congressional subcommittee suggests that even the choice between more goods and more leisure involves "something of an ethical challenge," for in this country there still are "substantial groups of comparatively underprivileged and lower-income groups who should be remembered before those in the more favored industries can conscientiously turn to a shortened work day or longer weekend."

Sooner or later, however, society will have to face the question: Is this country capable of developing a culture that does not depend on work to give meaning to our lives?

> **"Automation: Its Impact on Business and Labor,"**
> *Washington, D.C.; National Planning Association, Planning Pamphlet No. 106,*
> **May, 1959.**

Too often when we speak of automation and the speed with which it is being incorporated into our economy, we find ourselves hoping that this will be a slow transition — a gradual integration. This is likely to be the case, but in actuality, I suspect we ought to be thinking in terms of speeding it up rather than slowing it down. There are many reasons to adopt this avenue of thought, but the most compelling reason is the present divided state of the world. One does not need to be a mathematician to understand how greatly the free people of the world are outnumbered by the totalitarians. We must in some manner make up for this difference in manpower. Automation offers one possibility. If this alone were the only justification for automation, it would, in my opinion, be sufficient."

> **"Automation — Its Application and Uses,"**
> *address before the National Conference on Automa-*
> *tion, CIO Committee on Economic Policy,*
> *Washington, D. C.,*
> **April 14, 1955.**

Our position in international trade depends on technological supremacy. We pioneered in the technology of mass production, and this had much to do with the fact that we are now the richest nation in the world. The automobile assembly line, for example, created not only a tremendous export trade, but high wages and an unsurpassed standard of living. Today we can maintain this advantage only by pioneering in automation technology.

> **Testimony before the Subcommittee on Unemploy-**
> **ment-Automation,**
> *Committee on Education and Labor, U.S. House of*
> *Representatives, Washington, D.C.,*
> **March 8, 1961.**

We Americans look forward to an even better life than we enjoy today. We expect our children to have extra years of education. We want the safety of an expensive military-defense arsenal. We like the prestige of our $20,000,000 program to put a man on the moon. Each of us anticipates a yearly rise in personal income.

And yet we expect to gain all of these expensive benefits while working shorter hours, taking longer vacations, and retiring earlier in life. Through the use of our most potent economy expander — automation — we have been able to boost the production per man-hour enough to match the heavy demands. But unless we continue to automate intelligently, our productivity may not grow as fast as our needs. We will find ourselves working harder with fewer benefits.

> **"Facing Up To Automation,"**
> *The Saturday Evening Post,*
> **September 22, 1962.**

*Even more basic will be the ethical and public issues raised by some of the "far out"
technology discussed in Chapter 14, In this connection, John Diebold has said:*

A few moments' reflection upon almost any of the developments mentioned makes it clear that
there is a complete spectrum of problems with many of which we have no real basis for
coping — moral problems, legal problems, ethical problems, political problems. Worse, still, today
we do not even debate these questions.

What about the question of human experimentation? . . . It is needed, but do you do it without the
knowledge of the patient? . . . We are already beginning to see it happen. The scandal about cancer
experimentation in New York brought to public attention the fact that there is experimentation
every day in our hospitals, not related to therapy and without the patient's knowledge.

There is the problem of our ability to change and influence human behavior. Experimentation in
this area is already widespread. We are gathering new powers. But who is to decide on their use?
Who is to say what form mankind should assume? What conceivable guidelines can we develop for
such decisions?

**"Business, Computers and the Turn Toward
Technology,"**
*address at the Economic Club of Chicago, Chicago,
Illinois,*
February 24, 1964.

"BUT ARE WE AUTOMATING FAST ENOUGH?"

*Despite his full recognition of the problems posed by advancing technology, John
Diebold has never decried that advance, which in any event he has always seen as
irreversible. Quite the contrary — with his philosophy about the exciting new
dimensions of living provided by technology, he has felt emboldened to raise
questions from numerous forums not about the **threat** of expanding automation, but
rather whether it is, in fact, coming about **quickly enough** to fulfill its promise:*

Automation will play a crucial role in determining whether we can in the future maintain the high
standard of living we now enjoy. This standard of living, which is based on our magnificent
productive achievements, is one of the sources of our freedom. In the past few years, much
attention has been given to the potential threat of automation. Perhaps some attention should now
be given to the fact that we are not automating fast enough.

"Pitfalls to Business Data Processing,"
*address before the University of California Conference
on Automation, San Francisco, California,*
January 9, 1957.

Which Cause, Which Effect?

While John Diebold has found considerations such as the above compelling, he does not brush aside the vital questions of public policy and their impact upon business which must inevitably arise. However, before discussing the basic questions he raises and the direction which, in his view, constructive action must take, let us note the caveat he enters about apportioning the blame for some of the social consequences attributed to automation that have aroused the greatest concern. (However, as he has commented, the vehemence with which these issues have been discussed has varied in inverse proportion to the availability of pertinent factual information):

To attribute any inherent evils to automation or technological change is like aiming at the shadow instead of the object.

For years we have allowed the turn of phrases such as "automation causes . . ." erroneously to direct our approach to the subject. These phrases are really shortcut ways of saying, "When we *apply* a set of automation techniques, these sets of results occur." Our own actions or inactions actually *cause* the results.

It has frequently been said that "technological change causes unemployment"; but if a person literally believes this, it is like saying "atomic energy causes war." Atomic energy does not cause war and technological change does not cause unemployment. We know, for example, that the economy is going through a period when the unemployment rate for the unskilled, uneducated worker is much higher than the national average. This state is expected to continue for a long time to come. Is automation or technological change keeping the unskilled worker unemployed? Or rather is there the more basic problem of a failure to eliminate substandard education and training?

Testimony before the Subcommittee on Automation and Energy Resources,
Joint Economic Committee, of the Congress of the United States, Washington, D. C.,
August, 1960.

If normal technological change takes place in a rapidly expanding economy, only the benefits of change are usually noticeable: increased productivity, higher wages, new products, etc. When these same changes take place in a slow moving economy, disruption may occur. The basic issue in this case is not to attack the problem of "change." Clearly, the issue here is the slow growth of the economy.

This may seem like an academic point, but I believe that it is very important to realize this when dealing with the difficult problem of integrating technology in our highly complex economy. There have been times in history when technological developments were so potent and their introduction so rapid that normal economic growth could not accommodate the changes without much human suffering. But I would suggest that, in our case, we may not be suffering from too rapid an introduction of technology as much as we are experiencing too slow a rate of economic growth — the recent average of about 2.5 percent.

Testimony before the Subcommittee on Automation and Energy Resources,
Joint Economic Committee, U.S. Congress, Washington, D.C.,
August, 1960.

DIRECTIONS TO SOLUTIONS

*For problems of such magnitude, there are of course no pat answers. What must be done, however, John Diebold reiterates, is to develop a philosophy, a mental attitude, that will assure that the **directions** in which approaches are taken as problems evolve will work for the preservation and not the destruction of a free and healthy society. This calls first of all, he says, for intense involvement by business leaders in the human problems raised by technology:*

The result of inaction on the part of individuals will be a government solution. The farther this goes, the less likely it is that we are going to have a world in which we have individual freedom and enterprise.

The problems of today are new. The areas of genuine public action are different from those of a hundred years ago when education and public safety and the like were the extent of necessary public concern. Today the problems are more sophisticated, more complex, and very much larger. And it is clear that public action is going to be taken in many areas heretofore private. But do not let die the pluralistic nature of our society — this genius of the American system. Make *public* policy truly *public.*

Involve yourself. Involve yourself in testimony, in public debate, in action. The business response in this area has been poor. We should respond to these new problems in the manner of leaders of the private sector. This new technology is as great a gift as business could give to our society. Until now, we have been fighting a defensive position with respect to it. This need not be the case if we face up to the human problems and lead in social innovation to match the technological innovation.

Only by taking responsible and dynamic action in solving the myriads of problems raised by these new and rapidly changing technologies, can we preserve our society as we know it. Here again I

264

stress the importance to us as individuals and to us as business leaders that we realize that the *human* problems facing us are at the core of all of the solutions we must make.

"Business, Computers and the Turn Toward Technology,"
address at the Economic Club of Chicago, Chicago, Illinois,
February 24, 1964.

Continuing Assessment

As shown in the discussion of technological forecasting in the previous chapter, John Diebold had long called for an underpinning of factual knowledge about automation, as a solid indicator of the direction and intensity of further technological developments and of the shape of results to be expected. To this end he had on numerous occasions — at Congressional hearings and from other forums — called for large-scale studies funded by government or the foundations. More recently — this time in a dissertation on the occasion of the receipt of an honorary degree — he carried this proposal a step forward by urging a continuing assessment of the human consequences of technological change as a basis for business and public policy:

I should like to place before you a recommendation. There could be created an Institute for the continual assessment of the human consequences of technological change.

Such an Institute might be national at first, but surely should be planned along international — universal — lines:

It must not be exclusive, but inclusive.

It must not discourage the duplication of effort, but foster as many attempts to find answers to as many questions, or variations of the same questions, as possible.

It must be a center not of authority, but of light.

It must provide focus, but leave no area of investigation deliberately dark.

Above all, such an Institute should try to assess not only the immediate and obvious consequences of automation and related developments, but the impact of accelerated change itself . . . In the last generation, technology has overwhelmed the general practitioner, obliterated the mechanic's machine, forced the family farm into agricultural combines. Even though these technological manifestations were startling enough—in terms of hospitals, communications, production, economics, nations swept away, ideologies born — their fundamental human importance resides in the fact of change itself.

I do not propose how such an Institute should be financed, who its members should be, where it should be located. It should, though, be so structured and so financed that it can remain generally independent in its role and in its statements. This would dictate that it be at least quasi-public in nature — and I believe we should bear in mind that it is possible for an institution to be public without being an arm of the government. All too often we wish to leave such matters to the government, forgetting that many issues of public policy should be handled in part by government and in part by private groups as well — providing, of course, that they represent labor and education and the consumer, as well as business.

> **"Science, Technology and Man's Relation to the Universe,"**
> *address upon receipt of an Honorary Doctor of Laws Degree at the 80th Anniversary Convocation, Rollins College, Winter Park, Florida,*
> **February 22, 1965.**

PUBLIC POLICY AND YOUTH

*A discussion of technology's impact on public policy would hardly be complete without some consideration of social change and upheaval represented by those who must grapple with technology's problems and opportunities tomorrow — the youth of today. In his commencement address to the graduating class of 1970, upon the occasion of receiving an honorary Doctor of Engineering Degree, John Diebold took occasion to offer special congratulations to those who were "**graduating** rather than demonstrating." While decrying the excesses of student activists, he did, however, point out that there are two hopeful aspects of the student movement today:*

On the one hand one can only respect the ideals and unselfish motives underlying the concern of the great majority of today's activists — concern with our way of life and with our values. On the other hand, the interest in recent weeks in working within the political system to change our society is a development which, I think, is one of the most hopeful and welcome aspects of the entire phenomenon.

> **"Youth and Business,"**
> *commencement address upon receipt of an Honorary Doctor of Engineering Degree, Newark College of Engineering, Newark, New Jersey,*
> **May 27, 1970.**

Again he articulated his philosophy that the most efficient response to the imperatives of social change will come from the private sector:

As engineers, most of you will be employed most of your working lives within the institutions of private enterprise. In view of the fact that you are graduating rather than demonstrating, I think that it is with appropriate poetic justice to realize that private institutions are exactly where the action *is* going to be, and the graduates who work in these areas, rather than the demonstrators, are going to be the ones who in the next several decades are at the very center of one of the most interesting processes of social change . . . Business and youth have much to offer one another. It would be a tragedy for our society if we lost or wasted even a small part of the creativity and sparkle that today's graduates can bring to our times.

In the institution of private enterprise we have one of the most interesting and important social inventions of the West. In many ways it is the real *genius* of the West. It is through the combination of, on the one hand, the *organizational and managerial characteristics,* and on the other the *dynamics* of private enterprise that we have achieved what Norman Macrae of the London *Economist* has characterized as "the most productive use of resources that man has ever achieved."

In one sense it is because that success has been *too* great that we have the reaction of the activists today to "excess materialism." But even if we have become too preoccupied with material output, the mechanism — one of the few social institutions that works well — should not be thrown out as a result of confusing it with objectives. Let us rather apply it to areas that need more effective means of achieving results. Let us turn our attention to areas other than physical production. But, as a society, in doing this let us not throw out the one social mechanism we have that works — the organizing skill and the dynamics of the private sector.

"Youth and Business,"
commencement address upon receipt of an Honorary Doctor of Engineering Degree, Newark College of Engineering, Newark, New Jersey,
May 27, 1970.

Thus, says John Diebold, we can see the future and make it work!

BIBLIOGRAPHY: SELECTED WRITINGS OF JOHN DIEBOLD

"Automation, The Advent of the Automatic Factory." Princeton, New Jersey: Van Nostrand Company, Inc., 1952, 181 pages.   H1

"The Significance of Productivity Data." *Harvard Business Review,* Vol. XXX, No. 4, (July-August 1952), pp. 53-63.   H26

"Automation – The New Technology," *Harvard Business Review,* Vol. XXXI, No. 6, (November-December 1953), pp. 63-71.   H30

"The Challenge of Automation." Address presented before the American Society of Tool Engineers, Philadelphia, Pennsylvania, April 26-30, 1954. *ASTE Tool Engineering Conference Papers,* No. 22T39.   H34

"The Business Problems of Using Automation." Address presented at the Conference of Automation and Industrial Development, Syracuse, New York, May 12, 1954. *Minutes of Conference on Automation and Industrial Development.* Published by State of New York, Department of Commerce.   H35

"Automation – Its Impact on Human Relations." Address presented at the National Association of Manufacturers' Congress of American Industry, New York, New York, December 3, 1954.   H44

"Labor and Automation." Editorial, "Feedback," *Automatic Control,* Vol. II, No. 1, (January 1955), p. 48.   H45

"Automation – Will It Steal Your Job?" *This Week Magazine,* (June 26, 1955), pp. 7-27.   H57

"Automation." Address presented at the Twenty-Fifth Annual Meeting of the Textile Research Institute, New York, New York, *Textile Research Journal,* Vol. XXV, No. 7, (July 1955), pp. 635-640.   H59

"Automation: A Factor in Business Policy Planning." Based on address presented at the 2nd Annual Conference on Business and Tax Policy, Palm Beach, Florida, April 18, 1955, *The Manager* (England), (September 1955), pp. 1-3.   H61

"The Future of Automation." Panel Discussion at the Radio-Electronics-Television Manufacturers Association Symposium on Automation, University of Pennsylvania, Philadelphia, Pennsylvania, September 26-27, 1955. *Proceedings of the RETMA Symposium on Automation,* pp. 52-65.   H62

"Speaking of Automation: The Words, the Myths, and the Facts." Address presented at the Case Institute of Technology, Cleveland, Ohio, September 8, 1955.   H208

"What Is Automation?" *Management Record,* (September 1955), pp. 356-359.   H209

"Applied Automation: A Practical Approach." Keynote address presented at the Special Manufacturing Conference of the American Management Association, New York, New York, October 10, 1955.   H64

Congressional Testimony on "Automation and Technological Change," Hearings before the Subcommittee on Economic Stabilization of the Joint Committee on the Economic Report, United States Congress, 84th Congress, First Session, Washington, D.C., October 14, 1955. *Hearings, Automation and Technological Change.*   H65

"Automation – The Challenge to Management." Address presented at the British Institute of Management, Harrogate, England, November 4, 1955.   H213

"Management in the Age of Automation." Address presented at the Fifth Alumni Homecoming, New York University School of Commerce, Accounts, and Finance, New York, New York, December 3, 1955. *New York University Business Series,* No. 25, pp. 18-29.   H68

"What Is Automation?" *Collier's,* Vol. CXXXVII, No. 6, (March 16, 1956), pp. 38-44. H71

"The Effects of Automation on New Products." Address presented before the New Products Seminar, New York, New York, April 13, 1956. H72

"Report from America." Television interview with John Diebold, The British Broadcasting Corporation in cooperation with the United States Information Agency, London, England, April 19, 1956. H72

"Individuals in a World of Change." Commencement address presented at the East Contra Costa Junior College and West Contra Costa Junior College, San Pablo, California, June 20, 1956. H74

"Automation Pilots a New Revolution." *Challenge,* (November 1956), pp. 13-17. H76

"Pitfalls to Business Data Processing." Address presented at the University of California Conference on Automation, San Francisco, California, January 9, 1957. H80

"Impact of Automation on Control and Organization." Leader of panel discussion at the Roundtable on Innovation — New Management Concepts of the Society for Advancement of Management, Washington, D.C., April 11, 1957. H83

"Automation and the Manager." Address presented at the XIth International Management Congress, Comite International de l'Organisation Scientifique (CIOS), Paris, France, June 26, 1957. H87

"Education for Data Processing — The Real Challenge to Management." A Great Issues Lecture presented at Dartmouth College, Hanover, New Hampshire, November 11, 1957. New York: Management Science Training Institute, 1957, 13 pages. H78

"Electronic Computers — The Challenge to Management." Reprint of a paper presented at a five-day course for management on Automatic Data Processing, organized by John Diebold & Associates with the support of the British Institute of Management, London, England, January 20-24, 1958. H96

"Putting it to Work: Making the Most of Automatic Data Processing." Reprint of address presented at the 29th National Cost Conference of The Institute of Cost and Works Accountants, London, England, June 6, 1958, *The Cost Accountant* (England), Vol. 37, No. 2, (July 1958), pp. 52-56. H100

"Automation, 1958: Industry at the Crossroads." *Dun's Review and Modern Industry,* Vol. LXXVI, No. 2, (August 1958), pp. 36-96. H101

"The Economic and Social Effects of Automation." Address presented at the Second International Congress on Cybernetics, Namur, Belgium, September 3-10, 1958. Published by the Association Internationale de Cybernetique, Brussels, Belgium, 19 pages. H104

"A Review of Recent Experience of U.S. Applications." Address presented at a one-day conference of the British Institute of Management on 'Computers: Top Management Appraisal,' London, England, October 21, 1958. H105

"Electronic Data Processing — A Progress Report." Address presented before the Office Management Association, Nottingham, England, November 1958. H107

"John Diebold Answers Twenty Questions." Interview with John Diebold, *Automatic Data Processing* (England), (March 1959). H113

"Automation: Its Impact on Business and Labor." Planning Pamphlet No. 106, Washington, D.C.: National Planning Association, May 1959, 64 pages. H11

"Automation Needs a Human Approach." *Challenge,* (May 1959). H114

"What Is Really Promised by Automation?" *Chicago Sun-Times,* (June 22, 1959), p. 49. H116

"A Comparison of the Approach to Computers in Europe and America." Address presented at the Sixth Annual International Meeting of The Institute of Management Science, Paris, France, September 7-10, 1959. H118

"Automation as a Management Problem." Book chapter in Howard Boone Jacobson and Joseph S. Roucek (Eds.), *Automation and Society,* New York: Philosophical Library, 1959, pp. 310-329. H16

"A Review of Recent Experience of United States Applications." Address presented at a special conference of the British Institute of Management, Glasgow, Scotland, March 9, 1960. H124

"The Basic Economic Consequences of Automation." Working paper prepared for discussion at Governor's Conference on Automation, State of New York, Cooperstown, New York, June 1-3, 1960. H129

"Automation – The Need for a Positive Program." Address presented at the Commonwealth of Massachusetts Conference on Automation, Boston, Massachusetts, June 2, 1960. H130

Congressional Testimony, prepared at the request of the Subcommittee on Automation and Energy Resources of the Joint Economic Committee, Congress of the United States, August 1960. H132

"Life Under Automation." Interview with John Diebold, *Challenge,* (December 1960), pp. 20-25. H137

"Technology's Challenge to Management." Address presented before the Plenary Session, European Conference of The High Authority of the European Coal and Steel Community, The Commission of the European Economic Community, The Commission of the European Atomic Energy Community, Brussels, Belgium, December 6, 1960. H139

"Automation – Its Meaning and Impact." Address presented before the Industrial Relations Session of the 65th Congress of American Industry, sponsored by the National Association of Manufacturers, New York, New York, December 9, 1960. H140

"Automation as a Historical Development." Address presented at the annual meeting of the Society for the History of Technology held in conjunction with the annual meeting of the American Association for the Advancement of Science, New York, New York, December 29, 1960. H141

Summary of Congressional Testimony, Subcommittee on Unemployment – Automation, U.S. House of Representatives, Committee on Education and Labor, Washington, D.C., March 8, 1961. H144

"Urgent Need: All-Out Automation." Interview with John Diebold, *Nation's Business,* (July 1961), pp. 179-182. H150

"Industrial Applications of Heuristic Machines." Address presented at the Third International Congress on Cybernetics, Namur, Belgium, September 11-15, 1961. Published by the Association International de Cybernetique, Brussels, Belgium. H152

Roundtable discussion on "Effects of Computers on Personnel," Wayne State University, Detroit, Michigan, September 1961, as reprinted in *Data Processing,* Vol. 3, No. 11, (November 1961), pp. 8-24. H153

"The Application of Information Technology." *The Annals of the American Academy of Political and Social Science,* Vol. 340, (March 1962), pp. 38-45. H157

"Facing up to Automation." *The Saturday Evening Post,* Vol. 235, No. 33, (September 22, 1962), pp. 26-31. H164

"The Applicability of Programed Learning Techniques to Developing Countries." *Floor Statement of John Diebold,* United States Delegation to the United Nations Conference on Science and Technology for Less Developed Areas, Geneva, Switzerland, February 8, 1963. H168

"The Editor and Automation." Address presented before the American Society of Newspaper Editors, Washington, D.C., April 19, 1963. H171

"The Revolution That Fails to Take Place." Address presented before the National Machine Tool Builders' Association, Cincinnati, Ohio, May 3, 1963. H173

"Automation – Perceiving the Magnitude of the Problem." Address presented at the Fifth Annual Salute to the Alumni, Columbia University, New York, New York, June 3, 1963. H175

Congressional Testimony on "Manpower Development and Training Act," Hearings before the Select Subcommittee on Labor of the Committee on Education and Labor, U.S. House of Representatives, 88th Congress, Washington, D.C., August 5, 1963. H180

Congressional Testimony on "Nation's Manpower Revolution," Hearings before the Subcommittee on Employment and Manpower of the Committee on Labor and Public Welfare, United States Senate, 88th Congress, Washington, D.C., September 20, 1963. H181

"Management and Railroad Cybernetics." Address presented before the Plenary Session, Union Internationale des Chemins de Fer (UIC), UIC Railway Symposium on Cybernetics, Paris, France, November 4, 1963. H184

"Petroleum Industry Management in the New Era of Information Technology." Address presented before the Transportation Division of the American Petroleum Institute, Chicago, Illinois, November 11, 1963. H188

"Programed Learning: Its Role in Our World." Keynote address presented before the Society for Educational and Training Technology, San Antonio, Texas, April 1, 1964. H190

"ADP – The Still Sleeping Giant." *Harvard Business Review,* Vol. XLII, No. 5, (September-October 1964), pp. 60-65. H198

"New Concepts of the 'Foreseeable Future'" *Credit and Financial Management,* Vol. 66, No. 11, (November 1964), pp. 18-19. H201

"The Next Vital Step to Management Control Systems." Keynote address presented at the International Meeting of the Data Processing Management Association, San Francisco, California, November 1964. H202

"Science, Technology and Man's Relation to the Universe." ("In Apprehension How Like A God"), Address presented at the 80th Anniversary Convocation, upon receipt of an Honorary Doctor of Laws Degree, Rollins College, Winter Park, Florida, February 22, 1965. H203

"What's Ahead in Information Technology?" *Harvard Business Review,* Vol. 43, No. 5, (September-October 1965), pp. 76-82. H313

"The Impact of Science and Technology on the Development of Managers." Address presented at a Special Convocation upon receipt of an Honorary Doctor of Science Degree, Clarkson College of Technology, Potsdam, New York, October 12, 1965. H316

"Looking Bravely Back to 1948 or So." Book chapter in Rex Malik (Ed.), *Penguin Survey of Business and Industry,* Harmondsworth, England: Penguin Books, Ltd. 1965, pp. 26-39. H319

"Business, Computers and the Turn Toward Technology." Address presented at the Economic Club of Chicago, Chicago, Illinois, February 24, 1966. H324

"The New World Coming." *Saturday Review,* Special Issue on: 'The New Computerized Age,' (July 23, 1966), pp. 17-18. H331

"Marketing's Role in the Coming Age of Automation." Cover story interview with John Diebold, *Sales Management,* Vol. 97, No. 8, (October 1, 1966), pp. 58-70. H334

"Computers, Program Management and Foreign Affairs." *Foreign Affairs,* Vol. 45, No. 1, (October 1966), pp. 125-134. H335

"Impacts on Urban Governmental Functions of Developments in Science and Technology." *The Annals of the American Academy of Political and Social Science,* (May 1967), reprinted from 'Governing Urban Society,' Monograph No. 7 of the American Academy of Political and Social Science, Philadelphia, Pennsylvania, pp. 85-100. H355

"What Comes Next in the Computer Age.' Interview with John Diebold, *U.S. News & World Report,* Vol. LXII, No. 26, (June 26, 1967), pp. 311-312. H359

"How the Technology Gap Can Widen Even While Europe Possesses the Most Advanced Computer Technology." Abstract of address presented to a Meeting of the Senior Managers of Sponsor Firms of The Diebold Research Program – Europe, London, England, September 26, 1967. H361

"When Money Grows in Computers." *Columbia Journal of World Business,* Vol. II, No. 6, (November-December 1967), pp. 39-46. H365

"Is the Gap Technological?" *Foreign Affairs,* Vol. 46, No. 2, (January 1968), pp. 276-291. H370

"Needed: A Yardstick for Computers." Interview with John Diebold, *Dun's Review,* Vol. 92, No. 2, (August 1968), p. 40-42. H381

"Automation in the Future." Keynote address presented at the 37th International Conference of the Financial Executives Institute, New York, New York, October 25, 1968. H377

"Conversation with John Diebold." Script for Interview with Harry Reasoner – John Diebold, released with long-playing record by Listening Library, Record No. AA3321, 1968. H301

"Bad Decisions on Computer Use." *Harvard Business Review,* Vol. 47, No. 1, (January-February 1969), pp. 14-16 & 27-28 & 176. H388

"Obsolescence for the Printed Word?" Interview with John Diebold, *Think Magazine* (published by IBM), Vol. 34, No. 7, (January-February 1969), pp. 17-19. H390

"Tomorrow's Enterprise and Its Management." Speeches and Papers 1957-1969, in three volumes, New York: Praeger Publishers, Inc., 1970.

1. **Beyond Automation,** originally published by McGraw-Hill, Inc., New York, 1964 and republished by Praeger Publishers, Inc., New York, 1970, 220 pages. With Foreword by Peter Drucker.
2. **Man and the Computer,** Frederick A. Praeger, Inc., 1969, 157 pages.
3. **Business Decisions and Technological Change,** New York: Praeger Publishers, Inc., 1970, 268 pages. H404

"Youth and Business." Commencement address presented upon receipt of an Honorary Doctor of Engineering Degree, Newark College of Engineering, Newark, New Jersey, May 27, 1970. H407

"New Rules and Opportunities for Business – As We Enter the Post-Industrial Era." Keynote address presented at the Third Tri-Annual International Productivity Congress, Hofburg Palace, Vienna, Austria, October 28, 1970. H410

"Education, Technology and Business." (A case Study of Business in the Future – Problems and Opportunities) Diebold Group Position Paper No. 1 in a series entitled 'Private Enterprise in a Post-Industrial Society,' and published as one of the *Praeger Special Studies in U.S. Economic and Social Development,* New York: Praeger Publishers, Inc., 1971, 107 pages. H406

INDEX

International Minerals and Chemicals Company, 10; 72
International Productivity Congress, Third Tri-Annual, 55; 123; 221
International Railway Union, 7; 153; 154; 156; 157; 159; 160; 162; 165
International Social Science Bulletin, 113; 117; 169

J

Joint Economic Committee of the Congress of the United States, 62; 76; 119; 235; 238

K

Kaiser Steel Company, 226; 232
Kroger Co., 249

L

Labor, and technological change, 221-239
   and collective bargaining, 225
   and management-employee communication, 224
   management responsibility re., 222
Lockheed, 212
Long-range planning, 21

M

Machine tool industry, 32
"Man and the Computer," 169; 175; 177; 178; 179
Management, *by* the computer, 75-89
   of the computer, 91-106
Management-employee communication, 224
Management information systems, 81-89
   systems analysis for, 85
Management science, and marketing, 68
Management Today, 7; 75; 109
The Manager, 75
Managers, development of, 109-120
   entrepreneurial understanding of, 112
   role of higher education in, 118

Manufacturing, discrete, 42
Market concept, 31; 60
Marketing, administrative function of, 60
   data bank for, 63
   information systems for, 55-72
   models for, 68
Marketing risks, 18
Metropolitan Lithographers Association, 233
Models, of the economy, 250
Money and credit (*See* "Cashless society")

N

NCR, 36
The Nation, 12
National Association of Manufacturers, 1; 8; 223; 241
National Machine Tool Builders' Association, 7; 34; 35
National Planning Association, 43; 260
National Wholesale Druggists Association, 63; 71
New management sciences, 211
New product development, 17
Newark College of Engineering, 19; 259; 266; 267
New York Lithographers, 226
New York Stock Exchange, 142; 143; 145
New York Times, 50; 142
North American Aviation, 35

O

Office Management Association (England), 118
Office processes, 46

P

Pacific Maritime Association, 233
Panel, 13; 27
Petroleum industry, 34
Planning, long-range, 23
President's National Commission on Technology, Automation, and Economic Progress, 236
Printer's Ink, 12; 15; 23; 32; 35
Processing industries, 41

Managing Creativity

Too often management unconsciously assumes that spending a given percentage on research, or creating fine working conditions, will produce results. But the perquisites of genius follow – not precede – the essence of genius. Too often this fact is lost sight of. The fine equipment, campus-like plants, and company-paid university courses are but empty trappings if the human quality is not already present.

"Technology's Challenge to Management,"
address before the Plenary Session, European Confer-
ence of The High Authority of the European Coal and
Steel Community. The Commission of the European
Economic Community, The Commission of the Euro-
pean Atomic Energy Community, Brussels, Belgium,
December 6, 1960.

The solution to the creation of a viable and constructive relationship between the new breed of creative personnel and the rest of the organization, and one that will go a long way to solving the problem of retention of creative people, lies in the intelligent application of the insights of the behavioral sciences – the creation of an organization climate that induces recognition and acceptance rather than antagonism and resistence.

Remarks at a meeting of Sponsors of The Diebold
Research Program,
January 12, 1970

The "Cashless Society"

Automation will make it possible to render new, more comprehensive, and more economical services. It will, in fact, strengthen and further the trend toward acceleration of the service industries.

"Automation – The New Technology,"
Harvard Business Review,
November-December, 1953.

The current system of money-and-credit transfer could not support the needed expansion of national economic activity. To project a doubling of gross national product by 1983 on the basis of current means of financial transactions is like expecting the 1968 volume of telephone calls to be made through the 1948 telephone system, with its reliance on operators, limited local dialing, mechanical switching, and so on.

"When Money Grows in Computers,"
Columbia Journal of World Business,
November-December, 1967.

Education as a Market

I am convinced that the fundamental problem automation poses for management is the problem of education. On all levels of working and living we need more education. Beyond retraining those who already have jobs, or to prepare them for more highly skilled work, we must al face the larger problem of how we are to increase our resources of good engineers, scientists, and trained technicians. This problem will grow more acute in the years ahead.

"Automation as a Challenge to Management,"
International Social Science Bulletin,
June 1957.

The impact of educational technology on business, at least in the United States, is going to be phenomenal. It will change not only the markets business serves, but also the operation of business.

Education, Technology and Business, Alumni Day
Address,
Swarthmore College, Swarthmore, Pa.,
October, 1966.

Business, in meeting its own educational and training problems, is likely to lead the way in the application of advanced technologies for our educational institutions . . . it can (thus) serve a market of immense potential. In order to do so, business must ask, and seek answers to, the fundamental questions of education.

Introduction to the chapter, "Educational Technology
and Business Responsibility," in John Diebold's Man
and the Computer,
New York, Frederick A. Praeger,
1969.

Computer-Based Information Services as a New Business

The technology of computers and the rapid communications and information processing equipment which this technology makes possible will permit far more extensive analysis of our national economy and business, through up-to-the-minute market surveys and extensive research on distribution and transportation patterns.

Automation: The Advent of the Automatic Factory,
Princeton, New Jersey, Van Nostrand Company, Inc.
1952.

There must be more analysis of business needs and more imagination concerning practical business applications of computers – other than the sweeping concept of the totally automatic office.

"Automation – The New Technology,"
Harvard Business Review,
November-December, 1953.

A new industry is the one now being called the inquiry industry – it is in some ways the publishing field of the future. This development is one which allows the sale of proprietary data over a communication system in answer to a query placed by the customer from a unit on his desk . . . You key this request into the unit on your desk, see the answer on a screen virtually as you ask the question, and then go to ask another question and so on through a train of questions.

"Business, Computers, and the Turn Toward
Technology,"
address before the Economic Club of Chicago,
Chicago, Illinois
February 24, 1966.